Printing Statement:

Due to the very old age and scarcity of this book, many of the pages may be hard to read due to the blurring of the original text, possible missing pages, missing text, dark backgrounds and other issues beyond our control.

Because this is such an important and rare work, we believe it is best to reproduce this book regardless of its original condition.

Thank you for your understanding.

YALE STUDIES IN ENGLISH

ALBERT S. COOK, Editor

III

THE LIFE OF ST. CECILIA

FROM

MS. ASHMOLE 43 AND MS. COTTON TIBERIUS E. VII

WITH INTRODUCTION, VARIANTS, AND GLOSSARY

BY

BERTHA ELLEN LOVEWELL, Ph. D.

LAMSON, WOLFFE AND COMPANY
BOSTON, NEW YORK, AND LONDON
1898

PREFACE.

The pages that follow are the record of an attempt to present a small contribution to the general study of English Medieval Saints Legends, in as complete form as time and conditions have permitted. The legend here edited is in no sense peculiarly representative of medieval legends, yet it may serve to indicate the general tone of the species of literature to which it belongs.

Until, as Dr. Horstmann has observed, the combined intelligence of generations yet to come has been applied to the problem, many of the most vital questions relating to English Legendary must remain unsolved. Perhaps the best service which can now be rendered, is to continue to present, as Dr. Horstmann has so long been doing, accurate reprints of existing versions, together with textual studies of the kinds familiar to scholarship.

The texts, here printed for the first time, have been carefully transcribed from their originals and collated by scribes at the several libraries where the manuscripts are kept. I regret exceedingly that, owing to delay on the part of one scribe, this edition must go to press lacking the table of variants from MSS. Stowe 946 and Lambeth 223, which are the only existing versions of this legend not included. Moreover, many definitive results, which students of even a single legend have reason to expect, have been omitted but not overlooked. I shall hope to supplement these deficiencies as time and ability may permit.

In presenting this result of a few months' work, I wish to acknowledge, first of all, my great indebtedness to the strong, clear-sighted judgment of Professor Cook, under whose guidance my graduate work has received direction. I wish also to express my thanks to Professor Skeat, who sent me advance proof-sheets of the Ælfrician version of the Life of St. Cecilia, and at the same time gave suggestion and encouragement.

B. E. L.

New Haven, Conn., June 1, 1898.

TABLE OF CONTENTS.

THE LIFE AND ACTS OF ST. CECILIA.

From the long list of saints and martyrs whose acts are celebrated by the Western Church, there is separable a group of
Roman virgin martyrs. To this group, with St. Agnes, St.
Agatha, and St. Lucy (the two latter being undoubtedly of Sicil-
ian origin), St. Cecilia belongs. St. Cecilia is also frequently
associated in the modern mind with the Greek St. Katherine,
probably through the intensifying and relating of the emblematic idea, which gave to St. Katherine the province of literature
and philosophy, as it made St. Cecilia the patroness of sacred
music.

The attempt to reach conclusions concerning the historic St.
Cecilia is one full of difficulties, although the veneration paid
to the saint may be traced with considerable ease to a very early
period. The Roman church regularly interweaves the significant features of the legend into the celebration of the canonical
hours on November 22 and April 14, and the legend is also quite
generally included in the collections of Saints' Lives produced
in the monasteries of the 13th, 14th and 15th centuries.

From the medieval legends comes the following account of
St. Cecilia:

St. Cecilia was a maiden of noble blood—*ingenua, nobilis, clar-
issima,* who lived in Rome under the prefecture of Almachius,
and the spiritual rule of Pope Urban I. Although she had been
baptized and had lived a Christian from her infancy, she is
given in marriage to a rich young pagan named Valerian. St.
Cecilia, consecrated to God and to virginity by a secret vow,
withdraws from her friends on the night of the marriage feast,
and, in communion and prayer to God, hears heavenly music to
which she responds, singing in her heart, *in corde decantabat,* that
she may be preserved in her purity.

Valerian though skeptical as to the heavenly visitants which
Cecilia alleges to have seen, and toward the Christian faith in
general, is at last persuaded by her to rise from his bed and go
by night for instruction and advice to Pope Urban, who lives in
hiding among the Roman catacombs. Valerian's faith is con-
firmed during his interview with the Pope by a vision of an old
man who bears the roll of the Gospel in his hand and explains

2

its meaning. Valerian is baptized and returns to Cecilia, by whose side he finds a second spiritual visitant. This angel foretells their martyrdom, promises as a reward of Valerian's faith the salvation of his brother, Tiburtius, and places in their hands two wreaths of immortal flowers, which breathe a wonderful fragrance. The heathen, Tiburtius, hearing the rumor of his brother's conversion, appears shortly in a casual fashion at Valerian's house. His attention is, however, immediately arrested by the fragrance of the flowers, and the conversation is turned upon sacred things. Cecilia, according to some medieval versions, explains at length the doctrine of salvation, and finally Tiburtius consents to go with Valerian to Pope Urban. There he is baptized and the two brothers enter at once upon the active Christian career which is to lead to their martyrdom. They convert many pagans and at night seek for the cast-away bodies of martyrs to bury them. In this act of devotion they are at last detected and brought before Almachius, prefect of the city. Their own assurance in this ordeal is strengthened by Cecilia, who speaks to them from without the prison door and exhorts them to be stalwart knights in the service of God. Their conversation with the prefect at the time of their trial is variously elaborated in different versions, but is usually characterized by their introduction of the parable of the slothful and industrious husbandmen. At last, refusing to offer sacrifice, Valerian and Tiburtius are condemned to death, on which occasion many hundred people are converted, together with Maximus, the jailer, who sees the souls of the two martyred men borne aloft on the wings of angel messengers. Maximus speedily suffers death for his belief and the bodies of the three martyrs are cast without the city walls. Here Cecilia finds them and brings them to the catacombs for burial.

The wealth of the widowed Cecilia then appeals to the greed of the tyrant Almachius, and he sends messengers to possess themselves of all the property that can be found. Cecilia, however, convicts the messengers of sin, converts them to Christianity, and they go away empty handed, whereupon Cecilia proceeds to distribute her goods to the poor and Almachius finds his attempt baffled. He sends for Cecilia, who appears before him in all her Christian boldness and defies his power, which she asserts is as a "bladder blown full of wind." She claims her own high birth and announces her allegiance to God, who is the Lord of life, whereas Almachius is, at best, only *dethes lord.*

From the midst of a sorrowing group of men and women, Cecilia is led to her own house, where she is shut up in the *caldari-um* and placed in a boiling bath, yet she emerges, after a day and a night, in all content and without injury. Then the executioner is sent, who, according to the law of the country, is allowed three blows by which to strike off a head. By the intervention of some supernatural power the blows are only partly effectual, and Cecilia, though mortally wounded, lives three days, in which time she makes complete disposition of her property, consecrating her palace as a church and home for the maidens who have been under her guidance, and converting many hundred souls through her preaching. And this was, the legend tells us, two hundred and twenty-three years after that our Lord came to earth.

This legend is greeted to-day on the one hand by the popular conception of a mystical St. Cecilia vested with the emblems of music as her sole attribute, an estimate which modern art has done much to confirm; on the other hand, by the almost universal voice of skepticism on the part of the historical critic[1] as to the authenticity of her Acts.

The proof as to whether such a person as Cecilia ever existed at Rome, surrounded by the personages Valerian, Tiburtius, Maximus, Urban and Almachius, who provide the setting for the incidents of her life as set forth by monastic scribes after an interval of ten centuries, rests, so far as it can be at all determined, upon the testimony of four authorities:—First, the records of the saint as found in ancient calendars, martyrologies, and breviaries; second, the historic accounts of the early Church; third, the compilations of hagiographers, and fourth, the accumulating information of archeologists.

The Martyrologies were compiled from letters and brief records which were written, it may be supposed, under the same

---

1 Saint Cécile est honorée comme martyre dans l Eglise Latine depuis le 5e siècle, mais on ignore ce que concerne sa vie, ses actions, et sa mort. L'Advocat, *Dict. Hist-Portatif*.

Ses actes sont plus anciens, mais . . . non pas pour y donner une entière créance. Fleury, *Hist. Eccles.* lib. XLVI. § 41.

Ses actes qui ont peu d'autorite. Feller, *Dict. de Biog. et d'Hist.*

Of her life and history, however, hardly any authentic account has come down to us. C. H., *Dict. of Christ. Biog.*

The legendary accounts of her are not worthy of credence. McClintock and Strong, *Cyclop. of Eccles. Lit.*

The acts of St. Cecily are generally considered of very small authority. Alban Butler, *Lives of Saints.*

It is also unfortunate for Cecilia's claim to a footing on the solid soil of history that the earliest writer who makes mention of her, Fortunatus, bishop of Poitiers, represents her to have died in Sicily between the years 176 and 180. . . . It is absurdly stated in the *Biographie Universalle* that Cecilia's name is found in the most ancient martyrologies, whereas, as may be seen from Baronius, the earliest of these documents was compiled by Pope Clement I. who died A. D. 100. *Encycl. Brit.*

impetus as that which, in the early Christian church, collected
and preserved the Apostolic records. Many early documents
assure us of this activity.

Clement I. in 93 A. D. divided Rome into seven ecclesiastical
districts which he apportioned to faithful chuchmen that they
might search out with care the acts of the martyrs.[1] Another
record by Anastasius reports the continuation of this work
under the papacy of St. Fabian 236–249, shortly after the supposed time of our saint.[2] Of Pope Anteros, 235–236, we are told[3]
that "he diligently sought out the acts of the martyrs from the
notaries, and laid them up in the church, for which thing he
was made a martyr by the prefect Maximus." Cyprian[4] directs
his church officials to record the days of the martyrs, and says
that this custom has been practised by Tertullus. We know
from Sozomen[5] that municipalities under the same civil rule
frequently had their own feast days on which they celebrated their local martyrs.

These and similar records perished undoubtedly during the
Christian persecutions which accompanied and succeeded these
centuries, yet there is ground for belief that they provided the
first authentic step in the series which finally led to the Acts of
a St. Cecilia.

Eusebius in the early part of the fourth century affirms[6]
that with the judicial acts and records of the time, he has considered also the letters of the faithful in the compilation of his
Martyrology. Of this only the fragment containing the lives
of the Martyrs of Palestine[7] remains. A Latin compilation supposed to be based upon Eusebius[8] is preserved by the *Martyrologium Vetustissimum*[9] attributed to Jerome (330–420). It contains
references to the saints of the Cecilia legend, which show some
discrepancies and repetitions. These occur, as the more familiar

1 Hic fecit septem regiones dividi notariis fidelibus Ecclesiæ, qui gesta martyrum sollicite et curi-
ose unusquisque per regionem suam diligenter perquirerent. Anastasius, *Lib. Pontif.* iv. PATR. LAT.
127. Baronius, *Ann.* A. D. 95. Vol. I. 728, 729.
2 Hic regiones divisit diaconibus, et fecit septem sub diaconos, qui septem notariis imminerent, ut
gesta martyrum in integro colligerent. Anast. *Lib. Pontif.* xxi, PATR. LAT. 127.
3 De Rossi, *Rom. Sott.* II. 121.
4 Cypr., *Ep.* ix.
5 *Hist. Eccl.* V. 3. Paris, 1698.
6 πᾶσάν τε τὴν πρὸς τὴν σύγχλητον ἀπολογίαν ὅτῳ διαγνῶναι φίλον, ἐχ τῆς τῶν Ἀρχαίων
μαρτυρίων συναχθείσης ἡμῖν ἀναγραφῆς εἴσεται. *Hist. Eccl.* v. 21.
7 PATR. GR. 20, 1519.
8 For early allusion concerning the compilation of this work see Strabo, *de Rebus Eccl.* c. 28. PATR.
LAT. 114. 962; Bede, *Retract in Act. Ap.* 1. PATR. LAT. 92. 997; Cassiodorus, *de Inst. Div. Lect.* c.
32. PATR. LAT. 70. 1147.
9 Florentinius, PATR. LAT. 30. 455.

later records give us reason to expect, on 22 November, the day of St. Cecilia, 14 April, the day of Valerian, Tiburtius, and Maximus, and 25 May, the day of the martyr Urban.[1] Additional records are then given for 16 September and 21 April.

The reference to St. Cecilia on XVI Kal. October (September 16) is found again in the martyrology and breviary of Corbeiensus Dacherius. Also in the *Epternacensian* Martyrology the words "*Romæ Cæciliæ*" occur on this day, and the *Richenoviensian*, the *Augustan* and the *Labbeanian* calendars give here the name "*Cæciliæ*" without title or place. The frequent repetition of the date 16 September in these earliest calendars, gives rise to doubt concerning the authenticity of the now commonly accepted date, 22 November, for the commemoration of Cecilia's birth. The later date, some critics[2] believe, celebrates the consecration of the church of St. Cecilia in Trastevere in Rome. No evidence, however, is able to place this earlier than 434-440 (see p. 20). In the meanwhile the calendar of Fronto[3] (pope, 372-5), and most of the Latin collections[4] succeeding, mark Cecilia's festival on 22 November, and those of Valerian and Tiburtius, overlooking Jerome's second allusion on XI Kal. May (April 21), on 14 April.

The early Roman Sacramentaries, consist usually of a series of prayers for intercession and praise to the appropriate saint for the day, with vague allusion to the martyrdom and triumph of the one thus commemorated. Through these, the early veneration of St. Cecilia may be traced, and some intimation gained as to the character of her acts. The *Sacramentarium Leonianum*, which is the oldest of the accessible church uses, is attributed by Blanchini (1735) to Pope Leo the Great (440-461). It contains a long celebration of the martyrdom of St. Cecilia on 22 Novem-

---

1 X Kal. Decem. Romæ. Cæciliæ virginis, Valeriani, Tiburtii, Maximi.

XVIII Kal. Mail. Romæ, via Appia in cœmeterio Prætextati, natalis sanctorum Tiburtii, Valeriani, Maximi.

VIII Kal. Jun. Via Nomentana, milliaro nono, natalis Urbani episcopi.

These references are supplemented by the following repetitions: XI Kal. Mail. Romæ, in cœmeterio Calesti, via Appia, natalis sanctorum Valeriani, Maximi, Tiburtii.

XVI Kal. Oct. Passio Sanctæ Cæciliæ virginis. PATR. LAT, 30.

2 Das (Nov. 22) war ursprünglich nicht ihr Todestag, sondern der Kirchweihtag der Basilika in Trastevere. Das dieses Datum des 22 Nov. sich nach De Rossi auf die Translation unter Paschalis I. beziehe, berichtet Lipsius, *Chron. der Röm. Bish.* s. 182. Erbes, *Die Heilige Cäcilia, Zeitschr. f. Kirchengesch.* ix. 15.

3 Fronto, *Calendarium Romanum*, Paris, 1652, p. 140.

4 Kalendarium Floriacense, Antiquissimum (IX C),Stabulense, Verdinense, Martyrologium Insignis Eccl. Antissiodorensis, Mantuanum, Brixianum, Vallumbrosanum (two), Lucensis Kalendarii (fragmentum), Calendarium Anglicanum, and Veteres Litaniæ Anglicanæ. PATR. LAT. 138. 1186.

ber.[1] To Gelasius I. (pope 462-496), is attributed the authorship
of the *Liber Sacrementorum* in which *In Natalis Sanctæ Cæciliæ* is
celebrated with similar forms on 22 November and the preceding day.[2] It is a series of prayers on both days. Her martyrdom
is also celebrated in the important sacramentary of St. Gregory
I. (540-604), which is given in full.[3]

Parallel with the liturgical growth in the Roman church appear the independent liturgies of foreign churches. Such a
liturgy belonged to the church of Milan and has been ascribed
to Ambrose (334-397). This liturgy, which at all events was of
very early origin, commemorates Cecilia.[4] The office taken
from a service of about the year 1130, makes the instruction concerning the offerings suitable to the occasion its most prominent
feature.[5]

The *Gallican Liturgies,* which also preserved a distinct type
until, by the command of Charlemagne, the Roman order of service was instigated, have an independent celebration of St.
Cecilia. This service is believed by Thomasius[6] to have been
in use in Gaul in the sixth century. It contains little of the
history of St. Cecilia and is chiefly an ascription of honor to the
saint and supplication for her intercession.[7]

The *Mozarabic Liturgy,* supposed to be the ritual of Southern
France and Spain at the beginning of the eighth century, and
attributed to Isidore of Seville, who lived until the latter part
of the seventh century, contains an elaborate office of St. Cecilia

---

1 A part of this service is as follows: X Kal. Dec. In die festivitatis hodiernæ, qua sancta Cæcilia
in tui nominis confessione martyr effecta est. Quæ dum humanis devota nuptiis, thalamos temp-
orales contemneret, sponsum sibi, qui perpetuus esset, præsumto præmio castitatis adhibuit, & æterni-
tatem vitæ maluit, quam ut mundo procrearet originem. In cujus gloriam etiam illud accessit, ut
Valerianum, cui suerat matrimonii jure copulanda, in perpetuum sibi socians martyr casta confortium,
secum duceret ad coronam. Muratori, *Lit. Rom. Vet.* I. 456.

2 It begins, Sanctæ martyræ tuæ Cæciliæ supplicationibus tribue nos foveri: ut cujus venerabilem solemnitatem prævenimus obsequio; ejus intercessionibus commendemur. Per Dominum. Muratori, *Lit. Rom. Vet.* I. 672.

3 Deus, qui nos annua beatæ Cæciliæ martyris tuæ solemnitate lætificas: da, ut quam veneramur
officio, etiam piæ conversationis sequamur exemplo. Per &c.

Super oblata. Hæc hostia, Domine, placationis & laudis quæsumus, ut interveniente beata Cæcilia
martyre tua, nos propitiatione dignos semper efficiat. Per &c.

Ad complendum. Satiasti, Domine, familiam tuam muneribus sacris. Ejus semper intercessione
nos refove, cujus solemnis celebramus. Per &c. Muratori, *Vet. Lit. Rom.* II. 129; PATR. LAT. 78.

4 Erbes, *Die Heilige Cäcilia,* remarks, p. 11: "Ambrosius, Hieronymus und Prudentius, die so
viele anderen feiern, thun der Cäcilia keine Erwähnung."

5 In Sanctæ Cæciliæ, Ebdomadariis Solidi IV. & Denarii IV. Pro Calice cannata Vini. Custodi-
bus & Veglonibus, ut in Nativitate Sanctæ Mariæ. Muratori, *Antiquitates Italicæ,* (1741), IV. 930.

6 Josephus Thomasius, *Codices Sacramentorum.* Rom. 1680.

7 Venerabilem ac sublimem beatæ martyris Cæciliæ passionem, et sanctam solemnitatem pia devo-
tione celebrantes, conservatorem omnium Deum, fratres carissimi, deprecemur, etc. *Gallican Missal,*
Lib. III. XIV, in PATR. LAT. 72. 247.

for 22 November, both in the *Missale Mixtum* and the *Breviarum Gothicum.*[1] The former especially is more specific regarding the life and martyrdom of St. Cecilia than any church office yet considered. It mentions the penance of the hair-cloth garment, the attendance of the angels, the immortal flowers, the conversions of Valerian and Tiburtius, their martyrdom and ascent to glory. Urban's name is mentioned once, and St. Cecilia is recorded to have suffered martyrdom by fire. The place and time of her death are not mentioned.

Venantius Fortunatus (530-600?), one of Cecilia's earliest chroniclers, has placed her martyrdom in Sicily,[2] but has assigned no dates.[3] He also shows by his verses,[4] written at the consecration of the church of St. Andrew, by Vitalis, bishop of Ravenna, that Cecilia was commonly venerated in the sixth century. Brower[5] believes that Fortunatus received the impression that Cecilia had been born in Sicily from the fact that in his time she was held in especial veneration in that country.

Bede (673-735), was familiar with the life of St. Cecilia, and refers to her twice in the Ecclesiastical History.[6] Concerning his martyrology, which is of especial interest in this case, he says at the conclusion of Bk. V:—"A martyrology, concerning the festivals of the holy martyrs, in which all that I could find, not only on what day, but also in what form of strife and under what judge they prevailed over the world, I carefully wrote." The extracts from this martyrology are given in full.[7]

The Metrical Martyrology which was made in addition to this, in order to "imitate the method of the Holy Scripture

1 PATR. LAT. 85, 926; 86. 1051.

2 Cæciliam Sicula profert, Seleucia Teclam, *Carm. Lib.* VIII. 3. 171, PATR. LAT. 88.

3 " Fortunatus places her in Sicily *in the time of Commodus or Aurelius.*" *Dict. of Chr. Biog.*, Cecilia.

4 Sanctus Alexander felixque Cecilia pollent,
Quos meritis omnes una corona manet. *Carm. Lib.* 1, c. ii. 23-4, PATR. LAT. 88.

5 Forte in Sicilia, ætate Fortunati, sanctæ Ceciliæ memoria præcipuo honore colebatur quam cæteroquin Romanam matronam fuisse proditus est. *Fortun. Op.*

6 Cæcilia infestos læta ridet gladios, *Hymn to Virginity, Hist. Eccl.* IV. 18; also in the lines concerning the consecration of Wilbrord in the church of St. Cecilia at Rome. Ordinatus est autem in ecclesia sanctæ martyris Ceciliæ, die Natalis ejus, *Hist. Eccl.* V. 11.

7 XVIII. Kal. Maii. Romæ Tiburtii, Valeriani & Maximi, sub Almachio Urbis Præfecto: quorum primi fustibus cæsi & gladio sunt percussi, ultimus tamdiu plumbatis verberatus, donec spiritum redderet.

VIII. Kal. Junii. Romæ natale S. Urbani Papæ & Confessoris, cujus doctrina multi martyrio coronati sunt.

X. Kal. Decem. Natale S. Ceciliæ Virginis quæ & sponsum suum Valerianum & fratrem ejus Tiburtium ad credendum Christo ac martyrium perdocuit: & ipsa diende martyrizavit, ignem quidem superans, sed ferro occisa sub Almachio Urbis Præfecto.

Johannis Smith, Cambridge, 1722, *Martyrologium Bædae in 8 antiquis MSS. acceptum cum auctario Flori.*

in whose history poetical pieces in meter are often inserted,"
also refers to Cecilia.[1]

The English bishop Aldhelm (640?-709), mentions Cecilia
twice. His prose account[2] relates her musical powers, concerning which he approaches the modern conception of a Cecilia of
music and angels and flowers.

The *Liber Pontificalis* of Anastasius who died A.D.721, the sur-
viving document drawn from more ancient records and interest-
ing for its subsequent relations, mentions the martyrdom of
Cecilia[3] as one of the significants events of St. Urban's papacy.
The interdependence however of the Urban and Cecilia history
is such as to give to neither the value of separate and cor-
roborative testimony.

From the group of ninth century martyrologists,[4] when the
passion for investigation of church history was at its height,
Cecilia receives due and constant attention. From these sources
a connected story of her life in miniature begins to appear.

Rabanus Maurus (786-856), Archbishop of Mayence, who
compiled a martyrology based upon the *Liber Pontificalis* and
also upon the work of Bede, gives on X Kal. December the first
brief record of St. Cecilia.[5]

Odo, Archbishop of Vienna, toward the middle of the ninth
century compiled a calendar on the basis of the *Parvum
Romanum*, an old martyrology discovered by him and esteemed
of superior authenticity.[6] The account of Odo, since it elabor-
ates several points and adds some details, is of particular value

---

1 Cecilia merito decimis cum laude migravit. PATR. LAT. 94. 606.

2 . . . Quomodo Cecilia virgo sacratissima indulta jugalitatis consortia, ac pacta proci
sponsalia obtentu castitatis refutans, velut spurca latrinarum purgamenta laudabili spiritus fervore
contempserit, dispexerit, respuerit; quæ licet organica bis quinquagenis et ter quinis sonorum vocibus
concreparet harmonia. . . . Quamobrem . . . angelicis perfrui conspectibus fecit, quibus
cœlicola ab astris destinatus candidis ac purpureis contexta serta floribus obtulit: Istas, inquiens,
coronas immaculato et mundo corpore custodite, quia de paradiso Dei eas ad vos attuli. *De Laudibus
Virginitatis*. PATR. LAT. 89. 141.

3 Sanctus Urbanus. Anno Christi 226, Alex. imp. 4.
Urbanus, Natione Romanus, ex patre Pontiano, sedit annos octo, menses undecim, dies duode-
cim. . . . *Hic sua traditione multos convertit ad batismum et* credulitatem *etiam Valerianum*, nobilissimum virum, *sponsum sanctæ Cæcilæ*, quos etiam usque ad martyrii palmam per-
duxit, et per ejus monita *multi martyrio coronati sunt*. . . . *Qui* etiam *sepultus est in
coemeterio Prætextati, via Appia, VIII. Kal. Junias*. . . . PATR. LAT. 127. 1325.

4 For a discussion of the relation of these martyrologies to one another, see Preface to works of
Usuard. PATR. LAT. 123. 459-482.

5 Sanctæ Cecilæ, quæ et sponsum suum Valerianum, et fratem ejus Tiburtium ad credendum
Christo ac martyrium perdocuit, et ipsa deinde martyrizavit, ignem quidem superans, sed ferro occisa
sub Almachio urbis præfecto. PATR. LAT. 110. 1180.

6 The compilation was rendered further reliable he tells us, (Preface to Martyrology), from the
fact that manuscripts of the Acts of the Martyrs had been collected by him from all quarters.

in the study of the Acts of St. Cecilia. On X Kal. December is given an account which in abstract is as follows:

On the X Kal. December, Cecilia, the blessed virgin was born at Rome. She converted her husband Valerian and her brother Tiburtius to the faith, for which they endured martydom. Urban the Pope, moreover, as the result of her preaching, baptized no less than four hundred souls, among whom there was an illustrious man named Gordian.

Thereupon Almachius commanded that the blessed Cecilia be brought to him, and when she held true to the faith, he commanded further that she be conducted to her own home and burned to death in its bath.

Cecilia remained therein an entire day and night without injury, as if it had been a cold place. Hearing which, Almachius sent messengers who should behead her. These struck three blows but were not able to strike off her head. She lived after that for three days. Then St. Urban, bearing away her body by night buried it with the bodies of the popes. This blessed virgin lived during the times of the emperors Marcus Aurelius and Commodus.

On the XVIII. Kal. Maii in Rome, via Appia, in the cemetery of Prætextatus, the holy martyrs Tiburtius, Valerian, and Maximus under the prefect Almachius slain by the sword, (the last, beaten with leaden plumbets until he gave up the ghost).

On the VIII. Kal. Junii. In Rome, via Numentana, in the cemetery of Prætextatus. St. Urban, bishop and martyr, by whose teaching, in the time of the persecution of Alexander, many martyrs were crowned.

Usuard who compiled the martyrology which bears his name died in 876 or 877. The martyrology was adopted in most of the churches of France, Italy and Germany and is important since it became the basis of the Roman martyrology. He follows Maurus closely.[1]

During this period the Greek menologies continued to borrow the Latin legend. The great Menology of the Greeks,[2] and the Menology of Sirleti[3] follow Jerome's reference for 14 April and 22 November, and add that the martyr suffered under Diocletian (283-290).[4] The *Ephemerides*, the *Græcorum Metricus*,[5] and the *Martyologium Græcum* of Seberus also commemorate November 22.

The Greek Simeon Metaphrastes,[6] scribe to the emperor Leo VI. (886-911), in the tenth century compiled from many sources an important but unauthenticated[7] work which includes an elaborate account of St. Cecilia and her associates.[8]

1 Romæ, natalis sanctæ Ceciliæ virginis, quæ sponsum Valerianum et fratrem ejus Tiburtium ad credendum Christo ac martyrium perdocuit, et ipsa deinde martyrizata est, ignem quidem superans, sed ferro occisa. Passa est autem Marci Aurelii et Commodi imperatorum temporibus. PATR. LAT. 124.

2 *Menæa Magna Græcorum, die in textu notata*, Venetiis, 1528.

3 *Menologium Sirleti, ed.* Canisius Jac. Basnagius, *Thesaur. Monument.* III, p. 22, Nov. p. 400.

4 Lipsius, *Chron. der Röm. Bisk.* p. 51, observes that St. Cecilia was not first associated with the reign of Diocletian by the Greeks of the eleventh century, but that in the Latin Papal Records (MS. Berner 225) of the eighth or ninth century, Urban is mentioned in this connection.

5 X Kal. Dec. Δευτερί ἐιχᾶδι KIKIΛIAN τάμον ἀμφὶ λόετρον;—Ciciliam necat in balneo vicena secunda. Bollandus, *Acta Sanct.*1 Maii. Vol. 14, p. LIII. Henschen and Papebroke.

6 PATR. GR. 116. 3; Latin of Surius, *ed.* Lipomanus (see *Bibliography*).

7 Surius avoit de l'érudition, mais il donnoit tête baissée dan les fables, et manquoit de critique. L'Advocat, *Dict. Portatif.*

8 For a defense of the credibility of this compilation and its assignment to an earlier date, see Ceillier, *Hist. des Auteurs Sacrés*, Vol. II.

By Metaphrastus and Surius his translator, it is claimed that Urban I. was Bishop and Pope of the Christians at the time of Cecilia's death and consequently under the temporal rule of Alexander Severus (222-230). This in general is the accepted statement of the medieval legends.

Proceeding from the monasteries of England, in the time of Bede to the eleventh century there was a host of calendars and missals, in Latin, intended for the celebration of great festivals and fasts, Sundays and Saint's days. Of them all, only a few escaped the adversities of the time of King Edward VI (1547).[1]

The Sarum, York,[2] Bangor, and Hereford missals, drawn directly from the Sacramentaries of Leo, Gelasius, and Gregory, celebrate the office of St. Cecilia on her usual days.

The earliest English life of St. Cecilia is found in the martyrology attributed by Cockayne[3] and others to Alfred (849-901). The Old English text in full for both days is as follows:[4]

Nov. 22.

On þone XXII dæg þæs monðes byð sca cecilian þrowung þære halgan fæmnan. Seo wæs on hyre geogoðe æðelum were be weddod, *and* se wæs hæðen, *and* heo wæs cristen. Heo wæs ge gyred myd hæran æt hyre lychaman, *and* on ufan þære hæran heo wæs ge gyred myd golde awefenum hrægelum. *And* on þære nyhte þa heo wæs ingelæded on þone bryd bur, þa sæde heo þam brydguman þæt heo gesawe engel of heofenum, *and* se wolde hyne slean myd fær deaðe gif he hyre æfre onhryne myd unclænre lufon. Þa gelærde heo þone bryd guman, þæt he onfeng fullwyhte, *and* on god gelyfde. Þa he gefullod wæs *and* yn eode on þone bryd bur, þa stod se engel big hyre myd scynendum fyðerum; *and* hæfde twegen beagas on hys handa, þa glysnodon hwylum swa rosan blosman, hwylum swa lilian blostman; *and* þa sealde he oðerne þæra

---

1 Piper, *Die Kalendarien und Martyrologien der Angelsachsen*, Berlin, 1862, gives a valuable account of a group of these, including the Martyrologies of Bede.

2 The York Missal is as follows, (*Publ. Surtees Soc.*, 1872, II):

Sanctæ Cæciliæ, virginis et martyris. X. Kal. Dec.

Officium. Loquebar,

Oratio. Deus qui nos annua beatæ Cæciliæ martyris tuæ sollemnitate lætificas, da, ut quam veneremur officio, etiam piæ conversationis sequamur exemplo. Per Dominum.

Epistola. De virginibus præceptum.

Graduale. Audi filia. Alleluya *V.* Cantantibus organis Cæcilia virgo soli. Domino decantabat dicens. Fiat cor meum et corpus meum immaculatum ut non confundar.

Sequentia. Exsultemus, *ut in Communi.*

Evangelium. Simile est regnum cœlorum decem virginibus.

Offertorium. Offerentur, *majus.*

Secreta. Hæc hostia, Domine, placationis et laudis, quæsumus, ut interveniente beata Cæcilia martyre tua, nos tua propitiatione dignos semper efficiat. Per.

Communio. Confundantur.

Post communio. Satiasti, Domine, familiam tuam muneribus sacris, ejus semper intercessione nos refove, cujus sollemnia celebramus. Per.

3 We must conclude that this martyrology is of the age of Alfred; none of its materials are more recent; and it is further directly indebted to that king himself, and doubtless composed under his direction; it draws from Benedictine, Roman, English, and Syriac sources. Oswald Cockayne, *The Schrine*, p. 157.

4 For a translation see Skeat, *The Works of Geoffrey Chaucer*, Vol. IV. p. 489.

beaᵹa þære fæmnan, *and* oðerne þam brydᵹuman, *and* cwæð: "Healdað ᵹe þas beaᵹas myd clænlicum dædum, forþam ðe ic hiᵹ brohte ync of ᵹodes neorxna wanᵹe." Þeos fæmne ᵹeþrowode martyrdom for cryste. Almatheus hatte rome burᵹe ᵹerefa, he nydde hiᵹ þæt heo cryste wyð soce þa heo þæt ne ᵹe þafode, þa het he hiᵹ belucan on byrnendum baðe on þam heo wæs, dæᵹ *and* nyht, swa heo na ne ᵹeswætte. Þa eode hyre se cwellere to myd sweorde, *and* he hiᵹ sloh þrywa myd þam sweorde. *And* he ne myhte hyre þæt heafod of aslean. Ac heo ᵹe bæd hiᵹ to þam papan, se wæs haten urbanus, *and* þa, be foran þam papan, heo to dælde eall þæt hyre wæs, *and* hym ᵹesealde, *and* cwæð to hym: "Þyssa þreora daᵹa fæc ic me abæd æt dryhtne þæt ic þe þys sealde, þæt ðu ᵹe halᵹie myn hus to cyrcan." *And* þa on sende hyre ᵹast to ᵹode.

April 14.

On ðone feowerteoᵹðan[1] dæᵹ þæs monðes, bið þara haliᵹra ᵹebroðra tid. sče ualerianes *and* sče tiburties, ða allmachius rome burᵹe ᵹerefa nedde mid witum ðæt hi criste wiðsocan. Ða hi þæt ne ᵹeþafodan þa het he hi beheafdian. Þa se man ðe þæt sceolde behealdan þæt hi man beheafdade wepende *and* swerᵹende he sæde þæt he ᵹesawe heora sawle ᵹonᵹan ut of þæm lichoman fæᵹre ᵹefretwade. *And* þæt he ᵹesawe ᵹodes enᵹlas swa scinende swa sunne, *and* þa hi bæron to heofonum mid[2] hiora feðra flihte. *And* se mon ða ᵹelefde ᵹode, *and* he wæs [of] s[w]unᵹen on deað for criste, *and* his noma wæs maximus.

This, it will be seen, does not differ materially from the main line of Latin legends which have as their significant points Rome, Urban, Almatheus or Almachius, the attempted martyrdom of Cecilia by fire, her final execution, and her request that her home be hallowed for a church.

Just before the middle English period, and distinct in its literary qualities from the martyrologies and church uses which surround it, is the long account of Cecilia given by Ælfric (10th century)[3] in his Saints' Lives.[4] Cecilia is represented as a Roman virgin living in the days of the emperors "who cared not for Christ."[5]

Ælfric's version contains most of the material, including the theological arguments, of the finished legend as it appeared in the Middle Ages, in the Latin of Jacobus a Voragine, the French of De Vignay, the English of Caxton, Bokenam, and Chaucer, and the closely related family of monastic legends which overlaps both boundaries of the Middle English period.

---

1 ᵹ erased, MS.

2 Here begins an older copy in MS. Add. 23211 of two pages.

3 The date of Ælfric's birth is estimated as probably the year 955. c. II. p. 35, *Ælfric, A New Study of his Life and Works*, a doctoral thesis presented to the Philosophical Faculty of Yale University by C. L. White, Boston, 1898.

4 The life of St. Cecilia is to appear shortly (1898), in the fourth part (Vol. II) of *Ælfric's Saints' Lives*, edited for the E. E. T. S. by W. W. Skeat.

5 Iu on ealdum dagum wæs sum æðele mæden
Cecilia gehaten fram cild-hade cristen
On romana rica þa þa seo reðe ehtnys stod
On þæra casera dagum þe cristes ne gymdon.
—*Ælfric's Saints' Lives*, XXXIV, 1-4.

Among the ancient churches of Rome one of the first to be designated by a special title was the church of St. Cecilia across the Tiber, of which mention is made in the first Roman Synod held under Pope Symmachus in the year 499.[1] The church is mentioned again by Gregory the Great,[2] 590, in defining the movements of a great procession. It was dedicated under Pope Sixtus III (432-440),[3] and is supposed to occupy the site of St. Cecilia's house,[4] in compliance with her request.[5]

In 817 it became the duty of Pope Paschal to rebuild this church, which after three centuries was falling in ruins. In accordance with a not unusual custom, Pope Paschal celebrated the reconsecrating of the edifice by the translation of many bodies of martyrs from their first resting places in the now neglected catacombs, to places of more security and veneration. In this particular translation, the securement of the body of St. Cecilia for the church which bore her name became of peculiar moment.[6] Following the guidance of the old records, he searched for the body of the saint in the catacombs of Prætextatus on the Appian Way, but without success. He therefore abandoned the search upon the conclusion that her tomb had been rified during the invasion of Astulfus, king of the Lombards, in 755, but is said to have had a vision[7] of Cecilia which revealed to him the true locality of her resting place. "It is true," she said, "that the Lombards sought me, but the favor of my all-powerful friend, the mother of God, forever a virgin, protected me. She did not permit them to take me away, and I am now buried in the same place where I have always reposed." Again he sought, and this time *inter suos collegas*, in and about the papal crypt in the cemetery of Calixtus, and the explorations of De Rossi determine that the "Cecilian crypt," which abuts at its corner upon the papal crypt, was the place where Cecilia was found by Paschal in the year 821.[8]

1 Boll, *Act. Sanct.* 14 Apr. p. 203.

2 S. Greg. *Ep.* Lib. II. 2.

3 This is the conclusion reached by Erbes, *Die Heilige Cäcilia*, based upon De Rossi, *Rom. Sott.* II. 36.

4 La maison qu' habitaient les Valerii, et qui devait être celle des deux époux, était située en la XIVe région de Rome, dans le Transtévère. Guéranger, *Sainte Cécile*, p. 347.

5 . . . þat he scholde hire hous þat ȝe hadde woned Inne
    Halewen in oure louerdes name & þa churche þer higynne. ll. 249-50, MS. Laud 108.

6 The account of Paschal's work is preserved in the *Lib. Pontif.* of Anastasius. PATR. LAT. 128³, 1265.

7 Anast. *Lib. Pontif., Paschal*, § 437.

8 This is not the usual statement of hagiographers.
    . . . reperit in cœmeterio Prætextati situm foris portam appiam. Baronius, *Ann.* 821, § IV; Anast. *Lib. Pontif.* § 438.
    On raporte qu'il y fut trouvé . . . dans le cimetiere de Pretextat. Tillemont, III. 260.
    Il le trouva en effet dans le cimetiere de Pretaxtat en la voye Appienne. Fleury, Liv. XLVI. 41.
    Urban . . . buried her in the cemetery of *Calixtus;* . . . her body was found in the cemetery of *Prætextatus* adjoining that of Calixtus on the Via Appia. *Dict. of Chr. Biog., Cecilia.*
    She was buried in the same cemetery as her husband. Mrs. Jameson, *Sac. and Legend. Art*, II. 583.

The earlier archeologist Bosio (1629), endorses De Rossi.[1]

Anastasius' account[2] tells that the body was found uninjured by time, lying on the right side, the hands together, thrown forward and down, the knees slightly bent. She was clad in rich garments, her head enveloped in a covering which left only the chin and neck exposed, and linen cloths stained with blood were lying at her feet. Contrary to the custom of burial of that day, the body had been enclosed, Paschal asserts, in a cypress coffin. This he overspread with a covering of silk and deposited it incorrupt and beautiful in a marble sarcophagus under the new altar of the church of St. Cecilia in Trastevere, together with the bodies of Valerian, Tiburtius and Maximus, which he secured with little difficulty from the lately restored cemetery of Prætextatus' across the Appian Way, and the body of Pope Urban I, from the papal crypt of the cemetery of Calixtus.

In honor of these saints Paschal founded a monastery[4] near the church of St. Cecilia, where the sacred offices were celebrated day and night.

Gregory VII, in the eleventh century, revived the memory of the sacred relic by renewing the altar of the church and erecting a silver statue of the virgin (1075).

It was under this altar five centuries after the time of Paschal, that the body of St. Cecilia was found by Cardinal Sfondrati of the title of St. Cecilia, October 20, 1599.

The account of this discovery is given in a long description by Baronius who was commissioned by Clement VIII, pope at the time, to examine and report the remarkable occurrence. He alleges[5] that her body was taken from its place still incorrupt and answering perfectly to the description given by Pope Paschal five hundred years before. The body in its cypress case was carefully enclosed in a second case of silver and re-deposited with such supreme veneration that they forbore to touch even the tissue covering which Paschal had thrown over the figure. Above the altar was placed this inscription which may still be read :

1 Quella parte del cimiterio di Calisto, dove fù sepellito il corpo della gloriosa, e inuitta martiri Santa Cecilia. *Rom. Sott.* Lib. III. c. XV.

2 *Lib. Pontif.* §§ 438, 439, 440. PATR. LAT. 128[9].

3 . . . ecclesiam (cryptam) beati Tiburtii et Valeriani atque Maximi. . . . Martyrum foris portam Appiam uno cohærentes loco restauravit. *Lib. Pontif.* Adrian I. 772-795.

4 Fleury, *Hist. Eccl.*, Liv. xlvi. 841, and Bosio, *Rom. Sott.* p. 44: Monasterium b. Gregorii atque ss. virginum seu martyrum Agathæ et Cæciliæ juxta ipsius ecclesiam construximus.

5 Baron. *Ann.* 821. §§ xvi-xxv.

CORPVS S. CÆCILIÆ VIRGINIS ET MARTYRIS
A CLEMENTE VIII. PONT. MAX INCLVSVM
ANNO M. D. IC. PONT. VIII.

followed by an account from which these lines are taken:

'Hic requiescit corpus S. Cæciliæ virginis et martyris, quod a Paschali primo Pont. Max. ipsa revelante, repertum, et in hanc ecclesiam translatum. et sub hoc altari una cum corporibus SS. Martyrum Lucii et Urbani Pontificum, necnon Valeriani, Tiburtii et Maximi reconditum, iterum post annos fere octingentos, Clement. VIII, Pont. Max. cum iisdem SS. Martyribus lucem aspexit, die xx. Octobris, anno Dominicæ Incarnationis MD.IC.'

Over the saint's tomb was placed the celebrated recumbent statue of "St. Cecilia lying dead " executed by Stefano Maderno, a sculptor in the employ of the cardinal, who, according to the inscription,[1] had himself seen the body when it was exhumed.

Such is the ancestry of the Cecilia legend and the history of her relics, now traced to medieval times; a considerable body of testimony to, at least, the faithful acceptance of the story through these centuries and the long and continuous endeavor to secure its perpetuation. There can be little doubt from such witnesses, that the Acts of St. Cecilia rest upon a basis of fact. It is also doubtless the case that pious exaggeration and misapprehension, together with errors fixed by centuries of historical inaccuracy and insufficiency, have together conspired to produce a medieval account which, as it stands, is antagonistic to its own veracity. To disentangle the false from the true involves a piece of argumentation which might be a fruitless task, were it not that the facts of St. Cecilia's life involve closely matters and personages otherwise of historic interest.

St. Cecilia is reported by Fortunatus to have died in Sicily; by the Greeks, to have suffered in Rome under Diocletian (284-305); by Metaphrastes, in Rome under Alexander Severus (222-230); by Odo, Usuard, and Bede in Rome under the Emperors Marcus Aurelius and Commodus (176-180). The medieval legends, as may be seen, follow in these respects the general account of Metaphrastes and the majority of the Latin versions.

The first difficulty then is a chronological one.

As far as can be known, the assignment of a date is all inferential on the part of the several writers. The time of St. Cecilia's martyrdom is determined by the uniform reference to her close association with Urban, and this Urban whom the Acts designate

---

1 En tibi sanctissimæ virginis Cæciliæ imaginem quam ipse integram in sepulchro jacentem vidi, eandem tibi prorsus eodem corporis situ hoc marmore expressi.

as Pope, was Bishop of Rome under the Emperor Alexander Severus, who ruled from 222 to 235. Urban was elevated to his position about the time of Alexander's accession.[1]

The Acts maintain that at the time of St. Cecilia the Christians were undergoing severe persecution, so much so that the pope himself was obliged to live in hiding, the bodies of martyred Christians were refused burial, and an acknowledgment of the Christian faith was punishable with death. Now of such a persecution on the part of Alexander Severus, no record exists, though it must here be granted that the early accounts of his reign are inadequate. An auspicious calm is supposed to have been enjoyed by the Christians throughout Alexander's reign.[2] They were allowed to build churches[3]; many of the rules for the government of the church were esteemed worthy of incorporation into the law of the Empire[4], and even the household of Alexander was said to have included many who professed the Christian faith.[5] One of these was apparently[6] Mammæa herself, mother of the Emperor, and Alexander, from his desire to erect a temple to Christ,[7] seemed disposed to give the Christian God recognition among the pagan deities.

There must be admitted also to this examination, the probable character and influence of Alexander's counsel. Foremost among the advisors of the youthful Emperor and his mother was Ulpian, a man of integrity and power in the time of Septimus Severus (202–211). This man, it is held,[8] cherished a conservative spirit of unfriendliness toward the Christians, and it has been possible therefore to attribute to his influence the persecution and martyrdom, not of Cecilia and her associates alone, but of five thousand Roman Christians![9] Here our faith is something baffled, for while it is possible to believe that the spirit of the times during the life of Alexander would have given little heed to a local or temporary relapse to the old

---

1Tillemont, basing his conclusion upon Baronius, *Ann.* 226, §§ 1; 12; places Urban's accession in the year 223 or 224. See *Hist. Eccl.* iii, pp. 258, 682. Lipsius, *Chron. du Röm. Bish.* considers 222 the probable date. The Bollandists give the following: Tempus martyrii ex sede S. Urbani Papæ sciri potest, quem sedisse ab anno CCXXII, quo Callistus decessor passus est, usque ad annum CCXXX quo. S. Pontianus ei successit, alibi deducimus. *Acta Sanct.* May 25.

2Gibbon, *Decl. and Fall*, Vol. I. c. vi.

3Origin, *In Matth. hom.* xxviii, and Lamprid., *Alex. Aug. Hist.* 49. The subject is discussed by Fr. Görres, *Zeitschr. f. wissenschaftl. Theol.* xx. 68, and Erbes, *Zeitschr. f. Kirchengesch.* ix. 50.

4Lamprid. *Alex. Aug. Hist.* v. 230.

5Eusebius, *Hist. Eccl.* Lib. vi. 28, 228.

6Paulus Orosius, *Hist.* Lib. vii. 18.

7Lamprid. *Alex.* v. 129.

8 Lactant. *Divinar. Instit.*, Lib. v. ii.

9 Henschen, *Acta Sanct.* 14 April, 471, 474.

severity, the presumable gentleness and purity of the reign will not permit on any known ground, belief in the existence of a Christian persecution of such proportions.

That the matter could have remained unnoticed is the more improbable on account of the high rank of the *gens Cæcilia*[1] and the *gens Valeria*.[2]

There can be but little doubt that St. Cecilia "ibore," as the legend tells, "of noble kynde," and Valerian "of gret nobleye and of richesse," belonged to these families,[3] though a non-conclusive fact to the contrary, is the omission of her name from the list of 139 (15 women) names of this *gens* cited in a recent publication.[4]

These things being so, can the incidents of the Cecilia story, making allowance for some natural growth in the way of exaggeration, be considered an unofficial (as regards Alexander,) act of Alexander's reign?

The direct persecutor of the Christians according to the written acts, was not Alexander, (a circumstance which endorses the assumption that Alexander was recognized as disassociated from direct connection with the persecution), nor any of Alexander's known counsellors, but Almachius, according to the Bollandists, *Turcius* Almachius, prefect of the city of Rome during the Emperor's absence at one of the engagements of the Persian War[5] which was being waged intermittently throughout this period. The office of prefect during the reign of Alexander was one of authority. Forty chosen magistrates formed his counsel.[6] The names of many notable men of the time (among others, Gordian, who figures in some of the legends as a friend and convert of Cecilia's,) have been preserved by the compilations of Tillemont,[7] but error has perhaps connived with chance in leaving the name of this man, if he ever did

---

1 Cæcilus(ursprüngliche Form *Caicilios*,griechisch Καιχθιος und Κεχθιος),plebeisches Geschlecht, dessen bedeutendster Zweig die Metelli waren.   Die Sagen, die es auf Cæculus, den mythischen Gründer von Præneste, oder auf Cæcas, einen Gefährten des Æneas zurückführen (Fest. *cp*, 44), sind in später Zeit aufgebracht worden. Pauly, *Realencycl. d. Class Alterthw.* 5te *h.f. b.* 1897. p. 1174.

2 . . . . la gens Valeria, issue de Valérius Publicola, cette famille était une des anciennes gloires de Rome, et, plus d'une fois dans le passé, ses membres s' étaient unis aux Metelli. Dom Guéranger, *Saint Cécile*, p. 347, Paris, 1875.

3 She (Cecilia) was descended from a very ancient family which dated back to the time of Tarquin the Proud; she belonged to the same house as Metella, many of whose children were raised to the honors of triumph and the consulate in the heyday of the Roman Republic. Paul Lacroix, *Mil. and Rel. Life in the Mid. Ages*, p. 406.

4 Pauly, *Real Encycl. der Class. Alterthw. herausg. v. Georg Wissowa, Stuttgart*, 1897.

5 Not necessarily as late as 930, the date given in *Dict. of Chr. Biog., Cæcilia*.

6 Tillemont, *Hist, des Emp.* III. 178.

7 *Hist. des Emp.* III. 162.

exist, unknown.[1] The list of Roman prefects is broken at the point where this inquiry makes it available.

The prefect of Cecilia's time, whoever he was, did not recognize Cecilia for her high birth, nor, this being affirmed, did he hesitate to extend to her the penalty of the law. This in itself is not an unusual occurrence, for these virgin martyrs, whether reputed so to increase the dramatic features of the episode, or in accordance with fact, were often people of rank and distinction. Such martyrdoms are, of course, frequent in history. It is, however, a consideration worthy of attention, that this, an execution of some importance, failed to reach the cognizance of Alexander Severus, and of his biographers.

The martyrdom of Cecilia clashes certainly with no historic conditions of Christian favoritism if placed either earlier in the reign of Aurelius and Commodus, according to the testimony of Odo and Usuard, or later in the reign of Diocletian, according to the Greeks. The Greek account, probably more remote from the true sources and more subject to change through transmissions, is not sustained by later critics.

On the other hand critics of importance[2] are more and more overlooking the assertions of the medieval legend,[3] Latin and English, and on the authority of the ninth century martyrologists, transferring the authentic parts of the story to the time of the philosopher Aurelius and his son Commodus, when the persecutions of the Christians were, strangely, so prominent.

Tillemont combines the authority of Odo and Usuard with the old reference of Fortunatus, '*Cæciliam Sicula profert,*' and believes the saint to have suffered martyrdom in Sicily about the year 178, and that her body was later transferred to Rome.[4]

---

1 " Au P. Sirmond, (*Mercatorius, Opera,* I, 260), un nom suspect de faux, parcequ'il n'est ni grec, ni latin." Tillemont, *Hist. Eccl.* III, 688. Lipsius, *Chron. der Röm. Bisb.,* says that the name of the Turcian family was not associated with the persecution of Christian martyrs until about the end of the fourth century, and that at no time in their record does the name Turcius Almachius appear among them. Corsini, *De Præfectis,* p. 364, mentions a prefect about the year 492 who bore the name Turcius Rufius Apronianus Asterius, whom Erbes, *Die Heilige Cäcilia,* cites as a possible original of the prefect of the legend.

2 De Rossi, *Roma Sott.* XXXII-XLIII, 113-161 ; Erbes, *Zeitschr. f. Kirchengesch.* IX, *Die Heilige Cäcilia;* Fr. Görres, *Zeitschr. f. Wissenschaftl. Theol.* XX, *Alex. Severus und das Christenthum;* Northcote and Brownlow, *Roma Sott.,* London, 1879; Bosio, *Historia passionis S. Cæciliæ,* Rom., 1860; Laderchio, *Acta S. Cæciliæ,* Rome, 1722. Dom Guéranger, *Saint Cécile et la Société Romaine,* Paris, 1875. B. Aubé, *Les Chretiens dans l'empire Romain de l'an* 180-249, Paris, 1881, p. 252-317.

3 See NOTES, l. 257.

4 Nous ne croyons pas mesme qu'ils nous puissent assurer que Ste Cecile ait jamais vu S. Urbain, y ayant assez d'apparence, qu'elle a esté martyrisée en Sicile des le temps de M. Aurele et de Commode, vers l'an 178, *Hist. Eccl.* III. 260.

Il y a donc assez d'apparence qu'elle a souffert effectivement en Sicile, et que son corps ayant esté transporté à Rome des les premiers siecles, *Hist. Eccl.* III. 690.

To accept either of the theories, however, involves a new difficulty. Pope Urban I certainly lived at a later period and under the rule of Alexander Severus. To satisfy this point, these critics point out the fact that history shows two Urbans,[1] one a pope, the other a bishop of an outlying Roman district. The latter was undoubtedly martyred for the cause about the year 180,[2] and buried on the Nomentan Road opposite the Appian Way.[3] The proximity of the crypt of St. Cecilia to the papal crypt, where Pope Urban was interred, they consider a plausible reason for the later confounding of the two Urbans and the association of the name of Cecilia with that of the pope. The accounts of Pope Urban's martyrdom they consider a feature transferred to this from the Cecilia legends, and original with the Cecilia legends rather than with the history of Urban. The medieval legend of Cecilia, it is well to remark, does not in any extant form contain an allusion to Pope Urban's untimely death, though it does intimate that he was subject to such persecution,[4] and this confusion of names and circumstances, if confusion it is, has existed, as has been shown, in the martyrologies from a very early period.[5]

For the confirmation or rejection of their hypotheses, later critics are able to draw upon the the accumulating information of antiquarians and Roman archeologists. Two recently discovered itineraries may first be made of service. These itineraries record the topography of the streets and catacombs of Rome at about the seventh century, before the practice of transferring bodies from their original resting places began. These two notable records, the older probably the Itinerary found at Salzburg,[6] and the other incorporated by William of Malmesbury (1143) into the *Gesta Regum Anglorum*,[7] mention the tomb of Cecilia, and locate it close to the tomb of the popes.

---

1 Mais comme il y a eu tres peu de martyrs sous Alexandre: cette raison et d' autres encore, donnent lieu de croire qu'on l'a confondu avec un martyr de mesme nom. Tillemont, *Hist. Eccl.* III. 259.

2 Lipsius, *Chron. der Röm. Bisch.* objects to the theory of their having been an earlier bishop Urban, resident at Rome, as unsupportable and improbable.

3 Tillemont, *Hist. Eccl.* III. 686.

4 " Is þat Vrban,"quaþ tiburs, "þat so ᵹerne haþ be souᵹth
þat þare haþ be fleme *and* hud? *and* ᵹif he were forþ brouᵹth,
ffor-berne he scholde, *and* we also, ᵹif we wiþ him were: " *MS.* Laud 108, *ll.* 119-122.

5 See citations in this article from martyrologies of Jerome, Odo, Bede.

6 The Salzburg list is as follows: Primus Sixtus et papa martyr, Dionysius p. et m., Julianus, p. et m., Flavianus, m., S. Cæcilia virgo et martyr, LXXX martyres ibi requiescunt.
In eadem via (Appia) ad Aquilonem ad SS. martyres Tiburtium et Valerianum et Maximum. Ibi invenies S. Urbanum, episcopum et confessorem . . . Eadem via ad S. Cæciliam ubi innumerabilis multitudo martyrum. *Notitia Portarum, Viarum, Ecclesiarum, circa Urbem Roman., Rom. Sott.,* De Rossi, I. 155.

7 Via Appia ecclesia S. Cæciliæ martyris et ibi reconditi sunt (by name, 11) papa, (by name, 6) martyres, *Gesta Regum Anglorum, ed.* Hardy, Vol. II. p. 539; *ed.* Stevenson (1854), *Bk.* IV. § 352. p. 301.

These adjacent tombs have received most careful and scholarly
investigation through the explorations of De Rossi, who demon-
strates[1] that the Cecilian crypt, not later than the year 500, was
the resting place of one whom we have every right to believe
was St. Cecilia. He conjectures from inscriptions that the
tract of land occupied by the Calixtan cemetery had been in use
by the Cæcilian gens since the first half of the third century.
A vacant recess, in the wall opposite the papal side, he believes
to have been the spot where the saint was interred. By the
side of the recess is a painting which De Rossi attributes to the
seventh century. It represents a woman richly attired, a halo
about her head, her hands extended and in the background a
profuse decoration of roses. Near this is a fresco of the Lord
and a figure of a bishop with the name S. VRBANVS, inscribed
below. Certain *graffiti* on the walls of the tomb near the recess,
which record the names of priests of the ninth century, are to
be taken, De Rossi believes, as the official seal set at time of the
transferance of the body by Paschal I.

The Acts are generally agreed in saying that the bodies of
Valerian, Tiburtius, and Maximus, were taken to the cemetery of
Prætextatus for burial. De Rossi has discovered in the crypt
of St. Cecilia a tablet to the memory of a Septimius Prætextatus Cæcilianus, a Christian. The occurrence of this name, he
believes, suggests a relation between the families, and accounts
for the fact, that, while St. Cecilia of the blood of the *Cæcilii*
found burial in the tomb of her *gens*, her husband and his
brother were layed not far away, but in a tomb of less importance, where Cecilia's relationship gave her access.

The picture of Cecilia, however, was not the first with which
the tomb was decorated. Traces of older mosaic may be detected on the edges and underneath the present paintings.
This fact, together with the lateness of the date of the paintings, that of St. Urban being perhaps of the 12th century, points
to two conclusions,(1), that the tomb continued to be held in veneration even after, as is generally admitted, the bodies were re-
moved by Pope Paschal; (2),that the tomb was not the saint's first
resting place, and that the seventh century painting commemorates either directly or remotely some translation to this place
from Prætextatus or Sicily or wherever it might have been
that the saint was first buried.

On the basis of Odo's Martyrology then, and by the aid of later

---

1 *Rom. Sott.* III. 628, *et seq.*

explorations on the site of the legend, the following statement
may be secured. Cecilia died in 176-180 under the Christian
persecutions of Aurelius and Commodus. There is some historic foundation for an earlier Urban, who satisfies the requirements as to proximity and position sufficiently to have been
the friend and advisor of Cecilia. That on account of the fierce
persecutions of the time, a record of such individual martyrdoms as those of Cecilia, Valerian, Tiburtius, Maximus, and
Urban, were probably never made. That Almachius still
remains a historic enigma, and that many features of the legend
in the light of subsequent investigation, viz., a late emblematic
design on the tomb of Maximus, parallelism between the
theological arguments of the Acts and the writings of Augus-
tine and Victor Vitensis' (5th century), and the probably late
autocracy of the Turcian family, point to an origin later than
the second century, for certain features of the story.

To assume the composite nature of this, in common with
many similar legends, is probably the most legitimate solution
of the difficulties. The outline of the story, which may be regarded as reasonably authentic, has been modified and enlarged
by other items, perhaps historic in themselves, incorporated in
the whole through the natural inaccuracy of a scribe, who
writes at a distance from his subject and attempts to reduce
legendary material to historic form. Logic can probably never
smooth the present discrepancies of the legend. History may
some day contribute an element which will modify or enlighten.

To the modern mind St. Cecilia is well known in literature,
art and music. Perhaps along these lines the subject merits
a few words.

St. Cecilia is universally regarded as the patroness of musicians.[2] Her musical attributes as commonly accepted, are given
in their length and breadth by Mrs. Jameson.[3]

" As she excelled in music, she turned her gifts to the glory of God, and
composed hymns, which she sang herself with such ravishing sweetness, that
even the angels descended from heaven to listen to her."
" She played on all instruments, but none sufficed to breathe forth that
flood of harmony with which her whole soul was filled; therefore she invented
the organ, consecrating it to the service of God."

There is record of a musical society established in Louvain
in 1502 which bore the name of the Saint, and in Rome, an

1 See Erbes, Die Heilige Cäcilia.
2 A discussion on this subject was carried on in Notes and Queries, 3rd Series, II and III.
3 Sacred and Legend. Art, II. 202.

Academy of Music was dedicated to her patronage in 1584. Since 1571, the first authenticated occasion upon which St. Cecilia's day was celebrated by musical performances, many learned organizations have been formed for the same purpose. The practise was first adopted in England in 1683, when a musical society was incorporated which held a series of musical festivals on November 22. Similar musical celebrations became frequent throughout England, Italy, Germany, France, Scotland, and Ireland, until innumerable musical societies and celebrations have been and are being named in her honor.

For these occasions music has been adapted to Dryden's *Ode to St. Cecilia's Day*, and *Alexander's Feast*, to Pope's *Ode to St. Cecilia*, and to other less known poems, by such composers as Handel, Henry Purcell, and John Blow. Several full masses have also been composed for the Society of Artist Musicians at Paris by Adam, Niedermeyer, Dietsch, Gounod, and Ambroise Thomas.[1]

It is evident from the Acts that this idea has grown from a very casual reference. It is there related that when all were making merry "with mouth and menstralsy" at the wedding festivities, Cecilia went apart from the rest and sang in her heart the song of David, *Fiat cor meum immaculatum in tuis justificationibus ut non confundar* (Ps. 119, 80).

The versions, it is true, do not all assert that song was only in her heart and unexpressed, but at most, song with Cecilia was a passing and not essential characteristic of temperament,[2] suggestive, certainly, of no inventive activity on her part which would lead to the construction of the reed instrument known as the organ. It would indeed be a loss to much of the higher significance of the legend if the exalted, spiritual penetration of Cecilia were allowed to be devoted to so material ends.

Moreover the reference to music is quite as marked in connection with other saints of the calendar. It was the words '*cantantibus organis*,' undoubtedly, which originally gave the wrong impression and suggested the association of Cecilia with the organ as an instrument of praise.

Her miraculous power of drawing an angel from Heaven appears in the Acts as a power she held indeed, but not by

---

1 Grove, *Dict. of Music and Musicians*, I, 329. Mendel-Cossoni, *Musikal. Convers. Lex.* II, 270.
2. See NOTES, I. 11.
3 *cf. Berliner Musikztg. Echo*, 10, 1870.
4 The organ is mentioned in *Job* XXI, 12, and *Ps*. CL. 4. The Pandean Pipes, so called, record in their name a current Greek and Roman belief as to this primitive form of organ. An ancient organ consisting of a series of pipes and a wind chest is carved on a monument in the Museum at Arles with the date xx.M.viii. See Chappell, *Hist. of Music*.

reason of her gift of song, rather, on account of her purity of
life, which gave her command over things celestial.

To further establish the popular belief it may also have been
that the praises to Cecilia, inaugurated by Paschal at the com-
pletion of his act of veneration, were of a conspicuously musical character.[1] This might even have created the impression
that the services were chosen for their special significance
to the life of Cecilia. The most signal recognition of such
association is chronicled in art by Raphael about the close of
the 15th century. In this familiar painting, Cecilia is represented with a small reed instrument in her hands, while at her
feet lie the broken and rejected instruments of secular music.

Previous to the fifteenth century the early mural paintings
in the Catacomb of San Lorenzo (6th or 7th cent.), the niche of
St. Cecilia in the Catacomb of Calixtus, the colossal mosaic of the
Byzantine painters of about the time of Paschal I, the tryptich
of Cimabue in the chapel of St. Cecilia at Florence, and the
decorations of Fra Angelico, had portrayed the more dramatic
scenes from the life of the virgin martyr, and in portraiture had
given her the palm branch and book as distinctive emblems.

During, and after the fifteenth century, the pictures of St.
Cecilia with the organ or singing are frequent. One of the
earliest of these representations is by Van Eyck (1370), followed
by Garofalo, Van Leyden, Luini, Paulo Veronese, Salimbeni,
Giulio Campi, Guido Reni, Domenichino, Moretto, and Carlo
Dolci. Romanelli in the middle of the 17th century represented
her with a violin. Coincident with this, there continued to be
representations of historic scenes from her life. In these, the
wreaths of roses and lilies, the attendant angel, and the palm
branch betokening her victory are occasionally introduced.
Such are the paintings of Raphael, who treats the subject a second time, the fresco of Francia, and the paintings of Procaccini,
Pinturicchio, Spada, Poussin, Dominique, and Giulio Romano.[1]

In literature Cecilia first appears in the ascriptions of praise
to virginity and the like, of the Latin hymn writers. The
earliest of these poems is one attributed to Paulinus of Nola
(353-431), a writer of ascetic verse. Aldhelm, in the seventh
century, celebrates the holy Cecilia in verse in the *De Laudibus*

---

1 This is claimed by Baillet, *Vies des Saintes*, Nov. 22.

2 Mrs. Jameson, *Sac. and Legend. Art*, II. 202-210. Dom Guéranger, *Sainte Cécile*.

Virginitatis[1] and makes one of the earliest allusions to her musical powers.

From the ninth century a number of hymns have survived. One of these is in the *Breviarum Gothicum*.[2] In the same century, a Latin hymn by Prudentius of Troy (861) is recorded, and one by Wandelbert (813-870), poet and priest of Treves. The reference to Cecilia forms part of the so-called metrical martyrology[3] of the latter. In the tenth century there is a hymn of about two hundred lines written by Flodoardus.[4]

With an Italian poem entitled *La Trionfatrice Cecilia, Vergine e Matiri Romana*, by Castelletti, 1594, begins a more modern series of odes and lyrics. Santeuil (1630-1697), the most celebrated of modern Latin poets, has written three hymns to her honor. All of these have little to do with historic matters, but they preserve another slender line of perpetuity for the legend, until the time when the celebrated odes of Addison, Dryden, and Pope, with those of a host of minor poets, Shadwell, Congreve, D'Urfey, Hughes, Yalden, and Barry Cornwell, do much to immortalize but little to elucidate the name and fame of Cecilia. The Welsh poet, Lewis Morris, in a recent poem of some ascetic fervor,[5] follows the tradition quite closely.

Tennyson's picture in the *Palace of Art* must be chiefly an original conception:

> There, in a clear walled city on the sea
> Near gilded organ-pipes—her hair
> Bound with white roses—slept St. Cecily;—
> An angel looked at her!

---

[1] A part of the poem is given:

> Porro Cæciliæ vivacem condere laudem
> Quæ valeat digne metrorum pagina versu?
> Quamvis harmoniis præsultent organa multis,
> Musica Pierio resonent et carmina cantu;
> Non tamen illexit fallax præcordia mentis
> Pompa profanorum, quæ nectit retia sanctis,
> Ne forte properet paradisi ad gaudia miles.
> Angelus en, inquit, superis tranavit ab astris:

PATR. LAT. 89. 268.

[2] There are about eighty lines. It begins,

> Inclyti festum pudoris
> Virginis Cæciliæ
> Gloriosa præcinamus
> Voce prompti pectoris,

PATR. LAT. 86, 1252.

[3] It is in hexameters and runs as follows:

> Cæcilia illustrat denam mox sancta nitore,
> Perpetuo claris semper vulganda tropæis,
> Virgo hinc cognato, sanctoque hinc fulta marita.

PATR. LAT. 121. 619.

[4] Given in PATR. LAT. 135. 661.
[5] *A Vision of Saints*, London, 1890.

II.

HISTORY AND ARRANGEMENT OF THE VERSIONS.

The Cecilia Legend is preserved in the following Middle-English manuscripts:

MS. Ash(mole) 43	1300
MS. Stowe 946	1340
MS. Cott(on) Cleop(atra) D IX	14th C.
MS. Laud 108 (appendix)	15th C.
MS. Lamb(eth) 223	1400
MS. Trin(ity) Coll(ege) C(am)br(idge) R 3. 25	1400
{ MS. Cott(on) Tib(erius) E VII	1400
} MS. Harl(ey) 4196	1400
MS. Bodl(ey) 779	15th C.
MS. (Barbour, Cambridge Univ. Lib.) Gg. II. 6	15th C.

It is also found in the Early English of Alfred's *Book of Martyrs*, in Ælfric, *Saints' Lives* MS. Cott(on) Jul(ius) E VII, in the *Second Nonnes Tale* of Chaucer, 1373, in Osbern Bokenam's *Lives of Saints*, MS. Arundel 327, 1443–6, and in Caxton's *Golden Legend*, 1483. There is, besides these English Lives, the Greek of Simeon Metaphrastes in the translation into Latin by F. L. Surius, the Latin of Jacobus a Voragine (1290), the Medieval French of Jehan de Vignay (1300), and a Middle High German version in the editions of (1) Köpke, (2) Schönbach, and (3) Pfeiffer (prose), all of the 14th century.

This edition seeks to incorporate in some accessible form all of the Middle English versions. Of these MS. Ash. and MS. Cott. Tib. E VII are made the central texts, MS. Ash. for the reason that it is probably the oldest of existing versions, and MS. Cott. Tib. E VII because it represents the distinct type of the later Northern group. About these central texts the related versions or redactions are grouped. In cases where it has been practicable the hitherto unprinted versions are given in this edition as variants of the central text. The Latin of Voragine is given in full for comparison, since it may be considered a contemporaneous and independent version.

Of almost equal age with MS. Ash. is the mass of the collection in MS. Laud which as a whole is probably the older of the two. Horstmann assigns the date 1285–95 to the latter. Some estimates place it earlier. The life of Cecilia however which is given in the appendix to this manuscript is one of three *Vitæ* which are written in a later hand, assigned by Horstmann to the fifteenth century, making it therefore contemporary with MSS. Lamb., Trin. Coll., and Cott. Tib.

The authorship of MS. Ash. is sometimes attributed to Robert of Gloucester, and placed as early as the last quarter of the thirteenth century,[1] and is, therefore, the oldest and leading manuscript of this legend. It contains 94 legends including several readings from the *Temporale*.[2]

MS. Stowe 946,[3] formerly 669, is in the King's Library of the British Museum. It contains only the latter half of MS. Ash., 35 legends, beginning with *St. Michael*.

In point of date, MS. Vernon Bod. Lib. Oxf. (1380), which originally contained the Cecilia legend, should be next mentioned. An index of the MS. shows *'seynt Cecile virgyne'* for *fol.* 62. This unfortunately lies within one of *lacunæ* of the MS. (*fol.* 57–64) where leaves have been lost.

Only a fragment of MS. Cott. Cleop. D IX[4] containing the

---

1 Kölbing, *Eng. Stud.* I. p. 216.

2 Horstmann, *Einl., Alteng. Leg.* 1875, p. vii, gives the following description of the manuscript: MS. Ash. 43, in der Bodley'schen Bibliothek zu Oxford, früher dem Silas Taylor gehörig, Pergament, Quart., eine der werthvollsten Legenden-handschriften, ist gleichfalls im Anfang defekt, da die drei ersten Blätter, mit der *Circumcisio* und *Epiphania domini, Hillarius* und dem Anfang von *Wolstan*, ausgefallen sind; es beginnt mit *fol.* 4 und zählt 269 *fol.*, von denen jedoch *fol.* 151 doppelt numerirt ist. Die letzten Blätter, mit dem Schlusse von *Thomas Beket* und *S. Edward*, haben sehr durch Brand gelitten, *fol.* 265–269 sind fast ganz zerstört (nur kleine Läppchen sind noch übrig). Ueberschriften finden sich am obern Rande nur bis *S. Peter*, von späterer Hand; Bezeichnungen am Anfang der Legenden fehlen. Bei einzelnen finden sich Notizen am Rande von späterer Hand. Ein Inhaltsverzeichniss fehlt; doch findet sich ein solches zu MS. Ash. 43 auf einem Blatte im MS. Ash. 50 (welches jedoch keine Legenden enthält) von späterer Hand, und zwar von *S. Wolstan* an; es kann also erst nach dem Ausfalle der ersten Legenden angefertigt sein.

3 The legends contained therein have been discussed with extracts taken from the beginning and end of each, by E. Stiehler, Anglia, VII. 405. He believes the MS. belongs to an earlier period than the end of the 14th century, according to the Stowe catalogue notice. He discovers that the MS. is also undoubtedly the work of three different hands. The meter and general form show it to be closely related to MS. Ash. The MS. is not paged and contains, not 294 leaves (according to Stowe Catalogue) but 304. The titles of the legends, some in Latin, some in Old English are given on the top margin of each sheet. There are many glosses in Latin and modern English by the hand of Thomas Astle, Keeper of the Records in the Tower. Different parts of the MS. are not equally well preserved, many of the pages being torn and injured. There are only a few colored initial pages. Stiehler points out that the history of the separate legends of the collection varies considerably.

4 Vellum, XIV Century. Folio ff. 7, 40 l. to a page, Brit. Museum. The volume contains various chronicles and other historic documents including a fragmentary copy of the S. Eng. Legendary. Ward, *Cat. of MSS.* Vol. II. MS. Cotton Jul. D. IX in Brittischen Museum zu London, Pergament, in klein 8°, aus dem 15 Jhdt. Nichts weiter als eine (orthographisch freie Abschrift des MS. Ash. 43, mit derselben Ordnung der Legenden und mit ganz demselben Text, nur dass am Ende einige Legenden (zum Theil aus MS. Egert.) hinzugefügt sind. Das MS. is von Werth, einmal indem es, vollständig und ohne Lücken erhalten, auch die in MS. Ash. zu Anfang fehlenden Legenden (also mit dem Text des MS. Ash.) enthält, sodann weil es öfter den Text des MS. Ash., wo derselbe fehlerhaft erscheint, nach der gewöhnlichen Lesart verbessert. Es zählt (die Zahlen stehen in römischen Ziffern neben dem Anfange der Leg.) 107 Legenden (auf 305 Blättern, die Seite mit 32, später mit 40 Zeilen); . . . nur selten finden, sich Titel am Anfang der Legenden, niemals am oberen Rande. Auf dem 1ste Blatte steht als Titel der Sammlung von späterer Hand: *Tractatus festivalis in rythmo anglicano*. Ein Inhalts Verzeichniss fehlt. . . . Im allgemeinen liegt ihr Text in der Mitte zwischen MS. Harl. 2277 und MS. Ash. 43 (häufig mehr nach MS. Ash.hin), indem sie bald die Lesarten des einen, bald die des andern der beiden bieten, während die andern Versionen nur selten benutzt sind; in der Zahl und Ordnung der Legenden stimmen sie fast ganz mit MS. Harl., nicht mit MS. Ash. überein. Ausserdem verfahren sie mit dem Texte vielfach sehr willkürlich und nehmen keinen Anstand, denselben im Einzelnen zu verändern. Auch unter sich stimmen sie nicht völlig überein, doch stehen sie einander näher, als die verschiedenen Versionen. Horstmann, *Einl. Alteng Leg.* 1875, p. xxvi.

last eight verses of *St. John the Evangelist*, together with *Thomas Beket, Theophile*, and *Cecile*, remains. The legend of Cecilia is drawn from MS. Ash., though in the other legends the manuscript follows Harleian 2277, Egerton, and Laud. This edition gives the text in full.

MS. Lamb. 223[1], a Midland version, about 1400, contains texts peculiar to the Laud and Vernon MSS.

MS. Trin. Coll. Cbr. R 3. 25,[2] about 1400, is closely related to MS. Ash. It has 116 legends including selections from the *Temporale*. The order in the latter part has been changed. This edition gives it as a variant of MS. Ash.

MS. Bodley 779[3], Oxford, 16th Century, contains the latest version of the Cecilia legend. It has a long list of 135 legends increased from the original by the including of many new Pope's lives. The version is given in full in this edition.

The two Northern versions of this legend are next to be considered. Both of these are given in the succeeding pages. MS.

---

1 MS. Lambeth 223, perg., 4, ein dicker Band, aus dem Anfang des 15 Jhdts.; die *foll.* sind nicht numerirt; ein Index fehlt; Überschriften finden sich über den Seiten, nicht über den Legenden; die Schrift ist ziemlich gut und leserlich; die Seiten haben je 36 Verse. Das MS. ist ganz vollständig und ohne Lücken erhalten. Am Schlusse der Sammlung hat der Schreiber die seltsame Notiz hinzugefügt: *her endeþ* LEGENDA AUREA *writen by* R. W. *of þis toun To a gode man of þe came is cleped Thomas of Wottoun;* daher wird die HS. in Katalog fälschlich als *The Golden Legend in English verse by Robert de Wottoun, called also Thomas in the book*, aufgeführt; sie enthält mit nichten die Legenda aurea, sondern die sudenglische Sammlung. Unter jener Notiz steht von anderer Hand: *When lyffe ys most loffyt & dethe ys most hattyt, Dethe drawse hys draght & makys men full nakyt, quod Petrus Raynstroft.* Der Dialect der Hs. zeigt mittellandische Elemente (so die pron. *sho* ac. *hir*, *þai* ac. *hem*, die Endung 3 sgl. præs. ist *es*, die des plur. præs. *en*). Das Temporale ist vorn zusammengestellt. Horstmann, *Einl., Alteng. Leg.* 1881, p. xlvi.

2 MS. Trin. Coll. Cbr. R 3.25, klein *fol.*, perg., aus dem Anfang des 15th Jhdts., ganz von derselben Hand geschrieben, hat 276 Blätter, die Seite zu je 52 Versen, und ist vollständig und ohne Lücken erhalten. Am Ende folgt, von der Hand des Schreibers, ein Index, wovon unten ein Stück abgeschnitten ist. Diese Sammlung enthält nicht allein die gesammten Legenden des MS. Harl. ausser *Anastasia*, sondern auch die zusatzlegenden des MS. Ash. Sonst tritt der Einfluss der Laud-Version nicht hervor. . . . Die Ordnung der Legenden ist oft gestört in der Reihe ausgelassene Legenden sind später nachgetragen. Horstmann, *Einl., Alteng. Leg.* 1881. p. xlix.

3 Die letzte der grossen Legendensammlungen ist MS. Bodl. 779 zu angehörig, ein dicker Folioband, aus Papier, im Ganzen 310 Blätter enthaltend, obwohl nur 306 gezählt sind (2 Blätter sind doppelt gezählt). Titel am obern Rande der Blätter finden sich bis *fol.* 209; ausserdem stehen Ueberschriften in roth, oft aufgeklebt, über den meisten Legenden. *Fol.* 175 b und 176 sind unbeschrieben. Die Seite enthält durchschnittlich 56 Zeilen, später wird die Schrift kleiner und enger. Diese Handschrift ist vollständig erhalten. Diese Sammlung ist aus allen MSS. zusammengelesen, und dazu noch mit vielen neuen, nirgends sonst vorhandenen Legenden bereichert. Die Reihenfolge der Legenden ist ganz willkürlich und planlos; sie gehören meist nur nach einzelnen kleineren Gruppen zusammen. . . . Auch sonst zeigt dieses MS. die grösste Willkür. In den mit der ersten Version gemeinsamen Legenden steht der Text zwar auf Seiten dieser, inbesondere des MS. Ash. 43, doch zeigen sich auch Spuren der Einwirkung anderer MSS., besonders des MS. Laud L. 70, in welchem sich viele Lesarten wiederfinden. Dazu ist der Text noch häufig willkürlich verändert, und vielfach fehlerhaft und verderbt, und voll von Schreibfehlern. Auf dem ersten Blatt findet sich ein Inhaltsverzeichnis, von derselben Hand, auf der ersten Seite in rother, auf der zweiten in schwarzer Schrift. Horstmann *Einl., Alteng. Leg.* p. xxxiv.

Cott. Tib. E VII[1], 14th Century, believed to be older than its supplemental form in MS. Harl. 4196, is the central version of the short line group. The same text occurs in MS. Harleian 4196, *fol.* 191*a*–193*b* and is printed by Eugen Kölbing, *Eng. Stud.* I. 235.

With this is placed a version in the Lowland Scotch dialect, MS. Camb. Univ. Lib. Gg. II. 6, of about the year 1400. This is supposed to be the work of John Barbour, the author of the *Bruce.* There are about 50 legends in the collections containing in all 33,533 (Horstmann) verses. These legends have been recently edited for the Scottish Text Society and the editor's account of the MS. is given.[2]

MSS. Cott. Cleop. D IX, and Bodl. 799 are herewith printed for the first time, and the table of variants of the closely-related MSS. Laud 108, Camb. Univ. R 3. 25, Stowe 946, and Lambeth 223 reveals all essential differences between them and the foundational but not original Ashmolian manuscript.

There has been no attempt made in the present edition to determine the absolute inter-relation or chronology of these manuscripts, except so far as they reveal themselves in the mere presentation.

---

1 MS. Cott. Tib. E vii, perg., *fol.*, von fast demselben Format wie Harl., in ähnlicher Schrift von einer einzigen Hand geschrieben, hat 281 Blätter, die Seite ebenfalls 2 columnen, zu ze 46 Versen. Es enthält zuerst ein nördliches Gedicht über die Todsünden und deren Zweige, darauf die Homilien-sammlung *fol.* 101 b-244 auf der Rückseite von *fol.* 244 schliessen sich ohne besonderen Titel für die Sammlung und ohne die Einleitung des MS. Harl. die Legenden an, mit *Philip* und *Jacob* (1 Mai) beginnend. Das MS. ist leider durch einen Brand der Cottoniana sehr beschädigt, die Blätter sind verschrumpft und verdünnt, ihre rechte Seite grösstentheils zerstört, so dass nur die 1 Columne, auf der Vorderseite die linke, auf der Rückseite die rechte, bis auf die obersten 2-3 Verse enthalten ist, von der 2 Columne nur einzelne Streifen mit den Anfängen oder Schlussworten einzelner Verse. Es fehlt jedoch kein einziges Blatt so das die Lücken des MS. Harl. aus MS. Tib., soweit die versengten Blätter es gestatten, ergänzt werden können. Das MS. ist neuerdings sorgfältig gebunden, die Blätter in dicker Pappe befestigt. Die Überschriften sind genau dieselben wie in Harl. Horstmann, *Einl., Alteng. Leg.* 1881, p. lxxviii, Vellum, about A.D. 1400, Folio, ff. 5, in double columns of about 48 lines, but some lines at the top of almost every column are lost. With headings in red and initials in blue and red. Ward, *Cat. of MSS. Brit. Mus.*

2 The MS. is eleven inches in length, three and thirteen-sixteenths broad, and two and a half inches thick. The paper was once probably white; it is now of a dirty white or whitey-brown color, the combined effect probably of age and use. It is in a fair state of preservation, and has been tenderly dealt with by the binder. The original stamped brown calf binding of the fifteenth century, from which the clasp is wanting, still remains, but in a somewhat dilapidated condition, and bearing signs of ancient repairs. The sheets are loose and the binding is separate. At the beginning there is an index, with the names of the saints in Latin and the numbers of the Legends. On the last fly leaf of the MS. occur the words, "Katherine Greham with my hand, Finis," in the handwriting of the seventeenth century, which may perhaps justify the inference that a now unknown Catherine Graham was formerly its possessor.

The MS. appears to have had originally 364 leaves each of them written on both sides. . . . The handwriting belongs to the Scottish type of the 15th century, and is small, cursive, careless, and very difficult to read. In one or two places it is illegible. The greater part of the writing is by one hand. There are a number of lacunæ in the text. Metcalfe, *Scot. Text Soc., Lives of Saints,* Vol. 1, p. viii. (These lacunæ are all recorded by Metcalfe, and by Dr. Horstmann, *Einl., Alteng. Leg.* 1881, p. lxii.)

The Northern and the Southern groups are the provincial expression of the same faith, the same learning, and the same traditions. The Southern group, which subdivides itself into Southern and South-Midland types, shows the variation resulting from individuality in the person and in the monastery at work upon the transcribing of one or more primitive texts, to which MS. Ashmole stands probably more directly related than any extant version.

The two manuscripts which are taken as the central texts have been subjected to such emendation as the concurrence of the variants, and an examination of the grammatical forms of each unavoidably suggest. These emendations are all indicated by the italicized letter or letters within brackets, and the marginal notes. No change merely for the sake of uniformity has been permitted; only such as contribute to the intelligent reading of the version. The punctuation of the versions has not been made upon a uniform basis. That of MS. Ash. follows the manuscript pointing as given by Dr. Furnivall in the reprint of the Chaucer Society Publications. MS. Cott. Tib. follows in the main the punctuation of the Horstmann edition. MS. Gg. II. 6. is punctuated and capitalized according to the combined authority of Horstmann and Metcalfe. In the two new reprints, MS. Cott. Cleop. has been allowed to stand with simply the manuscript pointings, while MS. Bodl. which in the original is entirely without points, has been punctuated and capitalized according to modern methods.

III.

GRAMMATICAL OUTLINE OF THE CENTRAL VERSIONS.

The vocabulary of the earlier dialect, MS. Ashmole 43, contains less than 18 per cent of words of Romance origin; that of MS. Cott. Tib. E. VII, about 24 per cent. Grammatical inflections are extremely variable in MS. Ashmole, and in MS. Cott. Tib., reduced almost to the minimum of modern English. The context in both manuscripts is often the sole guide for constructions. Each has distinct marks of its respective Southern and Northern origin.

MS. ASH. 43.

NOUNS.

Declension.

The genitive case, singular, is formed in -s, or -es. *depes* 204, *godes* 231, *lordes* 105.

The dative and accusative singular are not distinguishable. The dative, sometimes independent of the nominative form, ends in -e, *ȝere* 89, *þinge* 62, but usually follows the form of the nominative. Examples of variations are the following: ds. *dep* (2 times), *depe* (3 times), as. *dep* (3 times); ds. *rede* 210, *red* 30, as. *rede* 112; ds. *lyue* 202, 206 (Laud *lyf* 202, *lif* 206); ds. *fure* 224, as. *fur* 218.

The plural is usually in -s or -es without distinction of case, np. *wreches* 158; gp. *frendes* 5; dp. *walmes*, 231; ap. *godes* 211; vp. *knyȝtes* 168.

Plurals are found in -n or -en in *breþeren* 134, *screwen* 182, *rosen* 71, *heden* 173, *soulen* 174, 176, *erthtilien* 152, *fon* 138, *lilion, lylion* 91, 71, *scourgen* 178.

Plural by vowel mutation shows *men*, 38, 254, and its compounds, *wimmen* 222; *fet* (Laud *feet*,) 49. *cloþes* ap. 7, and *good* dp. 245, have sg. and pl. alike. Proper names are uninflected.

PRONOUNS.

1. Personal.

The personal pronoun in this version is thus inflected: (A blank indicates that the form is omitted in the version).

Singular.

N.	Ich	þou, þe	he, heo, it, hit
G.	my, mi, myn	þi, þine, þin	his, hire
D.	me	þe	him, hire
A.	me	þe	him, hire it

Plural.

N.	we	ȝe	hi
G.	our, oure	ȝoure	hor
D.	———	ȝou	hem, þem
A.	ous	ȝou	hem

2. Demonstrative:

The demonstrative pronouns are *þat* and *þis*. *þat* has the instrumental form, *þe* - - - - *þe*, correlatives, 230. *þis* runs through ns. ds. as. np., uninflected. ap. has *þes* 60, but *þis* 180.

The definite article *þe* approaches the demonstrative signification in several instances (see Gl. *þat*). There is also the inflected *þen* of the as. 33, 42, 131, 189. *þulke* is used 83, 128, 237, 260.

3. Relative:

The relative pronoun *þat* is not inflected, save for the variant ns. *þet* 110. *Ho* has as. *wen* after *to*, 136. *Wat* is uninflected.

4. Interrogative:

Wat, wuch and *ho* are used as interrogative pronouns.

5. Indefinite:

The indefinite pronouns employed are *eche, eiþer, me, noȝt, noþer, noþing, oþer* (see Gl.). The disjointed *selue* 110, is used with reflexive force.

VERBS.

1. Weak Verbs.

The regular conjugation of the verb is as follows: (The blanks signify that no instance of the tense is given in the text). Pres. Ind. Sg.

1. — or *-e:* lif 212, kepe 207, mete 100, owe 183, sende 39.
2. *-st, xt,* or *-est:* axst 188, leuest 214, louest 25, bringest 163, luxt 200.
3. *-e* or *-eþ:* clepeþ 52, kepeþ 150, bihoueþ 104, comeþ 198.

Pl.

1. *-e* or *-eþ:* bidde 259, findeþ 3, 72.
2. *-eþ:* cupeþ 168.
3. *-eþ:* drinkeþ 151, liȝeþ 152, swynkeþ 152, sitteþ 151.

Pt.
1. — or -*de* : smulde 90.
2. -*e* or -*st* (*xt*).
3. -*ede* -*de* -*te* : burede 180, bileuede 235, sende 50, custe 113.
Pl.
1. ———
2. ———
3. *e* or -*ede* : caste 179, burede 139, bileuede 145.

The infinitives usually end in -*e;* several in *y* or *ie* : *burie* 136, *deie* 78, 216, *hie* 238, *crie* 38, *halwy* 250.

The past participle usually has *i*- as its sign, this being lost in several cases when the participle assumes an adjectival force.

The present participle has only one illustration in the text, *wepynge* 156. There is also *sepende* 229, a derivative adjective.

The imperative has *witeþ* 73, *fiȝteþ* 169, *sei* 39, *wepe* 225.

The optative shows the following forms, 1 sg. *ileue* 27, *ise* 31; 2 sg. *nost* 189, *grante* 16, *segge* 212; 3 sg. *seoþ* 25, *underȝete* 21; 3 pl. *teche* 39.

2. The following strong verbs may be clasified according to the OE. ablaut series.

Inf.	Pt.	Pp.
I.		
abide 133		
bringe 162		ibroȝt 13
scryue 17		
lese 124		
smyte 23	smot 235	ismyte 243
	aros 43	
		iwrite 3
II.		
	bed 4, bad 44	
	luxt 200	
iþe 158		
stonde 246	stod 88	
III.		
fiȝte 24		
grede 167	gradde 222	
vynde 38	vond 68	
begynne 250		
	gan 58, gon 179	
		ibound 178
	song 10, songe 9	

...... (drinkeþ 151)........ ....
...... (ʒelpest 197)...
....sucþ 9..............................
.........................worþ 36...............................

IV.

{ .... com 46...................icome 185
{ bicom(e) 116, 130..........bicom 65, 85......................
{ nyme 177 ....nom 58............................
{ by-nyme 23........ .....by nome 22.............inome 181
speke, 41, 87...
stele, 136....... ....
.........................ber 56, 174..........................

V.

ʒeue 83, 199............ʒaf 66 ʒef 173...............iʒeue 105
ise....................isei 57, 173..........................
....lay 253........ ....
....quaþ 15 ....
........................sat 231..............................
..... (swinkeþ 152)............................ ....
......(vnderʒete 21)........... ....

VI.

sle 32...slawe 238
vorsake 130...
...... (liʒeþ 152) ....

The preterite plural frequently adds *-e* to the preterite singular. *com* 46, *come* 140; *song* 10, 11, *songe* 9; *nom* 58, *nome* 140; *ber* 56, *bere* 174.

ADJECTIVES.

Weak adjectives show an inclination to take *-e* as their sign, but the usage is not uniform, strong: *good* 25, 115, 247; weak: *gode* 69, 128, 163, 171, 176, but *gode* 139, strong; strong: *old*, 46, 109, weak: *olde* 40, 45, 75, but strong: *olde* 47, and weak: *old* 55; strong: *schort* 201, weak: *scorte* 227, strong: *wit* 77, weak: *wite* 56, 65, 91, 184. Many words like *suete* show no variation, while *stalward* 168, and *stalwarde* 168, are both weak.

The vocative usually uses the sign of the weak adjective, *leue* 95, 99, 107, 113, 127, *stalwarde* 168. The plural cases apparently cling to the use of final *-e* though not invariably.

The comparative of the adjective is found in *briʒtore* 70; *bet* 64, *betere* 186; *mo* 182, 232; *soþer* 111; *woder* 112, *verisore* 92.

The cardinal numerals *o* 61, 62, 129, *on* 61², 71, *one* 84², *two* 76, 86, 257, *to* 70, *twei* 139; *þre, four, twenti, hondred,* are used; the ordinal *þridde* 253.

ADVERBS.

Terminations.

-liche: folliche 185, *stalwardliche* 169, *stilliche* 3, 10, *tristiliche* 18, *uol-liche* 236, *sodenliche* 94; *-e,* the most frequent suffix: *bi-hinde* 193; *dere* 236; *ȝare* 120; *ȝerne* 4, 119; *harde* 23, *lasse* 158, 159; *longe* 126; *-e (< en): bi-hinde* 193, *aboute* 88, *amidde* 219, *wiþþinne* 68, *wiþ-þoute* 179.

The old genitive derivation remains in *enes,* 190, 246 (Adj. *eny.*) The negative particle *ne,* frequently employed, appears *(-ny)* as a verb suffix in *wilny* 81. It is frequently agglutinated with verb forms as *n*ost, *n*olde, *n*ot, *n*ele, *n*abbeþ.

Þo (then, when); *þei* (although), 91, 145, 147, 148, are characteristic of the MS.

The frequent adverbial prefix *a-* is never written *o-* or *on-* as in Cott. Tib. E. VII., but *a*boute 88, *a*down 49, *a*midde 219, *a*riȝt 101; *-ward* is employed in *hamward* 238.

The comparative form of the adverb is given in *lengore* 230, *more* 54, *lasse* 158, 159; the superlative in *mest* 11.

PREPOSITIONS.

The prepositions with their dependant cases are to be found in the glossary.

To is frequently employed in this Southern dialect as sign of the genitive case. The prefix *a-* of prepositions, as in the adverb, is invariable in place of Tib. E. VII. *-o, on.*

MS. COTT. TIB. E. VII.

NOUNS.

Declension.

The genitive case is denoted by (1) the preposition *of, marterdom* 236, *chastite* 128, 208, *angell* 262; (2) ending *-s, -es, maysters* 388, *christes* 315, 319, 344; (3) without sign of case, *þroþer* 218. The dative and accusative singular show no inflexional sign. Plurals are formed without case distinction by (1) termination *-s, -es,-is,* or *-ys,* *angels* 358, *wordes* 80, *sawles* 356, *bodis* 355, *hertis* 202, *bodys* 202;

4

(2) vowel change, *men* 134, 321, *fete* 269, *breþer* 291, 308, *wemen* 6;
(3) alike in sg. and pl., *folk* 163, 359, *clathes* 32, 113, *sede* 128, 132,
paines 352, 434; (4) irregularly, *knese* 437, *heuides* 199, 354.

PRONOUNS.

1. Personal.

The personal pronouns are thus inflected in the text:

Singular.

N.	I	þow, þe, (t)ou, ou, ȝe	he, scho, it
G.	my, mi	þi, ȝoure, þine	his, hir
D.	me	þe, ȝow	him, hir, it, yit
A.	me	þe, ȝow	him, hir, it

Plural.

N.	we	þe, ȝow	þai
G.	oure	ȝoure	þaire
D.	us (vs)	ȝow	þam
A.	us	ȝow	þam

2. Demonstrative.

The demonstrative pronouns are *þat* or *þo* and *þis* with corresponding plurals *þa* and *þir*.

3. Relative.

The text shows the following forms for the relative pronoun; ns. *what* 118, 157, 170; gs. *whas* 260; ds. *wham* 462, *what* 281; as. *what* 211, 213, 290, etc. Plural throughout, *what.*

4. Interrogative.

This form of the pronoun occurs only in composition in *for-whi* 228.

5. Indefinite.

The indefinite pronouns used are *any* 67, *ilkane* 321, *no-man* 95, *none* 142, 430, *nowþer* 89, *oþer* 198, *sum* 433. Among these there is no instance of inflexion.

ARTICLES.

The definite article is *þe* with occasionally an apparent old neuter *þat* 198, 377. The indefinite article has the forms *a* 23, 60, 284, 420, 452, preceding a consonant, and *ane* 63, 87, 147, 418, preceding a vowel.

ADJECTIVES.

The adjective is irregular in its use of final *-e* to distinguish strong and weak forms, and, saving the occasional occurrence of *-e*, it is without case endings. Instances of variation occur in the following, ns. *mast*, gs. *moste* 126; dp. *maste* 384; ns. *both*, dp.

bathe 200, ap. *bath* 90, *both* 224; ns. *chast*, as. *chaste* 129, dp. *chast* 201.
Only one comparative form of the adjective occurs, *verrayer* 266.
The cardinal numerals *a* 162, 163, 164, 426, *twa* 81, 195, 308, *thre*
430, 431, 436, 438, 446, are employed.

VERBS.

I. *Weak Verbs.*

The inflexion of the verb is as follows:

Ind. Pres. Sg.

1. Usually without termination: *ȝern* 116, *luf* 66, *say* 103, *trow*
   173, *haue* 60.
2. } *-es: askes* 228, *dwelles* 168, *trowes* 167, *grantes* 181, *likes* 229,
3. }   *lufes* 82, 116, etc.

   Irregular, 2 sg. *sais* 80, 82, *will* 213; 3 sg. *multiplise* 133.

Pl.

1. }
2. } without termination, or *-e: lif* 450, *haste* 383.
3. }

The signs of the preterite, sg. and pl., are *-t: baptist* 178, 327,
comfort 331, *gert* 354, pl. 415, *left* 434, *sent* 443; *wirschipt* 397; *-d: cumand*
349, 371, 403, *entred* 247, *feld* 253, *had* 149, pl. 33, 310, *herd* 225, 267,
323, 348, 367, 399, 422, *mad, made* 45, 97, 215, 222, 459; *said* 46, 58,
78, 93, *willd* 338, *wond* 307, *answerd* 92, 226, *herd* 43, *honord*, 294; *-ed:*
pained 405, *granted* 318, *kissed* 248, 249, 269, *lifted* 156, *married* 23,
trowed 18, *turned* 319, *granted* 345, *lifed* 293, 309, 389, *trowed* 360, 396,
turned 360, 393: *-id, -yd; heuyd* 125, *sesid*, 16, 441, *lemid* 194, *prechid*
298, 315, *without ending: put* 352, *led* 240, 358, *fed* 38, *trow* 333; *irregu-*
lar: biliue 327.

The optative gives eight forms in the three persons of the
singular. They are without termination except *saue* 49, 144, and
file 68.

The imperative ending 2 sg. is *-e, -es* and sometimes without
termination, *greue* 62, 93, *luke* 62, *kepes* 201, *ask* 212, *mak* 452.

The infinite inclines to the dropping of final *-e*.

The present participle ends in *-and: assentand* 207, *brinand* 416,
calland 42, *kneleand* 191, *lifand* 438, *playand* 15, 421, *precheand* 308.

The past participle has the endings *-d, -t, -ed, -id, -de;* and *-n,*
-ne, -en.

The following, not derived from the umlaut series of strong
verbs, form their preterites and past participles regularly, but
with change of vowel.

Inf.	Pt. sg. and pl.	Pp.
bring 372	broght 195, 326, (pl.) 423	broght 39, 158

——— (teche 451)	———	———
tell 96, 288, 301, 303	tald (pl.) 30, talde 122, 444	tald 51, talde 231
——— (think 251)	thoght 55	———
seke 142	soght 325	soght 143, 401
wirk 318, 351, 451	wrogt 305, wroght 373	wroght 196

II. *Strong Verbs.*

The strong verbs are less numerous than the weak. Disregarding the seven verbs with irregular preterites just preceding there are thirty-eight. For these verbs eighteen infinitives are given in the text, twenty have been constructed on the analogy of other forms and related verbs. The termination for the infinite thus results, *-e*, eleven, without ending, twenty-eight.

Like the weak verb, 1 sg. of the strong verb takes no termination. 2 sg. shows only one form, *-e* instead of *-es, bede* 69. 3 sg. has three instances, termination *-es; thinkes* 381, *biddes* 423, *waxes* 133, also *tase* 159, *dose* 66. Uninflected, *gaf* 285, *tell* 323, 367, *wit* 67; impersonal, *think* 251; contracted, *bus* 61.

In the preterite sg., the sign continues to be *-de, talde* 242, and the similarity continues as in weak verbs between the forms of the 3 sg. and 3 pl.

The optative among strong verbs shows the forms 2 sg. *gifes* 124, 1 pl. *gif* 224, 3 pl. *fall* 365.

The imperative 2 sg. has *tak* 106, 131; *teche* 451; *tell* 107, 109.

The one case of pres. pt. is *schineand* 193.

The survivals of the OE. ablaut classes are as follows:

Inf.	Pt. sg. or pl.	Pp.
I.		
...........................rase 120..................................		
....(schineand)..		
strike 430..		
.....................................writen 174, wretyn 157, 160		
II.		
bed 428..		
bow 334...		
III.		
....boun 8, boune 297		
bygyn 190..		
..............................fand 191............................		
...........................gan 116, 362, 391, 427.................		
win 233..won 231		

IV.

.....................................bycome 284..

cum 235........come 184, 244, 314, 385, 440........ouer-cumen 339

V.

bid 281...................bad 156, 176, 245............................

gif 113, 341, 436.............gaf 285, 456.............. ...gifen 445

get 189...

...............................lay 154...................... .....

se 9, 14, 81, 94, 95.....saw 151, 192, 389 pl. 146.......sene 180, 417

.............................sat 437...............................

....spak 254, 392..............................

VI.

....ferd 123, 245................. ....

forsake 72, 144, 276, 332...forsoke pl. 395.........................

From the old reduplicating verbs we have the following, in *eo:*
bifell 324, 368, *byfell* 304, *fell* 153, 269, *knew* 13, 28.

In *e:* (*hete* 257).

From old preterite presents: *durst* 29, 76; *mot* 127; *may* 5, 9,
83, 94, 95, 110, 130, 376, *might* 170, 222, 265, 286, 289, 357, 448,
moght 56, 442; *sal(l)* 72, 86, 111, 117, 212, 279, *suld* 31, 311; *will*
79, 213, 241, *willed* 338, *wald* 142, 207, 219, 312, 351.

Anomolous verbs are represented in the text by the following
forms: inf. *be,* pt. *was,* pp. *bene;* inf. *ga,* pt. *ʒode;* inf. *do,* pt. *did.*

ADVERBS.

Adverbs usually end in -*ly: trewly, parfitely, smertly, stoutly, halily;*
once in -*i: wiseli;* frequently in -*e: wele, tite, rathe;* otherwise with
out ending or irregular.

PREPOSITIONS.

A list of the prepositions in their proper order may be found
with their respective case government in the glossary. Since
noun inflections in this text are so little to be relied upon, we
must decide in many instances the case employed by the methods of Mn. English, in general the dative being the case of the
indirect object, the accusative the case of the direct. The genitive is frequently expressed by means of the preposition *of.*
Source, possession (benefit, instrumentality, interest,) with the
preposition *of,* seem to convey a more distinctively dative than
genitive idea.

IV.

PHONOLOGY OF THE STRESSED VOWELS.

[The vowels and diphthongs here given are classified alphabetically according to their Middle English forms. The stem only of a word series is given, except in cases of compound words and where an inflection serves to make the placing of a word intelligible. There has been no attempt made to classify words according to their Middle English sounds. References given at the head of each group apply to the general type of the group, cases of special reference immediately follow the word under consideration. The abbreviations refer to the following authorities.]

Gr., Grammar of Old English. Eduard Sievers, ed. A. S. Cook. Boston. 1887.

Cosijn. Altwestsächsische Grammatik. P. J. Cosijn. Haag. 1888.

Morsb. Mittelenglische Grammatik. Lorenz Morsbach. Halle. 1896.

Schwan. Grammatik des Altfranzösichen. Eduard Schwan. Leipzig. 1893.

Murray. A New English Dictionary on Historical Principles. ed. J. A. H. Murray.

Kluge. Etymologisches Wörterbuch der deutschen Sprache. Strassburg. 1883.

Maetzner. Altenglische Sprachproben. Eduard Mätzner. Berlin. 1878-1885.

Fischer. The Stressed Vowels of Ælfric's Homilies. Frank Fischer; Publ. of Mod. Lang. Asso. Vol. IV. No. 2. 1889.

MS. ASH. 43.

MIDDLE ENGLISH *a*.

I. WEST GERMANIC.

1. WS. *a*, WG. *a* (*Gr.* 11):

ac, 25, 37, 75, 97, 134, 172, 202, 210, 226; habb, 95, 101, 144, 150, 154, 254, (*Morsb.* 102.2); knaue, 144; made, 53, 109, 138, 218; naked, 177; -sake, 130;-wake, 102.

2. WS. *a* (*æ* through umlaut), WG. *a* (*Gr.* 10; 50):

fader, 62;-gadere, 180; habbe 53, 74, 147, 255, hadde, 14, 67, 132, 145, 146, hast, 15, 24, 29, 97, 103, 111, 204, haþ, 105, 119, 120, haue, 128.

3. WS. *ǫ*, WG. *a*, before nasals (*Gr.* 51 2; 65):

an, 125; an (*Gr.* 65.2), 70; can, 118; fram, 2, 26, 35, 55, 190; gan, 58, 167, 178, 238; man, 5, 46, 130; name, 250.

4. WS. *æ*, WG. *a* (*Gr.* 49):

after, 30, 48, 65, 125, 253, 258; at, 1, 84; bad, 44; dawe, 142; quaþ (see Gl.); sat, 231; stalward, 168², 169 (cf. *Gr.* 202.3. Note 2); slawe (*Gr.* 50.2)238; þat (see Gl.); vaste, 21, 178; walmes, 231; war, 53; was, 1, 5, 13, 181, 221; wat, 80, 108, 137, 168, 182; water, 229.

5. WS. *ā*, WG. *ai* (*Gr.* 13):

a, 5, 16, 54, 55, 56, 154, 160, 188, 194, 196, 201, 218, 219, 220, 227, 239, 246, 250, an, 20, 31 46; axst, 188; hal-, 59, 250; ham-, 238.

6. WS. æ (umlaut of *á*, WG. *ai* (*Gr.* 17.1; 90):
ar, 2; clan-, 30; lad-, 129, 181, 221; lasse, 158, 159 (*Morsb.* 96.2);-last, 75, 220.

7. WS. æ, WG. *á*, Germ. *è* (*Gr.* 17.2; 90):
gradde, 222; radde, 60; war, 48, 65, 85, 88, 174.

8. WS. *ea*, Germ. *a*,
(*a*) before *r*+consonant (*Gr.* 79):
art, 116, 159, 204, 205, art-, 183, 185; hard-, 23, 138, 191; warde, 19, 165, wardeyn, 20.
(*b*) before *l*+consonant (*Gr.* 80):
al, 24, 30, 89, 195, 219, 229, 255, alle, 62, 166, 248, 252; as, 3, 13, 17, 26, 43, 46, 54, 72, 82, 88, 90, 97, 98, 118, 139, 188, 194, 216, 217; al-, 20, 91, 116, 118, 121, 196, 256; half, 238, 241, 243, 244³; halt, 24.

9. WS. *ea* (palatal+*æ*), WG. *a* (*Gr.* 75.1):
ʒaf, 66; schal, 41, 42, 162, 188, 196, 224, 227; schalt, 36, 42, 114, 116, 189, 190, 216.

10. WS. *éa*, WG. *á* preceded by palatal (*Gr.* 74):
ʒare, 120.

II. OLD NORSE.
caste, 76, 179, 219, 229, lawe, 141, take, 217.

III. CELTIC.
cradel, 2 (origin uncertain, *Murray*).

IV. ROMANCE (*Schwan*, 270).
belamy 149, 161, angel, 20, 28, 33, 42, 69, 83, 85, 105, 131, 174, 176; chambre, 68, 87, 132; chaste, 73; dame, 198, 207; grante, 16, 80; grace, 83, 231, 246; ianglinge, 161; alas, 223; maner, 76, 187; marie, 10; martir-, 78, 180, 253, 259, martred, 48, 135, 139; pal, 7 (*Morsb.* 107.5); place, 84, 232; sacrifice, 162, 172, 208.

MIDDLE ENGLISH *e*.

I. WEST GERMANIC.
1. WS. *e*, WG. *è* (*Gr.* 19.1):
beggare (?) (of uncertain origin, *Murray*), 160; helpe, 110; ne (see Gl.), quell-, 144, 233, 235, 237; queþe, 143, 163; speke, 41, 87; stele, 136; wel, 2, 44, 103, 147, 200, 201, 241.

2. WS. *e*, *i*-umlaut of *a* or *o*, WG. *a* (*Gr.* 89):
bedde, 13; bet, 64, 186; ende, 155, 189, 206, 227, helle, 35, 156, 216; -hered, 51; lete, 22, 164; lengore, 230; men, 38, 45, 47, 134, 139, 140, 163, 171, 176, 254, me, 47, 52, 85, 135, 137, 221, 229, 233, 242, me-, 48; sende, 39, 50, 228, 248; segge, 212, strengþe, 5; telle, 16, 36, þen, 31, 42, 54, 70, 92, 103, 111, 112, 158, 160, 186, 197, 232; þence-, 90, 92, 148, 149, 187, 203; wemmed, 12; wen, 9, 125, 135, 153, 156, 189, 198, 203, 205; wende, 44, 67, 85, 134, 156, 190, 247, 256; werede, 7.

3. WS. *æ*, later *ǽ*, WG. *a*, with ecthlipsis of *g* (*Gr.* 214.3):
sede, 29, 50, 51, 60, 73, 87, 89, 107, 111, 113, 149, 182, 209, 223, 255 (*Gr.* 89, Note 1).

4. WS. *eo*,

(*a*) breaking of *e* before *r*+consonant (*Gr.* 79.1):
-berne, 121, 122; derk-, 169; gerne, 4, 119; herte, 12, 190; verrore, 230; were, 109.

(*b*) by *u*-umlaut (*Gr.* 106.1):
clep-, 52, 192; henne, 37; heuene, 55, 59, 105, 122, 148, 174, 176.

(*c*) by *o*-umlaut (*Gr.* 109, *b*):
suere, 235.

5. Representative of WS. *ie*, palatal umlaut of WG. *e* (*Gr.* 75.3):
gelpest, 197; -gete, 21.

6. WS. *y*, *i*-umlaut of WG. *u*:
verst 102, uerst, 102.

7. WS. *y*, contraction of *i*+*u*:
þe, 230².

8. Contraction of WS. *e*+*i*, WG. *ô*:
nele, 32², 126, 215, nelleþ, 75, 76, 158.

9. WS. *é*, Germ. *è* (*Gr.* 21.1):
ber, 21, 63, 191; here, 90, 95, 122; het, 6, 165, 172, 173, 217; lette, 3.

10. WS. *é*, *i*-umlaut of WG. *ô* (*Gr.* 21.2, 94):
breþeren, 134; dest, 63, 79, 184; fet, 49; grepe, 154; suete, 15, 19, 33, 251, 259, twenti, 257; verde, 217; -uere, 96; -seche, 127; wep-, 156, 225.

11. WS. *é*, the result of secondary lengthening.
he, ge, me, þe, we (see Gl).

12. WS. *é*, representative of *ie*, *i*-umlaut of *éa* (*Gr.* 21.4; 97; 99):
geme, 26; kep-, 150, 161, 207; lef, 137, 212, -leue, 27, 32, 34, 61, 64, 98, 106, 115,130, 215, 241, leu-, 63, 141, 145, 214; repe, 153, 155.

13. WS. *æ*, *i*-umlaut of *á*, Germ. *ai* (*Gr.* 17.1):
clene, 25, 73, 86, 115; delede, 245; ech, 26, 62 (*Gr.* 347.1); enes, 190, 246; eny, 54, 70, 112, 124; er, 53, 103; euer, 75, 101, 186; lede, 58, 128, 170, 176, 218, leue, 74, 241; lere, 185; mest, 11; neuer, 75, 76, 90, 154, 158; teche, 39.

14. WS. *æ*, WG. *â*, Germ. *ê* (*Gr.* 17.2; 57.2):
ber, 56, 174, bleddore (*Kluge*), 194; drede, 57; grede (*Mätzner*), 167; here, 8; let, 12, 46, 130, 144, 177², 178, 234, met- 100², 101; nere, 123; red(e), 30, 59, 79, 112, 114, 118, 210; slepe, (*cf. Cosijn*, 82.3), 102, þer-, 56, 88, 140, were, 82, 88, 91, 120, 124, 217, 228, 234; 96, 121, 143; 134, 141; 48, 137, 139, 142, 170, 171, 186, 252.

15. WS. *éa*, by palatal umlaut (*Gr.* 101):
ge, 104; -gen, 24, 67, 131, 141, 160; ger, 89, 257 (*Gr.* 102); next (*Gr* 101, *a*), 8.

16. WS. *éa*, WG. *au* (*Gr.* 63):
bed, 59, 249, 254; bete, 178; ded, 244, deþ, 162, 199, 201, 203, 204, 205², 206, 208, 230, 233, 234, 236; eke, 157, 210; gret, 6, 36, 218; heued, 233, heden, 173; hewe, 240; led, 219; rede, 91; scewe, 28; screwe, 182, 217, 239.

17. WS. *éa*, WG. *a*+*o* (*Gr.* 111):
sle, 32.

18. WS. *éo*,

(*a*) WG. *eu* (*Gr.* 40. 1; 64):
dere, 236; lef-, 20, 27; lese, 224, 226, lene, 95, 99, 107, 113, 127; seke, 196; seþ, 220, 229².

(b) influence of *w* on WG. *e* (*Gr.* 73. 1):

　　heu, 76, 184; tre, 109, 211; trewe, 73; þreu, 47; -kneu, 48.

(c) contractions, *i+o* (*Gr.* 113); *e+o* (*Gr.* 114. 1); preterits of red. vbs.
be, ibe (see Gl.); frendes, 5; -þe (*Gr.* 403); 158, þre, 37, 180, 235, 257;
vel, 49, 57; -se, 28, 29, 31, 33, 35, 42, 63, 96, 98, 102, 189, 212. 213, 242.

II.　OLD NORSE.

hem, þem, (see Gl. *he*); reuþe, 244; verisore, 92; welluwe, 75.

III.　ROMANCE (*Schwan*, 271).

best, 112; certes, 158, 162, 200; cler, 170; emperours, 138, 140; gerlans, 8,
70, 95; ihesu, 4, 34, 38, 190, 247, 256, -leue, 169; menstrales, 9; menstrasie,
9; merci, 128; prechede, 231, 247, 254; semblance, 145, 146, 147; sergant,
204, 205; seruice, 251; trechours, 141; tresour, 8; vers, 11; vestemens,
56; werreour, 52.

MIDDLE ENGLISH *i*,

I.　WEST GERMANIC.

　1.　WS. *i*, WG. *i* (*Gr.* 23; 45; 54):

　　(a) in closed syllables,

　　　bidde, 259; bist, 80; ʒif, (see Gl.); ich, (see Gl. *I*); in, -inne, (see Gl.);
　　　it, hit, his, him (see Gl. *he*); is (see Gl. *be*); 220; midde, 219; prick,
　　　195; sitteþ, 151; still-, 3, 10, 44, 88, 225; swiþe, 7, 68; þis, (see Gl.);
　　　þridde, 253; wille, 30, 43, 255, wil-, 81, 151; witte, 94; wiþ, (see
　　　Gl.); write 56, 59; iwis, 28, 202, 206, 214.

　　(b) before *-nd* (*Gr.* 124.1.):

　　　find-, 3, 72; -hinde, 193.

　　(c) before *-ng* (*Gr.* 124.1):

　　　bring-, 162, 163, 260; þing, 62, 86, 110, 145, 213, 223.

　　(d) before *-nc* (*Gr.* 124. 1):

　　　drink-, 151;

　　(e) before *-ld* (*Gr.* 124. 3):

　　　milde, 54; wilde, 53.

　　(f) in open syllables :

　　　gidi, 209, 210, 214, 215, 216; -priked, 195; -tilien, 152; wit-, 4, 26, 35,
　　　73, 244; -write, 3.

　2.　Representative of WS. *y*, *i*-umlaut of WG. *u* (*Gr.* 31):
　　chirche, 250.

　3.　WS. *ie*, *i*-umlaut of *ea*, WG. *a* (*Gr.* 97):
　　liʒeþ, 152 (*Gr.* 98. *a*).

　4.　WS. *ie*, palatal umlaut of *ea*, WG. *a* (*Gr.* 82; 101):
　　miʒt, 18, 23, 35, 51, 92, 96, 98, 122, 201, 202, 203, 204, 212, 213, 233, 242, 246;
　　nyʒt, 13, 229. (*Gr.* 98, Note; 31, Note).

　5.　WS. *ie*, *i*-umlaut of *eo*, WG. *i* (*Gr.* 41. 1; 100):
　　hire (gs., ds., as. see Gl.) (*Gr.* 109. b).

　6.　WS. *ie*, palatal umlaut of *eo*, WG. *e* (*Gr.* 83; 101):
　　briʒt-, 70; fiʒt-, 24, 169; riʒt, 106, 140, 142, 203, 257; siʒt, 105.

　7.　WS. *ie*, WG. *e*, preceded by a palatal (*Gr.* 75.3):
　　ʒiue, 188.

　8.　WS. *ie*, *i+e* (*Gr.* 114.3):
　　hi (np. see Gl.).

9. WS. *io*, Germ. *i* (*Gr.* 38):
   quic, 244 (*Gr.* 71).
10. WS. *i*, shortened with gemination of consonant:
    blisse (*Gr.* 202.7), 148, 155; wimmen, 222.
11. WS. *i*, WG. *i* (*Gr.* 59):
    -bide, 133; idel, 151; liche, 8; lif (sb.), 24, 125, 178, 187, 199, 204, 224, 226,
    227; -ligt, 55, 258; mile, 37; riche, 7, 13,; wide, 134; wif, 183; wise, 42, 252;
    wite, 56, 65, 91, 184; wit, 77.
12. WS. *i* by secondary lengthening (*Gr.* 121):
    bi, 21, 69, 114, 167, 183, 203, 237; I, 12, 32², 81, 92, 94, 161, 212; mi, 226; siþ-
    (*Gr.* 122), 235; þi, 23, 30², 51, 80, 112, 115, 155, 161, 184, 187, 189, 192, 193,
    196, 197, 198, 202, 205, 207, 210; þin, 199, 211.

II. OLD NORSE.

   tristiliche, 186.

III. ROMANCE (*Schwan*, 274).

   biscop, 177, 129, 248; baptis- 3, 41, 61, 248; crist, 4, 34, 38, 190, 247, 256,
   crist- 34, 47, 50, 66, 82, 118, 130, 135, 166, 175, 232, 254; lil- 71, 77, 91;
   prison, 164, 167; priu-, 16, 17, 41; richesse, 6; seruice, 251; sire, 143, 200;
   strif, 124.

MIDDLE ENGLISH *o*.

I. WEST GERMANIC.

1. WS. *o*, WG. *o* (*Gr.* 55):
   bodi, 73, 179, 251; -bore, 1; corn, 153; god, 10, 62, 162, 207, 208, 211, 228,
   231, 239, 246, golde, 8; -morwe, 171; oþer, 100, 162, 208; ouer, 62, 219, 237;
   uor, 15, 22, 32, 57, 147, 148, 155, 156, 225, 259, -uore, 137, 181; uorþ, 44,
   58, 120, 179, 221; vor, 24, 124, 189; vor, 59, 144, wolde, nolde, (see Gl.);
   word-, 60, 85.
2. WS. *o*, WG. *a* (*Gr.* 51):
   of, off, (see Gl.); on, 34, 38, 210, -on, 78.
3. WS. *o*, WG. *a*, before nasals, (*Gr.* 65):
   honde, 245; lomb, 54; londe, 142; long, 126, mon, 14, 40, 45, 55, 65, 216, 248,
   mon-, 109, 128; mony, 247; -mong, 47, song, 9; stonde, 21, 69, 100, 246,
   strong, 178.
4. WS. *ǫ*, WG. *a*, with loss of nasal (*Gr.* 65; 185):
   -brogt, 13, 74, 94, 120, 137, 142, 170, 171, 184, 193, 208, 222, 234, 236, soþ,
   18, 292, 99, 111, 147, 148, 213; þogt, 11, 93.
5. WS. *u*, WG. *o*, before nasals (*Gr.* 70):
   com, 130, 191, 198, come, 2, 116, 185; wonede, 249 (*Morsb.* 65.7).
6. WS. *u*, WG. *o* (*Gr.* 55):
   lou-, 2, 15, 25, 31, 36, 73, 106, 115, vol, 91, 93, uol, 194, 219, 236; wolf, 54.
7. WS. *u*, WG. *u* (*Gr.* 56.):
   tonge, 36; þoru, 5, 97, 115, 116, 166, 224.
8. WS. *ū*, WG. *ū:*
   bote (e+ū), 96, 108, 123, 184, 194, 213; adon, 184.
9. WS. *ea*, WG, *a* before *l*+consonant (*Gr.* 80):
   bold, 160; old, 40, 45, 46, 47, 55, 75, 109; -told, 159.
10. WS. *eo*, preceded by *w*, WG. *e* (*Gr.* 72):
    worldes, 147; worþ, 146, 158, 184, 193, 197, 226.

11. WS. *eo*, *o*-umlaut of *e*, by contraction:

hor (OE. *heora*), 9², 76, 86, 144, 173, 174.

12. WS. *o*, *eo*, preceded by palatal, WG. *u* (*Gr*. 74; 75):

gong, 223, 224, 226; schort, 201, scorte, 227, scholde, 121, 157, 211, scholleþ, 84, 155. (*Gr*. 76.2. Note).

13. WS. *ō*, WG. *ō* (*Gr*. 60):

boke, 72; broþer, 82, 89, 95, 99, 107, 114, 115, 116, 127, 129; do, 30, 90, 92, 112, 114, 118, 164. 172, 184, 208; good, 25, 115, 245, 247, gode, 69, 125, 139, 163, 171, 176, moder, 258; mote, 16, 17, 78; most, 28, 34, 37, 40, 117, 133, 237; mowe, 102, 153, 154; inou, 86; -soȝt, 14, 119; suote (see *suete*), 68, 71, 77, 90, 97; to, (see Gl.); wod, 112, 149, 217.

14. WS. *ā*, WG. *ai* (*Gr*. 25.2), (*Morsb*. 134):

-blowe, 194; cloþes, 7; holiȝ. 107, 180, 225, 240, 243, 259; -hote, 18, 132; lord, 2, 12, 13, 43, 61, 74, 89, 83, 105, 250, 251, 258, 259; mo, 182, 232, more, 54; noþer, 31; o, 61, 62, 129; on, 61², 71, one, 84³, -on, 39, 43, 45, 49, 66, 113, 131, 136, 162, 164, 175, 177, 180; -om, (OE. *hām*), 133; oþer, 18, 64, 72, 86, 94, 99, 100, 103, 108, 129, 143, 184, 187, 191; owe, 183; smot, 235, 236; ston, 211; tok-, 77, 78; two, 76, 86, 257, to, 70; -ros, 43; þo, 55, 57, 67, 107, 131, 172, 179, 181. 217. 221; wo, 126, 150, 240, 241.

15. WS. *ō*, WG. *ā*, before a nasal (*Gr*. 68):

com, (*Morsb*. 93.2), 46, 49, 55, 65, 85, 87, 131, 166, 167, 232, 260, come, 140; -dom, 50, 260; don, 137; fon, 138; go, (*Gr*. 57.1. Note), 37, 55, 117, 154, gon, 40, 132, 135, 179; ido, 19, 103, 252, 255; nom, 58, 66, 86, 140, 165; sone, 14, 79 98, 181, 184, 193, -uonge, 125, 227.

16. WS. *ō*, (*e*+*ā*) by contraction:

non, 108, no, 36, 46, 146, 204, 237, 242, noȝt, 12, 24, 145, 147, 150, 161, 163, 202, 207, 212, 214, 224, 225, 233, 236, noþing, 22, 32, 64, 81, 111, 202.

17. WS. *ā*, by secondary lengthening, WG. *ā* (*Gr*. 121):

ho, 138, 242, hose, 150; so, 35, 36, 49, 53, 77, 81, 90, 93², 97, 100, 119, 122, 125, 126, 138, 160, 166, 185, 191, 228, 238, 240, 241.

18. WS. *ō*, contraction of *o*+vowel:

doþ, 26, 74, 98, 162, 168, 184.

19. WS. *ēo*, WG. *e*, preceded by *w* (*Gr*. 72):

wope, 222.

20. WS. *i*, WG. *i*.

womman, 133 (*Morsb*. 149.3).

II. OLD NORSE.

bone, 80, 97; both, 42, 84. 173; hondred, 232, 257; hor, 56; tok, 59, 71, 146.

III. ROMANCE (*Schwan*, 277).

conseil, 17, 41; fol, 14², 31, 124, 126, 130, 188, 192, 228; ioie, 30, 86, 126, 156, 260; noble, 1; poer, 189, 192, 193, 197, 252; robe, 7; rose, 71, 78, 91; soden, 94.

MIDDLE ENGLISH *u*.

I. WEST GERMANIC.

1. WS. *u*, WG. *u* (*Gr*. 56):

þus, 54; schull-, 125, 156, 256, (*Gr*. 76, 2, Note 2).

2. WS. *u*, WG. *o* (*Gr*. 29.2):

-fulle, 67 (*Gr*. 55).

3. WS. *i*, WG. *i:*
busemar, 152; muche, 81, 93, 148, 245; þuder, 50, 135.

4. WS. *i*, WG. *a*, contracted compound:
such, 158, 188, 233; wuch, 187 (*Gr.* 43, Note; 342).

5. WS. *e* (*y*), WG. *a:*
stude, 44, 46, 239.

6. WS. *ŷ*, WG. *u* (*Gr.* 95):
bur-, 47, 136, 139, 180, 251; custe, 113; dude, 240; gulte-, 240; kun, 185, 186; muri, 125; vuel, 239.

7. WS. *y*, WG. *e* (*Gr.* 81):
sulue, 110.

8. Representative of WS. *ea*, palatalization of WG. *a* (*Gr.* 75):
ichulle, 30, 256.

9. Representative of WS. *eo* preceded by *w*, WG. *e* (*Gr.* 28.3; 72):
wurþi, 143, 150.

10. Representative of WS. *ie, y*, WG. *eo* by palatal umlaut (*Gr.* 101; 100)
sucþ, 215, suxst-, 192, 214, suxt-, 103, 108, 109, 199.

11. Representative of WS. *eo* due to palatal influence on *o* (*Gr.* 101):
schulde (pt.), 249 (*Gr.* 76, Note 2).

12. WS. *i*, WG. *i:*
wule, 126, 220.

13. WS. *ŷ*, *i*-umlaut of WG. *ū* (*Gr.* 96):
cuþeþ, 168; fur, 218, 224; -hud, 120; lute, 16, 148, 196, 197; prute, 198.

14. Representative of *ie*, *i* umlaut of *ēo* (*Gr.* 101):
ʒut (*Gr.* 74, Note 1), 182; luþer, 52; luxt, 200.

15. Representative of *ēo*, the result of contraction:
huld, 65, 70, 88.

II. OLD NORSE.
puttes, 47; þulke, 83, 128, 237, 260; unknown origin, smul, 68, 90², 92, 97.

III. ROMANCE (*Schwan*, 277).
iugement, 142, 221; iustice, 137, 149, 157, 161, 164, 172, 175, 177, 181, 198, 207, 230; pur, 203.

MIDDLE ENGLISH *y*.

I. WEST GERMANIC.

1. WS. *i*, WG. *i*, in closed syllables (*Gr.* 124): gynne, 250; suyþe, 55, 56, 197; wynter, 151; before -*nd:* blynd, 210, 213, 216, bynd-, 38; wynde, 194; before -*nc:* swynk-, 152; scrynk-, 195; in open syllables: lyue, 197; -smyte, 243.

2. WS *i*, WG. *ĕ*, before a nasal (*Gr.* 69): nyme, 23, 177.

3. WS. *ie*, WG. *a* (*Gr.* 82): nyʒt, 13, 229.

4. WS. *ie*, WG. *e* (*Gr.* 83): knyʒtes, 168.

5. WS. *i*, WG. *i* :
lyve, (sb.), 202, 226; scryue, 17; smyte, 23, 173, 234, 237; tyme, 84, 89.

6. WS. *i*, by secondary lengthening:
my, 20², 22, 80, 82, 83, 93, 105, 114, 115, 192, 255, myn, 12, 190.

7. WS. *ie*, *i*-umlaut of *ēa* (*Gr.* 99): -lyue, 241.

II. OLD NORSE.
lym, 220.

III. ROMANCE (*Schwan*, 278).
pyne, 216.

DIPHTHONGS.

I. WEST GERMANIC.

1. WS. *æ+g*, WG. *a* (*Gr. 49*):
day, 253, 254, daie, 237, -dai, 114; lay, 253; mai, 29, 36, 110³, 199; maide 7, 10, 15, 19, 33, 44, 107, 123, 186, 188, 193, 199, 217, 225, 240, 243, 253, maiden-, 4, 22, 77; mayn, 235; vair, 56, 153, 223, 246.

2. WS. *ëo*, WG. *eu:* leome, 70.

3. WS. *ëo*, WG. *i+u:* heo (see Gl.) (*Gr. 114.1*).

4. WS. *eg*, WG. *ë:* weie, 170, -wei, 195.

5. WS. *æ+g* or *h*, (*Morsb.* 102.5): eiþer, 86; teiȝte, 45; pleide, 231.

6. WS. *ëa+g*, WG. *au:* eie, 119, 215, heie, 200, hei, 174.

7. WS. *a*, WG. *a:* sei, 39.

8. WS. *ëa*, WG. *a:* isei, 57, 173, 176, 222, 233.

9. WS. *i+e* (*Gr. 114.3*): þrie, 237.

10. WS. *i+ȝ* WG. *u:* hie, 238.

11. WS. *u*, WG. *u:* -bounde, 178.

12. WS. *e+u* by contraction: aboute, 88, 134, 152, 243.

13. WS. *û*, WG. *û:* out, 179, 218, 227; -doun, 49, 57, 154, 253; hous, 218, 249; loude, 167, 222; toun, 179.

14. WS. *û*, WG. *ô* preceded by *w:* hou, 89, 94, 109, 110, 182, 191, 198.

15. WS. *û*, lengthened from WG. *u*, with loss of *n:* our, oure, (see Gl.); ous, 35, 42, 163, 260.

16. WS. *û*, the result of secondary lengthening: nou, 92, 102², 103, 169, 224, 239, 255, 259; þou, (see Gl.).

17. WS. *ëo*, WG. *eu:* ȝou, 74, 162, 170, ȝoure, 77, 78.

18. WS. *ëo*, WG. *e*, by influence of *w:* four, 232.

19. WS. *â*, WG. *ai:* Louerd, 51; soul-, 174, 176, 260.

II. OLD NORSE.
deie, 78, 216, 224; trewe, 73.

III. ROMANCE.
OF. *ai:* gailer, 165; maister, 192; trauail, 155.
OF. *a:* maumet, 108, 171; sauter, 11; sergaunt, 205; tiraunt, 54.
OF. *ea:* creature, 223.
OF. *ai:* meseise, 154; seynte, 9; seyn, 40, 45, 51, 58, 63, 66, 67, 113, 167, 209, 248.
OF. *ei:* fei, 183.
OF. *ae:* doel, 242.
OF. *oi+g:* caroine, 196, 201.
OF. *i:* crie, 38.
OF. *o, ou:* confound-, 12; floures, 76, 96; honoure, 211; pouere, 38, 45, 245; scourgen, 178; soulement, 123; spouse, 5, 69; tresours, 8.

MS. COTT. TIB. E. VII.

MIDDLE ENGLISH *a*.

I. WEST GERMANIC.

1. WS. *a*, WG. *a* (*Gr. 11*):
bale, (*Gr. 105.1*), 218; made, 45, 97, 215, 222, 274, 459, mak, 45, 350, 427; -sake, 72, 144, 276, 332, 344, 408.

2. WS. *a* (*æ*, through umlaut), WG. *a* (*Gr. 10; 50*):
haue, 60, 117, 163, 229, 256, 289, 390, had, 33, 149, 310.

3. WS. *a* or *ǫ*, WG. *a* (*Gr.* 52.1; 65),

    (*a*)　before -*nc*, -*nd*, -*ng*, -*mb*, -*ld*:

        and (see Gl.); answer-, 92, 169, 226; band-, 234; fand, 191; hand, 125,
        149, 155, 195, land, 307; lang, 301; lamb, 40; omang, 45, 250, 302, 362;
        sang, 44, 46; stand, 415; thank, 188; wald, 142, 207, 241.

    (*b*)　in open syllables:

        bane, 322; fra, 184, 280; name, 394, 452; same, 458.

    (*c*)　in closed syllables:

        ban 88; gan, 116, 362, 391, 427; man, 23, 40, 87, 95, 147, 155, 166, 170,
        176, 256, 284, 384, man-; 2, þan (*Gr.* 65.2), (see Gl.).

4. WS. *æ*, WG. *a* (*Gr.* 49):

    at, 287, 353, 382; bad, 156, 176, 183, 332, 401, 410; fast, 258, 298; rathe, 199;
    sat, 437; slane (*Gr.* 50.2), 350, 380; spak, 254, 392; þat, was, what (see Gl.).

5. WS. *ea*, WG. *a.*

    (*a*)　before *r*+consonant (*Gr.* 79):

        hard, 34, 257, 352; harm, 317, -ward, 35.

    (*b*)　before *l*+consonant (*Gr.* 80):

        all, als, alls, all-, al- (see Gl.); ald, 147, 155, 166, 176; balde, 107; fall,
        365; hals, 432; tald-, 30, 51, 108, 122, 242, 444.

    (*c*)　before *h*+consonant (*Gr.* 82):

        saw, 151, 192, 379; waxes, 133.

6. WS. *ea* (palatal+*æ*), WG. *a* (*Gr.* 75.1):

    gaf (*pt. sg.*), 285, 456; sall, 72, 86, 89, 91, 103, 111, 117, 227, 279.

7. WS. *ā*, WG. *ai* (*Gr.* 13):

    a, 162, 163, 164; 23, 60, 284, 420, 452; ane 63, 87, 147, 244, 259, 321, 327, 328,
    363, 418; ask, 212, 215, 228; ay, 240, 287, 297, 342, 450; clathes, 32, 113; ga
    (*Gr.* 57.1), 183, 279; hal-, 12, 119, 122, 240, 246, 284, 421, 433; hame, 183;
    gast-, 119, 224, 456; lare, 14, 260; mare, 436; rase, 120; sare, 88; saw, 146;
    saw-, 128, 132; strake, 428, 430, 431, 436; takin, 266, tane, 197, twa (*Fischer*,
    WG. *ð*), 81, 195; whas, 260, wham, 462; wrathe, 75.

8. WS. *ǣ*, WG. *ai* (*Gr.* 17.1; 90):

    any, 67; are, 435; hathin, 27; last-, 342, 353; mast, 100, 384.

9. WS. *ǣ*, WG. *ā*, Germ. *ē* (*Gr.* 17.2; 91):

    bad (pl.), 387; lat, 81; war, whare, (see Gl.).

10. WS. *ēa*, WG. *a*+*o* (*Gr.* 111):

    sla, 90.

11. Contraction WS. *e*+*ā*.

    na, 317.

II. OLD NORSE.

    bath, 90, 200; baynley, 334; call-, 42; craue, 118, 211, 230, 290; frained, 405;
    haste, 120, 375, 383, 402, 455; lau, 435, law, 28, 54, 221, 319, 328; samen,
    235; scath, 89, schathe 76; slaughter-, 425; sogat, 267; tak, 71, 106, 131, 278,
    343, 407, tale, 120, 422, tane, 260, 296, 364; tase, 159, þam, (see Gl. *he*).

III. ROMANCE (*Schwan*, 270).

    angel, 44, 63, 84, 94, 95, 115, 193, 265, 267, 287[2], 364; armurs, 336; bargan,
    88; catell, 411; chamber, 41, 114, 187; charite, 293; chaste, 128, 129, 202, 208;
    cumand, 349, 371, 403; fare, 324, 368; grace, 119, 285; grant-, 181, 271, 318,
    345; maner, 47, 161; maried, 23; pape, 17, 443; paradis, 203; parfite-, 223;
    place, 160, 204, 286; sacrifice, 350; saue, 49, 144, 164, 255, 263; sauore, 250,
    253, 256; saluyng, 142, 143, 189; sawiowre, 461; solace, 72, 376; talent, 51.

MIDDLE ENGLISH *e*.

I. West Germanic.

1. WS. *e*, WG. *ĕ* (*Gr.* 19.1):

euyn, 86, 237, 453; feld, 298; fele (*Gr.* 106. 3. Note), 38; help 220; sene (pp. *Gr.* 73. 1), 180, 417; steuyn, 261, 454; wele, 6, 55, 66, 173, 331, 450.

2. WS. *ę*, *i*-umlaut of *a* or *ǫ* (*Gr.* 89):

bed, 53; better, 230, dwell, 135, 168, 453; els, 171, 350; end, 39, 109, 145; hende, 92; hent, 375; ken, 5; schent, 50, 355, schende, 92; sendes, 210, sent, 188, 313, 443; sett, 31, 414; stede, 153, 458; tell, 96, 104, 107, 109, 288, 301, 303, 323, 367, 448; wed, 31, 37, 54; wende, 40, 271, went, 41, 53, 117, 120, 186, 237, 356, 425.

3. WS. *æ*, WG. *a* (*Gr.*50):

efter, 241, 313, 438,443; geder, 382 (Gr.50. Note 2); when (see Gl.),whether, 84.

4. WS. *eo* (*Gr.* 72):

   (a) Breaking of WG. *e* before *r*+consonant (*Gr.* 79.1):

      beried, 458; erthli, 170; ȝern, 216; hert, 13, 48, 55, 168, 202, 421; smert-, 371; werk-, 335.

   (b) by umlaut (*Gr.* 106.1; 81; 108):

      heuyn, 63, 85, 115, 125, 172, 238, 262, 356, 364, 375; sen (*Gr.* 109, Note), 143, 252, 255, 277; self, 83, 90; werld, 196.

5. WS. *ie* (palatal+*e*):

get, 189 (*Gr.* 75.3).

6. WS. *a*, Germ. *a:*

-swer, 92, 169, 226 (Gr. 160.2).

7. WS. *ê*, Germ. *ē* (*Gr.* 21.1):

here, 4, 81, 95, 174, 250; mede, 236.

8. WS. *ê*, *i*-umlaut of WG. *ô* (*Gr.* 21.2):

bete, 218; dem , 282; fed, 38; feld, 252, 253; ferd, 123, 245, -fere, 26, 291; fete, 269; seke, 142; swete, 217, 253, 256, 270.

9. WS. *ê*, by secondary lengthening (*Gr.* 121):

he, ȝe, me, þe, we (see Gl.).

10. WS. *ê*, representative of *ie*, *i*-umlaut of *ĕa* (*Gr.* 21.4):

dede, 311; kepe, 56, 201; ȝeme, 450; here, 261; herd, 43, 124, 180, 225, 267, 323, 348, 367, 399, 422; leue, 61.

11. WS. *æ*, Germ. *ai* (*Gr.* 17.1):

clene, 48, 58, 69, 113, 148, 179, 202, 366, 419; er, 366; dele, 174, 332; euer, 12, 15, 99, 162, 332, 462; hele, 214; led, 240, 358; les, 388; leue, 335; left, 434; mene, 47, 161; neuer, 16, 252, 253; redy, 277.

12. WS. *æ* WG.*ā*, Goth. *ē* (*Gr.* 17.2):

dede, 70; drede, 74, 76, 153, 168; ferlis, 304; red(e), 165, 167, 171, 312; sede, 128, 132; teche, 451.

13. WS. *ĕa*, WG. *au* (*Gr.* 37.1):

ded (sb), 154, 304, 306, 374, 389, 457; grete, 43, 238, 310, 339, 386, 434, 457, 460; hede, 424, heuides, 199, 354; schewes, 3.

14. WS. *ĕa*, WG. *ā*, Germ. *e.*

nere, 43 (*Gr.* 57.2, d).

15. WS. *ēo*.

   (a) WG. *eu* (*Gr.* 64):

      bede, 69, 428; dere, 19, 119, 272, 292; lem-, 194; tene, 409.

(b) Influence of *w* on WG. *e* (*Gr.* 73.1):

knel-, 191; knese; 427, knew-, 13, 28; new, 112, neuyn, 116, 171, 376 *Gr.* 156.5.); trew- 18, 111, 278.

(c) The result of contraction (*Gr.* 40.3; 113; 114):

be, 31, 50, 61, 70, 99, 102, 127, 170, 263, 266, 281, 311, 340, 350, 401, 404. bene, 322, 418, 439; se, 9, 14, 81, 94, 95, 134, 261, 265, 286, 357, 363; -fell, 304, 324, 368; fre, 2, 10, 100, 209, 221, 232, 273; frend-, 23, 30, 36, 38, 272; thre, 430, 431, 436, 438, 446; wex, 75; -twene, 147, 201.

16. Variants of WS.*ā*, WG. *ai* (*Morsb.* 87.2):

cled 148, cleth, 34, 112², 336 (*Murray*); -hede, 73; hete, 257.

17. Variants of WS. *i* (*Gr.* 92):

es, 41, 174; mekill, 130, þedir, 326; wretyn, 157, 160; wemen, 6.

II. OLD NORSE.

meke, 139, 141; mele, 213; nec, 428; wenges, 365.

III. ROMANCE (*Schwan*, 271).

amen, 463³; amend, 110; assent, 207, 274; certayne 263; clere, 44; conuers, 361; eger, 405; descend, 146; entred, 247; entent, 42, 52, 426, 444; enuy, 310; erber, 418; fell, 136; fers, 136; gentill, 11; grefe, 373, greue, 62, 74, 93, Jhesu(s), 14, 18, 101, 127, 209, 219, 259, 338; lessons, 138, letters, 150; melody, 45; menge, 320, 330; mercy, 2, 100, 209; meruayles, 302; pete, 1; prech, 298, 308, 315; present, 314; rebell, 137; reches, 384, 387; reherce, 362; reuerence, 460; ses-, 16, 441; seru-, 65, 88, 232, 297, 398, 454; speciall, 64; spens, 459; tretice, 303; vengeance, 71; verray-, 84, 266.

MIDDLE ENGLISH *i*.

I. WEST GERMANIC.

1. WS. *i*, WG. *i* (*Gr.* 23; 45; 54):

    (a) in closed syllables.

    bid, 281, 423; -gin-, 98; his, him (see Gl.); if, 56, 59, 79, 87, 94, 96, 102, 105, 256, 312; in (see Gl.); ilk, 40, 174, 204, 286, 329, 332, 359 (from orig. long *i*, *Gr.* 43. Note 4); it, hit, yit (see Gl.); lif (wv.), 223, 328, 342, 450; still, 154; þis (see Gl., once þus, 210); will, 59, 79, 181, 213, 227, 241, 287, 318, 338, 345, 351, 448, 454; win, 131, 233; wit, 67, 173, 400; wist, 177; with (see Gl.); writen, 174.

    (b) before -*ng* (*Gr.* 124.1):

    bring, 372; thing, 97, 118, 157, 170, 216, 290, 378.

    (c) before -*ld* (*Gr.* 124.3):

    milde, 12, 22.

    (d) in open syllables:

    biding, 8, 182, 346; lif-, 190, 293, 309, 389, 438.

2. WS. *y*(*ū*) *i*-umlaut of WG. *u* (*Gr.* 31):

    did, 282, 320; fill, 182, 337, 346, 413; first, 383, 405; kirk, 452, 459; kit(?) (origin unknown, *Murray*), 432; mikell, 91; sin, 189, 234, 433; think, 251.

3. WS. *ie*, palatal umlaut of *ea*, WG. *a* (*Gr.* 82; 101):

    might, 3, 5, 100, 126, 276, 396, night, 16, 64, 137, 335, 420 (*Gr.* 98. Note).

4. WS. *ie*, *i*-umlaut of *eo*, WG. *i* (*Gr.* 100):

    brin, 412, 416, brint, 404, 410 (*Gr.* 79.2); hir, (gs., ds., as., see Gl. *scho*).

5. WS. *ie*, palatal umlaut of *eo*; WG. *e* by breaking (*Gr.* 83; 101):
betwix (*Gr.* 84.2 Note), 81; bright, 63. 115, 419; right, 108, 155, 241, 282, 360;
sight, 4, 151, 359; wirk, 318, 351, 451 (*Gr.* 79.1).

6. WS. *ie*, WG. *e*, preceded by a palatal (*Gr.* 75.3):
gif, 113, 129, 224, 341, 436. 445. 449; ȝing, 7 (WG. *u: Gr.* 74; 100, Note 1).

7. WS. *eo*, WG. *ĕ*, through influence of *w* (*Gr.* 72):
wirschip. 397, 460 (*Gr.* 72. Note).

8. WS. *i*, WG. *i*, shortened:
blis, 238, 342, 358; wikked, 377.

9. WS. *ā+i*, WG. *a*, contracted and shortened:
swilk, 70. 74; slike, 252, 285.

10. WS. *i*, WG. *i* (*Gr.* 59):
hid, 34; life, 109, 240, 301, liue (sb.), 446; like, 229, 251, 288, 366; rich-, 35;
schin-, 193; smite, 354, 424; strife, 386; strike, 430; time, 306; whils, 175,
450; whitte, 113; wife, 123, 186, 239, 385; wise, 37, 134, 397, 451.

11. WS. *i*, by secondary lengthening (*Gr.* 121):
bi-, 410; mi, 205, 209. 229, 452, 453, my, 48, 49, 64, 68, 173, 219, 220, 231, 272,
448, my-, 83, 90; sithes, 4 (*Gr.* 122).

12. WS. *ȳ (ü)* *i*-umlaut of *ū* (*Gr.* 31; 96):
bridal, 39; file, 49, 68; fire, 404, 416; king, 347, 377, 390; kiss-, 248, 249, 269;
pride, 33.

13. WS *ie*, *ēa* by *i*-umlaut (*Gr.* 99):
-liue, 327; hight, 125.

14. WS. *ie*, *ēo* by *i*-umlaut (*Gr.* 100.b):
light, 152, 194, 336.

II. OLD NORSE.

lift-, 156; lite, 353; mis, 110, 357; scill, 447; skin, 25; till, 23, 39, 106, 109,
158, 166, 170, 288, 317, 352, 428 (and see Gl. *until*); tite, 312; tiþ-, 348, 423;
þir (np., ap. of þis, see Gl.).

III. ROMANCE (*Schwan*, 274).

affied, 300; baptist, 27, 102, 178, 283, 327, 330, 394; baptime, 164, 296; bill,
157, 165; bisschop, 106. 121, 280, 283, 457; crist, 28, 42, 222, 315, 319. 341, 344,
393; desire, 413; gin, 67; lilyes, 251; lion, 136; min, 299, 411; prince, 307, 316,
329; sir, 59, 74, 93, 105, 277, 445, uirgins, 366.

MIDDLE ENGLISH *o*.

I. WEST GERMANIC.

1. WS. *o*, WG. *o* (*Gr.* 55):
body, 49, 68, 202, 355; bod- 210; born, 11, 252; folk, 20, 22, 38, 163, 359, 370;
for, 54, 70, 95, 133, 140, 153. 204, 246, 351, 389, 408, 435, for-, 72, 221, 229,
275, 317, 342, 346, 451, -for, 147, -fore, 192, 300, 402, -forn, 373; god, 52,
65, 85, 97, 115, 126, 241, 255, 262, 285, 287, 293, 297, 305, 421, 427, 445, 446,
god-, 94, 193. 265, 408; gold, 32, 150; morn, 371; oft-, 4; or, 69, 302; word,
77, 80, 92,107, 175, 225, 270, 362.

2. WS. *o*, WG. *a* (*Gr.* 51):
of (see Gl.); on, 47, 71, 121, 150, 161, 309, 333, 371, ·on, 199, 244, 437, on-, 69,
o, 176.

3. WS. ǫ, WG. *a*, with loss of nasal (*Gr.* 66; 185):
broght, 39, 158, 195, 203, 306, 326, 374, 402, 423; fro, 203, 296, thoght; 55.

5

4. WS. *æ*, WG. *a*, by *i*-umlaut (*Gr.* 90):
   most, 7, 126.
5. WS. *u*, WG. *o* before a nasal (*Gr.* 70):
   -com, 284, komen, 26; won, 231; wond, 307; wonders, 305.
6. WS. *u*, WG. *o* (*Gr.* 55):
   loued, 127; mornig, 391 (*Gr.* 389, Note).
7. WS. *eo* preceded by a palatal, WG. *u* (*Gr.* 74):
   gong, 25.
8. WS. *ó*, WG. *ó* (*Gr.* 60):
   blode, 11; boke 149; broþer, 218, 220, 234; do, 29, 66, 317, 345; -dome, 236; loke, 156; mode, 12, 22, 381, 405; moght, 56, 442; soght, 143, 325, 401; to (see Gl.); wode, 400.
9. WS. *á*, WG. *ai* (*Gr.* 25.2), (*Morsb.* 134):
   cloth, 148; lord, 48, 57, 144, 205, 219, 229; more, 172, 299, 376, 388, 411; oþer (*Gr.* 62, Note); 20, 29, 84, 198, 380.
10. WS. *ó*, WG. *á* before a nasal (*Gr.* 68):
    come, 184, 244, 280, 314, 385, 440; done, 227, 378; sone, 146, 176, 187, 192, 313, 318, 323, 356, 413.
11. WS. *ó*, contraction of *e+á*:
    no, 33, 76, 316, no-, 28, 77, 217, none, 29, 142, 216. 430; noght, 50, 62, 77, 93, 94, 141, 144, 152, 266, 343, 351, 432, 441; nowþer, 89.
12. WS. *á*, WG. *á*, by secondary lengthening (*Gr.* 121):
    so, 36, 82, 188, 193, 217, 253, 263, 355, 420.
13. WS. *éo*, Germ. *eu*:
    lose, 73; gode (contr. i+o, *Cosijn*, 38.2), 389.
14. WS. *i*, WG. *i* (*Morsb.* 149.3):
    woman, 79.
15. WS. *e+u*, WG. *u*:
    bot, 30, 33, 55, 96, 303, 312, 318, 399, 405, 430.

II. OLD NORSE.
   bone, 228; both, 21, 64, 137, 224; toke, 135, 155, 197; trow, 18, 79, 96, 102, 167, 172, 173, 179, 278, 333, 360, 396, trowth, 258, 278.

III. ROMANCE (*Schwan*, 277).
   coron-, 195, 201, 340, 341; dole, 311, flores, 419; honor-, 294, 462; kosyn, 272; nobill, 26; organs, 44; rose, 251.

MIDDLE ENGLISH *u*.

I. WEST GERMANIC.
   1. WS. *u*, WG. *u* (*Gr.* 56):
      cursed (Late OE. *u*, origin unknown, *Murray*), 347; durst, 29, 76; sum, 4, 433; sun, 101; sunder, 432, thurgh, 119, 232, 233; þus (see Gl.); un- (see Gl.).
   2. WS. *u*, WG. *o* (*Gr.* 29.2; 55):
      cum 235, -cumen, 339 (Gr. 70); ful, (see Gl.); luf, 66, 87, 259, luf-, 69, 82, 116, 273, 293; furth, 387, 428.
   3. WS. *u*, WG. *u* (*Gr.* 30.1):
      husband, 53.
   4. WS. *ú*, WG. *ú*, with loss of *n* (*Gr.* 185.2):
      us, 81², 250, 260.

5. WS. *ū*, by secondary lengthening:
up, 120, 156, 237, (but op-, (*opon*) 199, 244, 437).

6. WS. *ō*, WG. *ō* :
gude, 21, 42, 52, 62, 121, 181, 190, 250, 361, 382, 390, 406, 426: luke, 150, 152, 245; bus (OE. *bihofian*), 61.

7. Variant of WS. *i*, WG. *i:*
þus, 210.

8. Representative of WS. *eo*, due to palatal influence on *o* (*Gr.* 101):
suld, (pt.), 31, 311, 401, 404, 410, 430, 436.

II. CELTIC. put, 352.

III. ROMANCE (*Schwan*, 277).
cuntre, 429; custom, 429; multiplise, 133; turmentes, 373.

MIDDLE ENGLISH *y*.

I. WEST GERMANIC.

1. WS. *y*, *i*-umlaut of *u :* kyn, 26; syn, 50, 68.

2. Representation of WS. *i*, WG. *i:* -gyn, 190.

3. Representative of WS. *i*, WG. *i:* lynnen, 148.

4. Interchangeable with *i :* bi, by; mi, my (see Gl.).

II. OLD NORSE. lym, 140.

III. ROMANCE (*Schwan*, 278). syr, 62, 63, 103.

DIPHTHONGS.

I. WEST GERMANIC.

1. WS. *æ* before *g*, WG. *a* (*Gr.* 49):
day, 16, 64, 137, 420, 438, 446; faire, 21, 25, 419; may, 5, 9, 83, 94, 95, 110, 130, 376; mayster- 388; mayne, 185; mayden, 7, 10, maiden- 439, 449, 453; said, 46, 58, 78, 93, 126, 166, 200, 206, 216, 227, 249, 264, 270, 311, 337, 407, 435, 445, 455, saydē, 78.

3. WS. *e*, WG. *ē:* way, 106, 176, wai, 40.

4. WS. *ę*, *i*-umlaut of WG. *a* (*æ* or *ǫ*,) (*Gr.* 89.1):
lay, 154, 387; say, 103, 175, 267, 316, sais, 80, 82.

5. WS. *ēa*, lengthened from *ea*, palatalization of WG. *a:*
ogain, 183, ogains, 138, 152, 299, ogayne, 186, 264.

6. WS. *ā*, WG. *ai:* sawl-, 130, 140, 164, 356, 363, saul, 375.

7. WS. *u*, WG. *u:* boun, 8, 297.

8. WS. *ū*, WG. *ū:* bow-, 281, 334; down, 269; hows, 194, 247, 383, 403, 411; out-, 89, 98, 234, 353, 357, 400; toun, 298.

9. WS. *ū*, WG. *ō* preceded by *w:* how, 123, 177, 245, 324, 358, 368, 369, 370.

10. WS. *ū*, lengthened from WG. *u* -with loss of n: mowth, 171.

11. WS. *ū*, the result of secondary lengthening:
now, 61, 80, 131, 233, 257, 271, 277; tou, þou, þow. (see Gl).

II. Old Norse. þai, þaire, (see Gl.); **trewe,** 73.

III. Romance.

   1. OF. *ai, ay, ey, ei:*
      abaist, 343; assay, 83, 105; array-, 35; availe, 130; bataile, 339; faith, 163;
      lay, 138, 267, 315; payde, 77; place, 160, 204, 286; pray-, 15, 421, 427, prai-,
      145, 191, 447; saint, 10, 323, 331, 380, 391; traitur, 389; uaines, 433.

   2. OF. *a:* ensaumple, 9, maumet-, 276, 309, 395, mawmet, 299, 333.

   3. OF. *au:* bycaus, 21.

   4. OF. *ie:* conciens, 178.

   5. OF. *ou:* cours, 337; pouer, 408; pouste, 3; power, 316; spows, 135, 248;
      stoutly, 386; vowches, 255.

   6. OF. *o:* counsail(l), 86, 208, cownsail, 60, 129; flowre, 73.

   7. OF. *oy:* noyis, 43.

   8. OF. *ui:* fruit, 131.

V.

METRICAL ANALYSIS OF THE VERSIONS.

The metrical analyses here given of the central versions of this edition are in the main illustrative, each, of a group of legends. The Southern and Midland type is represented by MS. Ash. 43, the prevailing type in the Northern legends by MS. Cott. Tib. E. VII. In contrast to the uniformity of the long-line couplets of the South, is the variety in line length, stress, and strophaic arrangement, of the later Northern group. For this reason the meter of MS. Cott. Tib. E. VII. does not stand as an analysis of so characteristic a form for the legend, though it was an easy and therefore a popular rime-form for a great variety of literary productions of the 14th century.

MS. ASHMOLE 43.

I. METRE.

1. *Latin Septenary* (Schipper, *Eng. Met.*, I. §§ 113–115), iambic, 4+3 stress, in couplets with an equal proportion of masculine and feminine end-rime; usually masculine cæsura. Several lines in this version are French Alexandrine (Schipper, I. § 54), 3+3 stress, usually masculine cæsura, riming, masculine or feminine, with its adjacent septenary.

The standard line, most free from irregularities of contraction and elision, reads as follows:

> 8 Gerláns & trésours ál of gólde‖þe hére néxt hirẹ líche.
> 110 þing bét ne mái him sílue hélp‖hou mái it hélpe þê.
> 133 Cecíle, vor héo wómman wâs‖atóm heọ môst abíde.
> 134 Ac þís breþéren þát werẹ mén‖abóute wénde wíde.
> 135 & wén me mártred crístenmén‖þudér he wólde gón.
> 136 & stélẹ to wén hi míȝte bést‖& búrie hém anón.

so also *ll.* 7, 16, 36, 40, 41, 63, 64, 68, 72, 95, 96, 97, 98, 100, 111, 114, 123, 126, 128, 129, 133, 137, 144, 173, 175, 177, 190, 193, 194, 195, 196, 197, 210, 220, 227, 235, 240, 243, 245, 251, 254, 255, 256.

Beside the lines reducible by slurring and elision to the above type, the following have an irregular number of syllables, *ll.* 31, 58, 75, 104, 106, 119, 124, 126, 127, 151, 152, 153, 161, 162, 171, 180, 201, 203, 205, 207, 228, 253. These vary from five *l.* 27, and six (*ll.* 58, 104, 127, 153, 180, 203), to eleven (*ll.* 75, 152) syllables in the first hemistich, and from three (*l.* 153) to nine (*l.* 126) in the second hemistich.

Probable Alexandrines are the lines:

27 Lif þou wólt, lefmón‖þat ích ileúe þís.
58 Seyn Vrban hím nom vp‖& gan hím uorþ léde.
104 "Le" séde valérián‖wel mé bi-hóueþ só.
107 þo séde þis hóli máide‖tybórs leué broþér.
138 Ho máde hem só hardí‖to bén þeempérours fón.
146 & tóke þat wás awórþ‖& no sémblance nídde.
180 þis þré holi martírs‖to-gádere heo búrede anóu.
203 Wén þou miȝt deþ ȝúue‖me þénch bi pur ríȝt.
257 þis wás two hóndred ȝér‖& þré & twénti ríȝt.
258 Aftér þat oúr lord wás‖In is modér alíȝt.

Also 153, 204, 207, 232. Some of these (_ll._ 27, 58, 153, 173, 180, 203,) MS. Laud. enlarges to septenary form.[1]

2. _The cæsura:_ The principal cæsura occurs regularly after the fourth foot, immediately following an accented syllable. Not infrequently a final -_e_ that may or may not be elided occurs before the cæsura. See _ll._ 1, 3, 5, 6, 8, 13, 15, 16, 19, 23, 33, 36, 39, 41, 48, 51, 61, 68, 69, 70, 71, 73, 81, 88, 90, 94, 100, 105, 107, 108, 110, 115, 122, 123, 124, 128, 130, 132, 142, 147, 148, 153, 156, 157, 161, 172, 173, 174, 178, 185, 186, 188, 193, 194, 195, 196, 198, 200, 202, 203, 206, 215, 220, 221, 222, 225, 227, 231, 233, 237, 239, 240, 241, 243, 250, 260.

An extra syllable other than -_e_ at the end of the first hemistich, forming a feminine cæsura is found in,

31 Lif ich ise þat in folie lóuest‖an noþer þen me.
50 & sede þat cicile him sende þúder‖to esce cristendom.
102 Non we beþ verst of slepe awáked‖nou we mowe uerst ise.
192 To clepe me fol þat am þi máistre‖ne suxstou my poer.

A secondary cæsura may be detected in the following, in the first member:

1 Séyn Cecíle | of nóble kúnne‖ibóre wás at róme.
15 "Suéte héorte" | quáþ þis máide‖" uor loúe þat þou hást to mé.

There may be two cæsuras in the first member:

73 "Witeþ þís" | he séde | In tréwe lóue‖wiþ chást bodí & cléne.
89 "Broþér" | he séde | "hóu geþ þís"‖þis týme óf þe ȝére.

One cæsura may occur in the second member:

92 I né miȝte hém verísore smúl‖me þénch | þen ích nou dó.
113 Séyn cecíle him cúste anón‖" léue tybórs " heo séde.

These examples may be multipled.

1 27. "Lif þóu wilt," séyde Valérián,‖þat ích I-léue þís,
58. Seint úrban nóm him vp aȝén,_lánd_ gan hím forþ léde.
153. In héruest whán þe swýnkeres mówe‖ffair schéf _and_ goód _and_ rype
173. Opón þe mórue, to þé mauméts‖þis ȝóde mén were bróuth
180. Þesé þre hóly mártíréal‖ȝe búrede to-ȝýdere anón
203. Seþe þóu myȝth ȝíue deþ ánd no tíftme þínkþ bé pur ryȝtte.

3. *Enjambement:* There is apparently little effort to lighten the metrical effect of the poem by the running-on of the first to the second hemistich, or of line to line. One probable example of the run-on line is,

> 143 "Sírę, we wólde," quebę þís opér, "þát we wúrþí wére
> 144 Hor knáues uórte hábbę íbé þat ӡé lette quélle þére.

and the following may fairly be regarded as examples of the running-on of the first hemistich.

> 153 In héruest wén hi mówe váir corn répe
> 258 Aftér þat oúr lord wás in ís modér alíӡt.

The poem is somewhat lightened by the inversions of the conversational passages. Considerable shifting of word stress is unavoidable, in words both of Germanic and Romance origin. An incomplete list follows:—Jústice, 137, Jústicé, 161, Justíce, 149, 172, 175; Cécile, 167, Cecíle, 67, 69, 133, Cécilé 113; bróþer, 95, 114, broþér. 82, 107; léfmon, 27, lefmón, 20; Vrbán, 40, 51, 66, 129, Vŕban, 58; Týbors, 82, 87, 107, 131, Tibórs, 111, 127; Valérián, 52, 60, 79, 81, 95, Válerían, 57, 117; þorú, 97, þóru, 5; schollép, 155, schúllep, 156. The metre allows the retention of the French pronunciation in richesse, 6.

4. *Arsis and Thesis:* The acephalous line is a frequent type produced by the omission of the first thesis:

> 21 Váste hé stont hér by mé‖& íf he únderӡéte.
> 23 Þát he nólde hárde smyte‖& bý-nymę þé þi míӡte.
> 56 Hór wiþ wíte vésteméns‖a súyþę uair wrít he bér.

so also *ll.* 1, 14, 15, 19, 21, 23, 27, 33, 39, 46, 56, 61, 66, 82, 87, 93, 99, 119, 124, 127, 131, 140, 143, 156, 157, 159, 163, 165, 166, 168, 169, 182, 185, 198, 200, 206, 207, 212, 224, 228, 242, 244, 250, 256.

By the omission of the first thesis of the second hemistich, two accented syllables come together:

> 30 In clánnessę ichúlle þi wílle dó‖ál aftér þi réd.
> 34 Þou móst byléuę on ihésu críst‖& icrístned bé.
> 54 & móre tiraúnt þen ény wólf‖ás a lómb þus mílde.

So also *ll.* 31, 44, 53, 58, 60, 61, 75, 81, 82, 105, 107, 108, 109, 121, 127, 139, 143, 145, 146, 149, 152, 153, 164, 186, 187, 189, 206, 209, 213, 215, 218, 222, 237, 238, 239, 241, 247.

An arsis and a thesis are wanting in the second hemistich of the following lines:

> 124 Fól he wérę þat ít woldę lésę‖vor ény stríf.
> 153 In héruest wén hi mówę‖váir corn répe.
> 201 A wréchę caróinę þou míӡtę ӡeuę déþ‖þat wél schort ís.
> 205 & wén þou déþes sérgaunt árt‖deþ þi lord ís.
> 252 Vpe ís poer þér-Innę wérę idó‖In álle wíse.

A trisyllabic measure, produced by doubling the thesis, must frequently be employed to reduce the redundancy of the line. (Ellis, *E. E. Pron.* p. 334.)

    5 Þóru híre fréndes strēngþe|ispóus*ed heo* wás *to* a mán.
    12 Let lórd myn hérte un-wémmed bē|þ*at* þné *be con*foúnded nógt.
    93 Só vol ícham óf þis smúl|ĵŏ⸱ *so* múchẹ *it is* ín my þógt.
    125 An wén þer ís so múri lif|þ*at we* schúllẹþ her-áfter auónge.

Other instances may be found in *ll.* 13, 28, 31, 33, 35, 40, 45, 5², 57, 62, 67², 70, 77, 78, 86, 91², 93², 106², 112, 118, 119, 120, 125², 130, 131, 152², 154, 155, 163, 170, 171, 174, 183, 187, 188², 191, 202, 207,² 208², 215, 216, 219², 226, 228, 230, 233, 234, 237, 248, 250, 253.

5. *Elisions:* A final vowel occurring before a vowel or aspirate *h* before a vowel, in another word, is usually elided. Syncope is illustrated in the metre by the following: werdẹ 7, trist-iliche 18, togadere 180, carọine 196, 201, creature 223, louẹst 25, seoþ 25, clepeþ 52, ouẹr 62, liljon 71, welluwe 75, tokẹneþ 77, 78, scholleþ 84, neuẹre 90, poẹr 189, 252. Syncope in preterite endings in *ll.* 5, 48, 102, 135, 145, 180. *Heo* is frequently slurred as in *ll.* 2, 3, 5, 180, 230, 231, 233. Diæresis is found in conseïl 17, wardeÿn 20, vestëmens 56, emperoürs 140, sergäunt 205, þenc˙þ 203, iugë-ment 142, 221.

Final -e:

The following classification of the use of final -*e* in MS. Ash. 43 is made on the basis of Ellis' enumeration and suggestions for the study of Chaucer. (*E. E. Pron.* p. 339-42.)

In many cases an allowance must be made for a possible double reading of the lines. In doubtful cases the choice here given has been influenced by grammatical and rhetorical stresses, and by reference to MS. Laud, 108.

(a) Final -*e* was elided before a following vowel: *ll.* 7, 12, 19 (89 times).

Doubtful cases: *ll.* 29, 173, 218, 237, 253, 260.

(b) Final -*e* was elided before *h*: *ll.* 3, 32, 50 (47 times).

Doubtful cases: *ll.* 4, 14, 19, 33, 53, 110, 132, 166, 184, 222.

(c) Final -*e*, when the sign of an oblique case, was elided before a consonant: *ll.* 1, 3, 10 (68 times).

Final -*e*, when the sign of an oblique case, was not elided before a consonant: *ll.* 12, 13, 14 (39 times).

(d) Final -*e*, when the sign of verbal inflection, was elided: *ll.* 2, 3, 4 (66 times).

Final -*e*, when the sign of verbal inflection was not elided: *ll.* 7, 27, 28 (39 times).

(e) Final -*e* is elided in the nominative case: *ll.* 7, 10, 36 (12 times).

Final -*e*, in the nominative case is not elided: *ll.* 44, 113, 150², (10 times).

(f) Final -*e*, in *hire*, elided: *ll.* 3, 4, 8 (25 times).

Final -*e*, in *hire*, probably not elided: *ll.* 13, 235.

(g) Final -*e* in *hadde, habbe*, not preceding a vowel or *h*, elided: *ll.* 14, 67, 132, 147, 254.

Probable exceptions: *ll.* 74, 132, 150.

(h) Final -*e* in adverbs and prepositions, elided: *ll.* 3, 14, 18 (19 times).

Final -*e*, in adverbs and prepositions, not elided: *ll.* 4, 7, 10 (18 times).

(i) Final -*e*, at the end of first hemistich, permitting a possible pronunciation: *ll.* 1, 3, 5 (76 times).

(j) Medial -*es*- is pronounced: *ll.* 5, 7, 9, 47², 60, 76, 105, 144, 147, 157, 158, 168, 183, 204, 205, 208, 231, 250.

Medial -*es*-, pronounced as *s*: *ll.* 86, 96, 108, 109, 149, 231, 251.

II. RIME.

1. Masculine end-rimes in this version number 66, feminine, 64. With four exceptions,—broþer : oþer, 108; ibe : ise, 102; isoȝt: ibroȝt, 120; drinkeþ: swynkeþ, 152, and one case where two words are employed, it nys : it is, 148, the feminine endings are secured in the final -*e's*. These final -*e's* exist in infinitives in twenty-five cases. In five cases, the infinitive rimes with an infinitive, 41:42, 75:76, 177:178, 187:188, 217:218. Twice the infinitive rimes with a participle, 3:4, 243:244; twice with an opt. sg. 21:22, 187:188; three times with a pt. sg. 59:60, 175:176, 219:220; ten times with substantives, ns. 239:240; gs. 37:38; ds. 57:58, 155:156, 161:162, 35:36; as. 23:24, 167:168, 169:170, 189:190; twice with an adjective, ds. 73:74, ap. 237:238; once with an adverb, 125:126.

The rime in this version is practically pure. A difference in quantity which is to be detected in some word-pairs, is too slight to warrant citation since the short vowels allow of being lengthened. There is difference of consonance in cleue : ȝe[m]e, 25-6, and (?) seruice: wise, 251-2.

Words from West Germanic sources rime with those of Norse origin in, take:make, 217-18; lawe:dawe, 141-2, laste:caste, 75-6, 219-20, sone:bone, 79-80, 97-8, toke:boke, 71-2, fulle:smulle, 67-8.

Words of West Germanic origin rime with Romance words in the following: man:-an, 5-6, 45-6, 81-2, 129-30, -an:can 117-18, 15-16, 17-18, her:poer, 191-2, rome:come 1-2, mahon:adon, 183-4

-ture:fure, 223-4, -tise:wise, 41-2, lif:strif, 123-4, seruice:wise, 251-2.

2. *Alliteration:* Alliterative passages are distributed quite evenly throughout the poem, and are of sufficient distinctness and frequency to noticeably bind the lines, though their introduction is not coincident with logical or rhetorical stresses. The following are examples.

> 85 þe angel *w*ende *w*iþ þis *w*ord!
> 143 " Sir*e, w*e *w*olde," queþ*e* þis oþer! "þat *w*e *w*urþi *w*ere.
> 173 *H*or *h*eden *h*e *h*et boþ*e* of smyte!
> 194 Vor it nys *b*ote as a *b*leddor*e*! i*b*lowe uol of wynde.

So also; *ll.* 2, 10, 38, 59, 68, 220, 238, 240, and others. Alliteration between words of the same root is found in

> 9 Wen þe *menstrales songe* hor *song* of hor *menstrasie,*

and lines 14, 34, 90, 187, 195.
Assonance:

There is one case of end-assonance, *clene: ȝeme* (MS, ȝene) 25-6.

MS. COTT. TIB. E VII.

I. METRE.

1. *French short couplet:* (Schipper, I. §§ 117-124), each verse consisting of four (usually) iambic feet; a masculine cæsura occurs regularly after the second stress. Correct masculine rime is the rule, the possibility of feminine rime being secured, for the most part, through the final *e's.*

The first lines represent the prevailing type of scansion.

> Jhésus Crist, ful óf peté,
> To mánkind ís of mércy fró
> And schéw*es* his póuste & his might
> Of(t)-síthes her*e* únto súm men síght
> 5 So þát we máy his míghtes kén,
> Als wél*e* in wémen íls in mén,
> And íll-þermóst in máydens ȝíng
> Þat will be bóun to his bíding.

2. *The Cæsura:*

The cæsura may be strongly marked by rhetorical stresses as

> 31 Þe day was sett‖þai suld be wed

and *ll.* 1, 10, 16, 27, 56, 63, 66, 127, 307, etc.

The cæsura may be felt most strongly after the first stress:

> 48 Lórd‖þou mák my hért all cléne
> 363 He sáid:‖I só, þair*e* sáwl*es* ilkâne,

so also *ll.* 59, 79, 105, 212, 216, 218, 231, 363, 413.

Or after the third stress as

> 148 All cléd in lýnnen clóth|ful cléne
> 343 Þarfóre besę nóght abáist,‖to táke.

Occasionally two cæsuras are introduced:

> 93 Gudę sír|scho sáid|greué noght þé
> 136 A spóws|scho tóke‖with hír to dwéll.

Also *ll.* 227, 311.

The verse is but slightly retarded by cæsura in *ll.* 11, 15, 21, 26, 33, 36, 46, 60, etc.

Rhetorical pauses often are not coincident with metrical pauses as in ll. 62, 63, 74, 104, 147, 148, 343, 445.

3. *Enjambement:*

A pause in the thought usually occurs at the termination of the line. There is frequent skilful illustration, however, of the run-on line.

> Þan say I, syr, þat þou sall se
> 104 Þe Angell,—þat I tell to þe

> Woman, if þou will þat I trow
> 80 Þir wordes þat þou sais me now,
> Bitwix vs twa here lat me se
> 82 Him þat þou sais so lufes þe,
> So þat I may my-self assay
> 84 Whether he be angell uerray

So also *ll.* 29-30; 117-18, 120-21, 146-7, 156-7, 211-12, 217-18, 229-30, 261-2, 275-6, 286-7, 289-90, 332-3, 337-8, 359-60, 363-4-5, 387-8, 393-4, 407-8, 441-2, 455-6.

4. *Arsis and Thesis:*

The omission of the thesis gives an acephalous line in

> 1 Jhésus Críst, ful óf peté

and *ll.* 16, 25, 29, 48, 55, 58, 85, 97, 112, 117, 120, 134, 140, 173, 176, 180, 212, 219, 221, 232, 233, 255, 257, 269, 279, 291, 313, 316, 325, 344, 348, 397, 400, 411, 414, 419, 424, 426, 433, 437, 440, 446, 456, 458.

A double thesis must be read in *ll.* 130, 132:

> 130 Þat tó þairę sáwl may me*kill* aváil,
> 132 *Of* þe sédę þou hás in Cícill sáwn—

also *ll.* 23, 27, 136, 156, 174, 178, 198, 199, 226, 239, 243, 250, 252, 254, 266, 272, 274, 283, 318, 339, 383.

5. *Elisions:*

Elision or slurring takes place in *ll.* 63, 64, 80, 82, 125^2, 136, 151, 159, 196, 347, 364, 372, 399, 408. Medial *-e-* is syncopated in

richęly 35, halęly 122, parfitęly 323, wisęly 451, reuerence 460.
e in the preterite suffix *-ed* is syncopated in *ll.* 18, 149, 127, 263,
269, 300, 209, 321, 393, 396, 398², 405, 447, 458. *-id*, 282, 298, and *-yd*,
125. As exception to this we have *-ed* in *ll.* 156, 248, 249, 263, 293,
319, 360², 441; *-id* in 16, 24, 194, 315, *-*(t)*ed* in 318, 345.

Other vowels than *-e* being chiefly the essential vowels of
pronouns, are not agglutinated to the succeeding word beginning with a vowel, or vowel preceded by *h.* As illustration of
this non-elision before vowels, note in *ll.* 8, 15, 46, 114, 209, 235,
277, 333, 418, 420, 442; vowel before *h* + vowel, *ll.* 116, 122, 125,
132, 186, 224, 373, 375, 382, 417, 434, 444. Diæresis is not noted
except in the possible case of sawñ, 132. Word accent is subject to fluctuation, throughout, through the exegencies of
metrical stress. In proper names this becomes particularly
noticeable, *Cicíll* and *Cicill; Valírián* 24, *Válirían* 406, *Váliridn* 178,
Valíriąn 159, *Úrban* 106, *Urbán* 124, 120.

-es as a substantive termination is pronounced *-ęs, ll.* 32,42,94,
103, 116, 125, 164, 175, 224, 234, 251, 299, 302, 326, 335, 352, 354, 362,
363, 380, 436, 438; *ís*, 355.

-es, verbal, occurs *ll.* 3, 128, 129, 230, 423. Elsewhere *e* is not
elided in *-es*.

-es (substantively), 5, 23, 30, 36, 77, 80, 107, 182, 193, 199, 225,
265, 270, 319, 344, 356, 365, 384, 408, 409, 419, 430, 431; (verbally),
133, 167, 168, 181, 201, 210, 228, 229, 255, 328, 381.

Final -e:

1. Final *-e* is usually elided in any position as shown in the
following enumeration.

   (a) Elided before a vowel: *ll.* 6, 12, 14, 21 (62 times).
   Exceptions: 71, 112, 166, 261, 286, 242, 289.

   (b) Elided before *h* + vowel; *ll.* 66, 76, 122 (21 times).

Final-*e* before a consonant is elided:

   (a) Before case forms: *ll.* 37, 43, 62 (49 times).
   (b) Before verbal inflections: *ll.* 49, 62, 68 (23 times).
   (c) Adverbial *-e: ll.* 13, 55, 66 (23 times).
   2. Final *-e* before a consonant is not elided:
   (a) Before case forms: *ll.* 38, 109, 219, 386.
   (b) Before verbal inflections: *ll.* 108, 420.
   (c) Adverbial *-e: l.* 158.

The possessive pronouns furnish the following additional
cases of elision:

oure, 14, 224, 259, 461; ʒowre, 59, 61, 73, 337; þaire, 40, 130, 199, 240, 299, 301, 304, 312, 318, 354, 355, 356, 363, 365, 382, 395.

II. RIME.

1. The normal rime for version Cott. Tib. E vii. is the masculine. From a total of 231 couplets, 120 are masculine, and 11 are feminine (*ll.* 15-16, 85-6, 115-16, 131-2, 171-2, 237-8, 261-2,375-6, 423-4, 433-4, 453-4). Besides these feminines there is a considerable number which admit the possible pronunciation of final -*e*. This final -*e*, as shown above, was rarely pronounced when medial in the line. There are indications, however, that final -*e* at the end of the line was sometimes retained for euphony, since it must be remembered that the Saints' Lives were intended for the ear of the listeners, not to satisfy with well matched words the eye of the priest who read. *Mak* (inf.) occurs twice medially, *ll.* 350, 391 but *make* (inf.) *l.* 427, final, rimes with *strake; man* rimes with *Valirian, ll.* 169-70, 233-4, 253-4, but *Valiriane: allane* 243-4, *Valiriane: tane* 295-6, *Ualiriane: slane* 379-80. Opposed to this, note the variableness in *dede* (ppl. adj.): *stede*, 457-8, and *stede: ded* (ppl. adj.) 153-4; also of unmistakably silent -*e* in *cum: martirdome* 235-6, and *convers: reherce* 361-2. There are 74 of these quasi-feminine rimes. It is safe to say the pronunciation was variable, and left to the individuality of the officiating monk.

Of the 74 couplets in -*e*, 23 rimes are made by combination with infinitive endings, classified as follows:

Infinitive: infinitive.......................... 7
Infinitive: other verb forms. 3
   "   noun (oblique cases)............. ... 9
   "   adjective (strong)..................... 4

The remaining 20 of the rimes employed, 16 masculine, 4 feminine, require a transferred or "hovering accent" (*Schwebende Betonung*, Schipper, §119), to satisfy the metrical requirements. They are, (*-ing*-rimes), ʒing: biding, 7-8; thing: beginning, 97-8; asking: thing, 215-16; king: tiþing 347-8; *e*-rimes; pete: fre, 1-2, be: chastite, 127-8, 207-8, charite: degre, 293-4; he: menʒe, 319-20, cuntre: thre, 429-30; participial (*-and*-rimes), land: precheand, 307-8, stand: brinand 415-16. Others have varying formations, *ll.* 101-2, 225-6, 235-6, 313-14, 387-8, 397-8, 409-10, 439-40.

The rime is usually pure, even where it involves secondary lengthening of Middle English forms. The following list includes all the cases of difference in quality. cum: -dome, 235-6;

ȝode: gude, 389-90; gude: mode, 21-2, 381-2, 405-6; boke: luke, 149-50, knew: Jhesu, 13-14.

Words of West Germanic origin rime with the following Norse derivatives: wrathe: scathe, 75-6, gaste: haste, 119-20, 455-6, allane: tane, 259-60, ilkane: tane, 363-4, haste: maste, 383-4, take: sake, 71-2, 275-6, 343-4, 407-8; haue: craue, 117-18, 211-12, 229-30, 289-90, rathe: bathe, 119-200, meke: seke, 141-2, mele: hele, 213-14, wed: cled, 31-2, lite: smite, 353-4, mis: blis, 357-8, skin: kyn, 25-6, will: untill, 59-60, 287-8, 317-18, 351-2, hym: lym, 139-40, scill: will, 447-8, toke: boke, 155-6, done: bone, 227-8.

West Germanic rimes with Romanic; tane: -ane, 197-8, -ane: allane, 243-4, haue: saue, 163-4, 255-6, -ane: slane, 379-80, mayne: ogayne, 185-6, certayne: ogayne, 263-4, man: -an, 23-4, 169-70, 253-4, -an: þan, 121-2. leue: greue, 61-2, he: menȝe, 319-20, nere: clere, 43-4, reches: les, 387-8, knew: Jhesu, 13-14, be: chastite, 127-8, 207-8, cuntre: thre, 429-30, went: entent, 41-2, 425-6, end: amend, 109-10, end: descend, 145-6, sent: present, 313-14, sent: entent, 443-4, angell: tell, 95-6, wise: seruise, 397-8, multiplise: wise, 133-4, desire: fire, 413-14, wist: baptist, 177-8, gin: syn, 67-8, hows: spows, 247-8, -us: þus 329-30.

Words of Romance origin in some cases rime with those from Norse, tase: place, 159-60, -ane: tane, 295-6, bill: till, 157-8, 165-6.

3. *Alliteration:*

Alliteration is a frequent though not essential feature of the verse. It occurs for best illustration in the following lines:

> 38 *F*ull *f*ele *f*olk þaire frendes *f*ed.
> 45 Scho *m*ade hir *m*elody o*m*ang.
> 100 *M*ast of *m*ight and of *m*ercy fre.
> 112 *Cl*eth þe all in *cl*ething new
>   Whitte *cl*athes and *cl*ene shall he gif þe
> 125 He *h*euyd *h*is *h*andes to *h*euyn on *h*ight
> 246 Þor *h*alines *h*e of *h*im *h*erd.
> 278 To tak his *tr*owth & *tr*ewly *tr*ow
> 375 His saul was *h*astly *h*ent to *h*euyn

also *ll.* 5, 8, 18, 89, 110, 111, 112, 143, 148, 149, 196, 218, 276, 299, 326, 357. Alliterative phrases like the following occur: *m*ilde of *m*ode, 12, 22; *m*oste of *m*ight, 100, 126; *f*ers and *f*ell, 136; *l*emid of *l*ight, 194; *m*ede of *m*arterdome, 236; *b*aynly *b*ow, 334; gaf þe gaste, 456.

VI.

TEXTS AND VARIANTS.

ASHMOLE MS. [*fol.* 185 *back to* 188 *back*].

    S Eyn Cecile of noble kun*n*e ! ibore was at rome.
      Our lord crist heo louede wel ! ar heo f*r*am c*r*adel come
    Heo lette hir*e* baptise stillich*e* · as we fi[n]de*þ* iwrite.
    Ľerne heo bed ih*e*su c*r*ist ! hir*e* maidenhod to wite.
  5 *þ*oru hir*e* frendes streng*þe* ! ispoused heo was to a man.
    Of g*r*et nobleie & richesse ! *þa*t het valerian.
    *þ*is maide wer*e*de robe of pal ! & clo*þ*es swi*þe* riche.
    Gerlans & tresours al of golde ! *þ*e her*e* next hir*e* lich*e*.
    Wen *þ*e menst*r*ales songe hor song ! of hor menst*r*asie. f. 186.
 10 *þ*is maide stillich*e* song of god ! & seynte marie.
    Of *þ*e saut*er* heo song *þ*is v*er*s ! *þa*t mest was In hire po*ʒ*t.
    'Let lord myn herte vn-we*m*med be ! *þa*t Ine be *c*onfounded
      no*ʒ*t.'
    As heo was any*ʒ*t in rich*e* bedde ! wi*þ* hir*e* lord ibro*ʒ*t.
    Sone hadde *þ*is fole mo*n* ! of folie hir*e* biso*ʒ*t.
 15 "Suete heorte" qua*þ* *þ*is maide ! "uor loue *þa*t *þ*ou hast to me.
    G*r*ante *þa*t ic*h* *þ*e mote telle a lute p*r*iuete.
    & *þa*t ic*h* me mote scryue to *þ*e ! as *c*onseil p*r*iue"
    "Tristilich*e* *þ*ou mi*ʒ*t" qua*þ* *þ*is o*þ*er ! "to so*þ*e ic*h* bihote *þ*e."
    "Suete heorte" qua*þ* *þ*is maide ! "In warde icham ido.
 20 An angel is my wardeyn ! & my lefmon also.
    Vaste he stont h*er* by me ! & *ʒ*if he vnder*ʒ*ete.
    *þ*at *þ*ou by-nome my maidenhod ! uor no*þ*i*n*g he nolde lete.
    *þ*at he nolde harde smyte ! & by-nyme *þ*e *þ*i mi*ʒ*te
    Vor al *þ*e nobleie *þa*t *þ*ou hast ! *þ*e ne halt no*ʒ*t a*ʒ*en hi*m* fi*ʒ*te
 25 Ac *ʒ*if he seo*þ* *þa*t *þ*ou louest me ! In good lif & clene.

Legenda Aurea.

   Cæcilia, virgo præclarissima, ex nobili Romanorum genere exorta, et ab ipsis cunabilis in fide
Christi nutrita, absconditum semper evangelium Christi gerebat in pectore, et non diebus neque
noctibus a colloquiis divinis et oratione cessabat, suamque virginitatem conservari a domino exorbat.
Cum autem cuidam juveni, nomine Valeriano, desponsata fuisset, et dies nuptiarum instituta esset,
illa subtus ad carnem cilicio erat induta, et desuper de auratis vestibus tegebatur, et cantantibus
organis illa in corde soli domino decantabat dicens: "fiat, domine, cor meum et corpus meum immaculatum, ut non confundar;" et biduanis et triduanis jejuniis orans commendabat domino, quod
timebat. Venit autem nox, in qua suscepit una cum sponso suo cubiculi secreta silentia, et ita eum
alloquitur: "o dulcissime atque amantissime juvenis, est mysterium, quod tibi confitear, si modo tu
juratus asseras, tota te illud observantia custodire." Jurat Valerianus, se illud nulla necessitate
detegere, nulla prodere ratione. Tunc illa ait: "angelum Dei habeo amatorem, qui nimio zelo custo-
dit corpus meum. Hic si vel leviter senserit, quod tu me polluto amore contingas, statim feriet te, et
amittes florem tuæ gratissimæ juventutis, si autem cognoverit, quod me sincero amore diligas, ita

MSS. Laud 108; Cmb. R. 3. 25.

   1. L. seinte Cecilie, C. seint Cecelie (reg.) ; L. kynde, C. kunde; L. I-bore, C. bore | 2. L. oure,
C. oure; L. louerd (reg.) L.*ʒ*e (reg.); C. loued; C. or; | 3 L. let, C. lete; C. hure (reg.); L. bapti*ʒ*e, C.
baptyse; L. C. Stilleliche (reg.); L. fynden; L. I-wryte, C. ywryte; | 4. L. bad, C. bade; C.-hode (reg.);
| 5. C. *þ*orwe; L. pp. I-(reg.), C. spoused; C. suy*þ*e (MS. su*þþ*e?) | 6. C. gr*e*te; L. nobleye, C. nob-
ley; L. his name was, C. hete; | 7. C. wered; C. palle; | 8. L. garlaundes, C. garlouns; L. tressoures, C.
trassoures; C. nexte: | 9. L. whane *ʒ*e herde menstrales song, *ʒ*e song in hire menstralcie, C. wan myn-

MS. Bodley 799. [*fol.* 286a–288b.]

S eint Sisile of nobil kin bor*e* was at Rome ;
  Our*e* Lord C*r*ist ʒhe louid wel er ʒhe fro cradil come ;
  ʒhe leet her*e* baptise stillelich, as we finde write,
  ʒerin ʒhe had Ih*e*su Crist her*e* maydinhood to kepe
5 þorwʒ her*e* frend*us* strengþe, spousid ʒhe was to a man
  Of gr*e*t nobley *and* ryches, þat heet Valerian.
  þis mayde was cloþid in pal þat wer*e* swyþe ryche,
  Garlond also of gold, *and* her nex her*e* lyche.
  Whan mynst*ralus* song her*e* song of her*e* mynstralsyʒe,
10 þis mayde stilleliche song of God *and* Seint Maryʒe.
  Of þe saut*er* ʒhe song a vers þat mest was in her*e* þouʒt,
  "Leet, Lord, myn herte vnwem*m*ed be, þat I comfou*n*de be nouʒt."
  As ʒhe was anyʒt be her*e* lord in ryche beed I-brouʒt,
  Sone þis fool mon of foly her*e* be-souʒt.
15 "Swete hert," q*uod* þis mayd, "for loue þou hast to me,
  Gr*a*nt me þat I telle alyte pr*e*uite,
  And þat I mowe schriue to þe as conseyl pr*e*ue."
  "Tr*e*wly þou myʒt," q*uod* þis oþ*er*, "to soþe I be-hote þe."
  "Swete lem*m*on," q*uod* þe mayd, "In ward I am do,
20 An au*n*gel is my wardeyn, *and* my lem*m*on al-so,
  ffast he stont her be me, *and* ʒif he oundir-ʒete
  þat þou be-nome my maydinhood, for noþing nold he lette
  þat he nold þe hard smyt, *and* be-neme þe þi myʒt.
  For al þe nobley þat þou hast, þou no myʒt aʒen him fyʒt ;
25 But ʒif he se þat þou louist me in good lyf *and* clene,

C 39.
[*originally*
cxxvij]

MS. Cotton Cleopatra D ix. [*fol.* 155b–158b.]

Seint Cecile of noble kinne. ibore was at Rome,
  Oure louerd crist ʒeo louede wel. er ʒeo fram cr*a*del come
  Stilliche ʒeo let hire cristne. as we findeþ iwrite
  Lurne ʒeo bad oure lord crist. þat he scholde hire maidenhod wite
5 Suþþe þoruʒ strengþe of hire frendes. ywedded ʒeo was to a man
  Of grete nobleie *and* richesse inouʒ þat het Valerian.
  þþis maide werede robe of pal. *and* cloþes swiþe riche
  Gerlauns *and* tressours al of gold. þe her next hire liche
  Whan þis minestralles songen her song*es*. in hire minest*r*ancie
10 þþis maide stilliche gan singe. of god *and* seint marie
  A uers of þe saut*er* heron songe was. *and* þeron was mest hire þouʒt
  Let lord min hert wiþoute wem beo. þat ỹ ne beo confou*n*ded nouʒt
  A niʒt as ʒeo was in hire bed. mid hire lord ibroʒt.
  Son he hadde of folie. þis clene þinge bisouʒt
15 Swete hert þis maide seide. for loue þat þou hast to me
  Graunte me þat ich þe mot telle. a lutel in pr*i*uete
  þþat ich me mowe þerof schriue to þe. *and* þat þou hit wole hele
  Certes lemman þis man seide. to noman telle ic*h* nele
  Swete lemman þis maide sede. in warde icham ido
20 An angel of heuene is mi wardein. *and* mi lem*m*an also
  Wel faste he stod here bi me. ʒif he hit unde*r*ʒete
  þþat þou binome min maidenhod. for noþint he nolde hit lete
  þþat he þe nolde wel hard smite. *and* binime þe al þin miʒte
  Of þi strengþe *and* of þin noble stat. for þou miʒte nouʒt wiþ him fiʒte
25 Ac ʒif he seoþ þat þou louest me. in gode loue *and* clene

f. 155 b.
("Sanct*a* Cecilia.")

f. 156. (at top
of the page, "De
Sanct*a* Cecilia.")

stralis songen of menstralcie | 10. C. L. stiliche; C. songe; L. moder marye; 11. I̶ psalter; L. hire song
was; C. fers; L. wer-on; L. mast, C. moste; L. þout; | 12. L. lat, C. late; C. hert; L̶ wiþout wem; L. it,
C. ic; L. confundet; L. naut; | 13. L. a-nyʒt, C. a nyʒt; L. bed; C. myd; L. i-brouth; | 14. L. man; C.
foly; L. be-sout; | 15. L. C. swete herte (reg.); L. seyde, C. sede; C. haste; | 16. L. y, C. ic (reg.); L. mowe
(reg.); L. litel; | L. schryue, C. schryuen; L. þt þou it wille hele, C. conceil; | 13. L. "certes lemman," þis
ʒungman seyde, "noþing telle I nele," C. truliche; | 19. L. C. lemman; L. seyde, C. sede; C. i am; | 20. L.
Aungel (reg.); L. of heuene; L. lemman, C. leman; L. þer-to, C. also; | 21. L. C. faste; L. stant, C. stante;
C. here; | 22. L. be-nome; C. nold; | 23. L. ne wolde, C. nold; L. bè-nyme, C. bynym; L. myʒtte, C.
myʒt; | 24. L. C. of; L. ʒungness & of noble state, C. nobley; L. ne myʒth, C. ne myʒt; L. wiþ; L.
fyʒtthe, C. fyʒt; | 25. L. wiste, C. sey; L. louedest, C. loue; L. gode, C. goud; L. C. loue; | 26. L. wolde;

6

He wole þe wite as he doþ me : & ech vuel fram þe ӡe[m]e "
"Lif þou wolt, lefmon : þat ich ileue þis.
þe angel þou most scewe me : þat ich him ise iwis.
Lif ich mai þat sope ise : þat þou hast þat sope ised
30 In clannesse ichulle þi wille do : al after þi red.
Lif ich ise þat In folie louest : an noþer þen me.
I nele bileue uor noþing : þat I nele him sle & þe."
"Swete heorte" quaþ þis maide : "ӡif' þou wolt þen angel ise.
þou most byleue on ihesu crist : & icristned be.   (1 MS. þ ӡif)
35 Lif þou wolt so þou miӡt him ise : & wite he wole ous fram helle
& so gret Ioie worþ of our loue : þat no tonge ne mai telle.
Ac þre mile henne þou most go : to þe wei of apie.
þou schalt þere vynde pouere men : on ihesu crist crie.
Sei þat ich þe to hem sende : þat hi þe teche anon.
40 To Seyn Vrban þe olde mon : vor þou most to him gon
& priue conseil wiþ him speke : uor he þe schal baptise.
þen angel þou schalt þenne ise : & he schal ous boþe wise."
Valerian aros anon : as our lord him ӡef wille.
To þe stude þat þis maide bad : uorþ he wende wel stille.
45 þis pouere men him teiӡte anon : to þe olde mon Seyn Vrban.
In an old stude uor-let : þer as ne com no man.
Among olde puttes & burles : as me cristene men þreu.
After þat hi Imartred were : ware me eny 'ikneu. (1MS. meeny.)
To is fet he vel adoun : anon so he to him com.
50 & sede þat cicile him sende þuder : to esce cristendom.
"Louerd Ihered be þi miӡte" : sede Seyn Vrban.
"Is þis þe luþer werreour : þat me clepeþ valerian.

quoque diliget te sicut me, et ostendet tibi gloriam suam."
    Tunc Valerianus, nutu Dei correctus, ait : "si vis, ut credam tibi, ipsum angelum mihi ostende, et
si vere probavero, quod angelus sit, faciam quod hortaris ; si autem virum alium diligis, te et illum
gladio feriam." Cui Cæcilia dixit : "si in Deum verum credideris et te baptizari promiseris, ipsum
videre valebis. Vade igitur in tertium milliarium ab urbe via, quæ Appia nuncupatur, et pauperibus,
quos illic invenies, dices : 'Cæcilia me misit ad vos, ut ostendatis mihi sanctum senem Urbanum,
quoniam ad ipsum habeo secreta mandata, quæ perferam.' Hunc, dum tu videris, indica ei omnia
verba mea; et postquam ab eo purificatus fueris et redieris, angelum ipsum videbis." Tunc Valerianus
perrexit, et secundum signa quæ acceperat, sanctum Urbanum episcopum intra sepulchra martirum
latitantem invenit; cumque ei omnia verba Cæciliæ dixisset, ille manus ad cœlum expandens cum
lacrymis ait: "domine Jesu Christe, seminator casti consilii, suscipe seminum fructus, quos in Cæcilia

L. wytte, C. wyty; L. als; L. deþ, L. al; L. C. yuel; L. fro; L. ӡene, C. ӡeme; | 27. L. wilt; L. seide V.;
C. lemman sede he; C. leue; | 28. L. þen; L. angel; L. C. scewe; L. I (reg.); L. C. se; L. I-wis, C.
ywys; | 29.L.wanne; C.so[y?]: L. i-se, C. yse; L. i-seyd, C. ysede; | 30. L. clenesse; L. for-soþe, C. ic
wole; C. alle; C. þy; C. rede; | 31. L. C. se; L.anoþer, C. & oþer; L. C. þan; | 32. L. no-þing ne schal
ӡou helpe, C. nelle leue for; L. ne, C. nelle; | 33. L. seyde, C. guod; L. & þou wile þe aungel se, C.
þan; | 34. L. bileuen, C. moste lyuen; C. ybaptiӡed; | 35. L. wilt; L. C. schalt; L. sen, C. se; L. he wile
wytte, C. wele wyten þe; L. fro; | 36. C. such; L. ioye; L. C. oure; L. tunge; | 37. L. henne ouer; L.
gon; L. C. wey; | 38. C. þer; L. C. fynde; L. [þore], C. poure; C. man; C. in; L. faste, L. ӡeme; | 39. C.
hym; L. he, C. ic; C. tell; | 40. L. Whar is; L. þe holi old man, C. þe holy man; C. moste; | 41. L. ffor,

He wole þe loue as he doþ me, *and* ech euil fro þe ʒeme."
" Lif þou wolt, le*m*man," q*uod* þis oþer, " þat I be-leue þis,
þe aungel þou most schewe me, þat I hy*m* se, I-wis,
And ʒif I may þe soþe se, of þat þou hast I-seyd,
30 In clennesse I wole do þy wille, *and* aft*er* þy reed,
And ʒif I se þat þou in foly louist oþer þan me,
I nele leue for noþing, þat I nele sle him *and* þe."
" My swete hert," q*uod* þe mayde, "ʒif þou þe aungel se,
þou most be-leue oñ Ih*e*su Crist *and* I-cristenyd be;
35 Lif þou wolt so þou myʒt hym se, *and* he vs wole kepe fro helle,
So gret ioyʒe worþ of oure loue þat no tonge may it telle.   f. 286 b.
But þre myle þou most henn*us* go, to þe wey of appyʒe,
þou schalt finde þer*e* por*e* men, oñ Ih*e*su C*ri*st ʒerne cryʒe ;
Sey þat I þe to hem sent, þat þey þe teche anon
40 To Seint Vrban, þe holy man, for þou most to him gon,
Apr*eu*e conseyl w*ith* him to spek, for he þe schal baptyse ;
þe aungel þou schalt þanne se, *and* he schal vs boþe wyse."
Valerian roos. a-non, as our*e* Lord hym ʒaf þe wille,
To þe stede as þe mayde bad, *and* wente forþ wel stille.
45 þe por*e* men hy*m* tauʒte anon to þ*e* old man Seint Vrban,
In añ olde stede al forlete, þ*er* ne com no man*er* man,
Among old pitt*us* *and* berielus, þ*er* me c*ri*stin men þrew
Aft*er* þat þey martrid wer*e*, wha*n* me any of hem knew.
To his feet he fel doun anon, þo he to him com.
50 *And* seyde þat Sicile him sente þedir, to lerne Cristindom.
" Lord, heryid be þy myʒt." seyde Seint Vrban,
" Is þis þe liþ*er* verrour, þat me clepiþ, Valerian ? "

Wite he wole þe ! as he doþ me. *and* al uuel fr*a*m þe ʒeme
Lif þou wolt seide ualerian. þat ich ileoue þis
þþen angel þou most schewe me. þat ich seo him iwis
And ʒif ic*h* mai þe soþ iseo. þat þou hast soþe isede
30 In clannesse ichulle þi wille do. al af*ter* his rede
And ʒif ich seo þat in folie. þou louest anoþer þan me
Noþinge schal hit me binime. þat y nelle slee hi*m* *and* þe
Swete hert seide þis maide. ʒif þou wolt þe angel iseo
þþou most bileoue on iesu c*ri*st. *and* icristned also beo
35 Iseo him þou schalt ʒif þou wolt so. *and* wite he þe wolle fr*a*m helle
So grete ioie schal of oure loue beo. þat no tonge þerof mai telle
Ac henne ou*e*re þreo miles þou most go. to þe hulle of apie
Pore men þou schalt þer finde. *and* on iesu c*ri*st ʒurne c*ri*e
Seie þat ich þe to hem sende. *and* hi þe teche anon
40 Whar is seint Vrban þe holi man. for þou wolt to hi*m* gon
For priue conseil þou woldest wiþ hi*m* speke. *and* he þe schal baptize
And þan þou schalt þen angel iseo. *and* don as he þe wole wise
Valerian þo aros anon. as oure lord him ʒaf wille
To þe stude as þis maide bad. he wende hi*m* forþ wel stille
45 þþis pore men him tauʒte anon. to þe holi seint vrban
He fonde him in an old forlete stude. þ*er*as noman ne com
To his fet he fel adoun. anon þo he to him com
And seide þat Cicilie him þider sende. to ask*y* c*ri*stendom
Whar þis beo þe luþ*er* werrour. þat me clupeþ Valerian

C. & in; L. counseil, C. conceyl; L. þou wilt; C. myd (reg.); L. ʒ, C. for; L. C. baptiʒe; | 42. L. þan
C. þe; L. þanne, C. þan; L. & do as he þe wile wise, C. boþ; | 43. L. a-ros; L. a-non; L. oure louerd, C.
god; L. C. ʒaf; | 44. L. C. stede; L. þe, C. as heo sede; L. forþ; C. welle; | 45. L. pore, C. poure; L.
taute, C. teyten; C. man; | 46. L. C. stede; L. for-late, C. forlete; L. þat wonede neuere man; | 47. C.
amonge; C. old; L. burieles, C. buryeles; L. as, C. þer as; L. men, C. cristen; C. yrew; | 48. L. he, C.
hŷ; L. martired, C. martred; L. men anye kneu, C. wan me any knew; | 49. L. feet, C. fete; L. ful, C.
felle; L. a-doun, C. adoune; L. als-sone as [he], C. þo he; L. C. come; | 50. L. seyde; L. cesilie, C. cecele;
L. send; L. þider, C. þude[þ ?]; L. asken, C. habbe; L. dome; | 51. C. lord; L. I-herd, C. yheryed; L.
myʒtte, C. myʒt; L. C. seyde; | 52. L. Weþer þis be þat, C. ne ys þis þe; L. Luþere; L. werreor, C.
werreoure; L. men; L. clepuþ, C. clypeþ; | 53. L. were, C. where; L. haue y-mad, C. made; | 54. L.

"I ne wilny noþing so muche" : sede ualerian.
"As þat tybors my broþer : were cristeneman."
"My lord wole." quaþ þis angel : "ȝeue him þulke grace.
þat boþe ȝe scholleþ at one tyme be : Imartred In one place."
85 þe angel wende wiþ þis word : me nuste war he bicom.
þis two clene þinges wiþ Ioie Inou : hor eiþer to oþer nom
Tibors com to þe chambre : to speke wiþ is broþer þere
He stod stille & bihuld aboute : as he nuste war he were.
"Broþer" he sede "hou geþ þis : þis tyme of þe ȝere.
90 So suote smul ne smulde ich neuere : me þencþ as ich do here
þei þis hous were vol of rede rosen : & of wite lilion also
I ne miȝte hem verisore smul : me þencþ þen ich nou do.
So vol icham of þis smul : & so muche it is In my poȝt.　*l. 187.*
þat I not hou icham sodenliche : In oþer witte ibroȝt."
95 "Leue broþer" quaþ valerian : "gerlans we habbeþ here.
Of floures þat þou ne miȝt ise : bote þou were our Iuere
Ac so as þou hast þem suote smul : þer-of þoru our bone.
Gif þou wolt bileue as we doþ : þou miȝt hem ise sone."
"Leue broþer" quaþ þis oþer : "weþer is it soþ þis
100 Oþer ich stonde in metynge : & mete þat it so is."
"In metynge" quaþ valerian : "we habbeþ euer ibe.
Nou we beþ verst of slepe awaked : nou we mowe uerst ise."
"Suxton bet nou" quaþ þis oþer : "þen þou hast er ido."
"Le." sede valerian : "wel me bi-houeþ so
105 Vor my lordes angel of heuene : haþ iȝeue me siȝt
& vor our loue he wole þe also : ȝif þou wolt bileue ariȝt"

que volueris, et consequeris." Cui Valerianus: "nihil mihi in hac vita exstitit dulcius, quam unicus fratris
mei affectus, peto igitur, ut et veritatem ipse mecum agnoscat." Cui angelus: "placet domino petitio
tua; et ambo cum palma martirii ad dominum venietis." Post hoc, ingressus Tiburtius, frater Valeriani,
cum nimium rosarum sensisset odorem, dixit: "miror, hoc tempore roseus hic odor et liliorum unde
respiret; nam si ipsas rosas vel lilia in manibus meis tenerem, nec sic poterant odoramenta tantæ mihi
suavitatis infundere; confiteor vobis, ita sum refectus, ut putem me totum subito immutatum." Cui
Valerianus: "coronas habemus, quas tui oculi videre non prævalent, floreo colore et niveo candore
vernantes; et sicut me interpellante odorem sensisti, sic et, si credideris, videre valebis." Cui Tiburtius:
"in somnis hoc audio, an in veritate ista tu loqueris, Valeriane?" Cui Valerianus: "in somnis usque
modo fuimus, sed jam nunc in veritate manemus." Ad quem Tiburtius: "unde hoc nosti?" Et
Valerianus: "angelus domini me docuit, quem tu videre poteris, si tu purificatus fueris, et omnibus
ydolis abrenuntiaveris." (Huic miraculo de coronis rosarum Ambrosius attestatur in præfatione sic
dicens: 'sancta Cæcilia sic cœlesti est dono repleta, ut martirii palmam assumeret; ipsum mundum est
cum thalamis exsecrata; testis est Valeriani conjugis et Tiburtii provocata confessio, quos, domine,
angelica manu odoriferis floribus coronasti; viros virgo duxit ad gloriam, mundus agnovit, quantum
valeat devotio castitatis.' Hæc Ambrosius.) Tunc Cæcilia evidenter ostendit ei, omnia ydola esse

L. wille; L. þe; L. C. graunte; L. sone; | 8t. L. wille, C. wylne; C. no þyng; L. miche; L. seyde, C.
seide; | 8a. L. Bote, C. but; L. Tiburst; L. wiþ me; C. cristen man; | 83. C. sede; L. aungel, C. þe a; L.
wile ȝiuen þat ilke, C. ȝyue hym suche; | 84. L. C. &; C. boþ; L. schulle, C. schullen; L. C. o; L. I-
martired, C. martred; L. o, C. a; | 85. L. aungel, C. angle; C. þat; L. he, C. hy nust; L. wher, C. ware; L.
be-com, C. bycome; | 86. C. þes twey; L. þingges, C————; L. ech of oþer; C. nome; | 87. L. C. Tiburs; C.
come; L. spak, C. spake; C. with; L. C. his; C. þer; | 88. C. stode; L. beheld, C. byhelde. L. al-a-

" Wher, Sysile haue mad him, þat was so wilde,
Amore tyraunt þan a wolf, as alomb, mylde."
55 þo þer com an old man, fro heuin he alyȝt þer,
Cloþid in whit vestementus, and a fayr writ ber.
þo Valerian him seyȝ, he fel adoun for drede.
Seint Vrban nom him vp, and forþ gan hym lede.
þe Halw of Heuin took him þe writ, and bad him rede,—
60 " On lord is on to be-leue, and on baptysing,
On God and Fadir of alle, þat beþ, and ouer al is, and ech þing"
" Leuistow her-on," quod Seint Orban, "þat þou dost here se,"
" þer is noþing," quod þis oþer, "þat bet to leue may be."
After þis whit mon he be-held, he nyste wher he be com.
65 Seint Vrban hym nom anon, and ȝaf hym Cristindom.
To Sycile he wente aȝen, þo he hadde be þer his fille.
He fond here chaumbir lyȝt with-inne, and of sote smelle,
He fond Sysile his spouse, and aungel wiȝt here stond
Bryȝter þan eny sonne ; to garlondus he bar an hond
70 Of rosis and of lyliis soot ; þat on, Sysile, he took.
And þe oþer, Valerian, as we finde in book,
" Kepiþ þese," he seyd, " in trewe loue, wit chast body and clene,
I hem haue fro Heuin brouȝt, oure Lord hem ȝow doþ lene ;
For falwe, ne elde, neuer þey nele, but euer I-lych laste,
75 þe two maner of flourus þat beþ þer-on, nele neuere here heu caste."
" þe lyly be-tokeneþ ȝoure maydinhood, þat is so whit and sote,
þe rose be-tokenyþ ȝoure martirdom, forþ on deyȝe ȝe mote ;
And, for þou dedist, Valerinan, Secilis reed so sone,
What þou of my lord biddist, he wil grant þy bone."

50 Louerd þat Cicilie haþ imad. him þat was so wilde   49-50 Blank line in MS.
And more tiraunt þan eni wolf. as a lombe so milde
þþo com þer gon a swiþe old man. alite fram heuene þer[1]   (1 MS.per.)
Al hor wiþ white uestemens. and a wel faire writ he ber
Anon so ualerian iseiȝ him come. adoun he fel for drede
55 Seint vrban him nom vp anon. and forþ he gan him lede
þþis halwe of heuene him toke þis writ. and bad he scholde hit rede
Valerian anon radde þis writ. þat þes wordes sede
O god is and on bileone. and on cristendom
And fader and lord of alle þinge. þat flesshe and blod among ous nom.
60 Ileouest þis seide seint vrban. þat þou dost þere iseo   f. 156 b
þþer nis þinge in þis world þe oþer seide. þat betere ileoued mai beo
He biheolde after þis old man. he miste whar he bicom
Seint vrban þo him nom anon. and ȝaf him cristendom
To Cecilie son he wende aȝen. þo he hadde ibeo þer his fulle
65 He fonde hire chambre wel liȝt wiþinne. and swiþe swote smulle
And founde Cecilie his trewe wif. and an angel bi hire stond
þþat was briȝtore þan eni leom. tweie gerlauns he hulde an hond
Of rose and lilie hi weren imad. þat on Cecilie he tok
þþat oþer he tok ualerian ! as we findeþ in bok
70 Witeþ þeos he seide in trewe loue. wiþ chaste bodi and clene
Ich hem habbe fram heuene ibrouȝte. oure Lord hem doþ ȝou lene
þþe lilie tokneþ ȝoure maidenhod. þat is so white and swote
þþe rose tokneþ ȝoure martirdom. for þerinne deie ȝe mote
For þat þou dost ualerian. Ceciles red so sone
75 What so þou of mi lord dost bidde. he wole graunte þi bone.

sede; C. louynȝ; | 65. L. whyte, C. þe whyt; L. beheld, C. byhold; L. wher, C. ware; L. be-cam; C.
by-come; | 66. L. a-non; C. nome; | 67. L. sein Cecilie; L. was þare (reg.) is fulle, C. he þer his fulle; |
68. L. fond, C. founde; C. Schaumbre; L. lyȝth; L. wiþ-inne, C. with In; C. ful of swete smylle; | 69. C.
fonde; | 70. L. bryȝttere, C. bryȝtur; L. C. þan; L. C. any; L. lome; C. lyȝt; L. twey, C. two; L. gar-
londes, C. garlauns; L. hadde, C. held; L. on; | 71. L. rose, C. swete ros; L. lilie, C. lyly; L. tok; | 72. C.
þe; L. fynden; L. bok; | 73. L. in, C. myd chaste loue; L. chaste body; | 74. L. i-brouȝth, C. broȝt; L.
C. oure; L. C. hem; | 75. L. flor-falewe, C. falewy; C. olden; L. wille þei nat; L. euere he wille þ. laste,
C. more laste; | 76. L. manere; L. beþ on, C. beþ here on; L. nelle; L. neuere; L. hor; C. hewe; | 77. L.
be-tokneþ, C. bytokneȝ. L. whyt, C. whit; L. C. swote; | 78. C. marterdom; L. for (reg.); C.
deyȝe; | 79. C. dyst; C. Cecilijs; C. rede; L. C. so sone; | 80. L. what; C. oure; L. be-sekest, C. beste;

"I ne wilny noþing so muche": sede ualerian.
"As þat tybors my broþer : were cristeneman."
"My lord wole" quaþ þis angel : "ȝeue him þulke grace.
þat boþe ȝe scholleþ at one tyme be : Imartred In one place."
85 þe angel wende wiþ þis word : me nuste war he bicom.
þis two clene þinges wiþ Ioie Inou : hor eiþer to oþer nom
Tibors com to þe chambre : to speke wiþ is broþer þere
He stod stille & bihuld aboute : as he nuste war he were.
"Broþer" he sede "hou geþ þis : þis tyme of þe ȝere.
90 So suote smul ne smulde ich neuere : me þencþ as ich do here
þei þis hous were vol of rede rosen : & of wite lilion also
I ne miȝte hem verisore smul : me þencþ þen ich nou do.
So vol icham of þis smul : & so muche it is In my þoȝt.   f. 187.
þat I not hou icham sodenliche : In oþer witte ibroȝt."
95 "Leue broþer" quaþ valerian : "gerlans we habbeþ here.
Of floures þat þou ne miȝt ise : bote þou were our Iuere
Ac so as þou hast þem suote smul : þer-of þoru our bone.
Lif þou wolt bileue as we doþ : þou miȝt hem ise sone."
"Leue broþer" quaþ þis oþer : "weþer is it soþ þis
100 Oþer ich stonde in metynge : & mete þat it so is."
"In metynge" quaþ valerian : "we habbeþ euer ibe.
Nou we beþ verst of slepe awaked : nou we mowe uerst ise."
"Suxtou bet nou" quaþ þis oþer : "þen þou hast er ido."
"Le" sede valerian : "wel me bi-houeþ so
105 Vor my lordes angel of heuene : haþ iȝeue me siȝt
& vor our loue he wole þe also : ȝif þou wolt bileue ariȝt"

que volueris, et consequeris." Cui Valerianus: "nihil mihi in hac vita exstitit dulcius, quam unicus fratris
mei affectus, peto igitur, ut et veritatem ipse mecum agnoscat." Cui angelus: "placet domino petitio
tua; et ambo cum palma martirii ad dominum venietis." Post hoc, ingressus Tiburtius, frater Valeriani,
cum nimium rosarum sensisset odorem, dixit: "miror, hoc tempore roseus hic odor et liliorum unde
respiret; nam si ipsas rosas vel lilia in manibus meis tenerem, nec sic poterant odoramenta tantæ mihi
suavitatis infundere; confiteor vobis, ita sum refectus, ut putem me totum subito immutatum." Cui
Valerianus: "coronas habemus, quas tui oculi videre non prævalent, floreo colore et niveo candore
vernantes; et sicut me interpellante odorem sensisti, sic et, si credideris, videre valebis." Cui Tiburtius:
"in somnis hoc audio, an in veritate ista tu loqueris, Valeriane?" Cui Valerianus: "in somnis usque
modo fuimus, sed jam nunc in veritate manemus." Ad quem Tiburtius: "unde hoc nosti?" Et
Valer'anus: "angelus domini me docuit, quem tu videre poteris, si tu purificatus fueris, et omnibus
ydolis abrenuntiaveris." (Huic miraculo de coronis rosarum Ambrosius attestatur in præfatione sic
dicens: 'sancta Cæcilia sic cœlesti est dono repleta, ut martirii palmam assumeret; ipsum mundum est
cum thalamis exsecrata; testis est Valeriani conjugis et Tiburtii provocata confessio, quos, domine,
angelica manu odoriferis floribus coronasti; viros virgo duxit ad gloriam, mundus agnovit, quantum
valeat devotio castitatis.' Hæc Ambrosius.) Tunc Cæcilia evidenter ostendit ei, omnia ydola esse

L. wille; L. þe; L. C. graunte; L. sone; | 81. L. wille, C. wylne; C. no þyng; L. miche; L. seyde, C.
seide; | 82. L. Bote, C. but; L. Tiburst; L. wiþ me; C. cristen man; | 83. C. sede; L. aungel, C. þe a.; L.
wile ȝiuen þat ilke, C. ȝyue hym suche; | 84. L. C. &; C. boþ; L. schulle, C. schullen; L. C. o; L. I-
martired, C. martred; L. o, C. a; | 85. L. aungel, C. angle; C. þat; L. he, C. hȳ nust; L. wher, C. ware; L.
be-com, C. bycome; | 86. C. þes twey; L. þingges, C——; L. ech of oþer; C. nome; | 87. L. C. Tiburs; C.
come; L. spak, C. spake; C. with; L. C. his; C. þer; | 88. C. stode; L. beheld, C. byhelde. L. ala-

80 " I ne desire no þing so moch," seyde Valerian,
　　" As Tyburs, my broþer, were wit me in Cristindam."
　　" My Lord wille," *quod* þe aungel, " ȝeue hym þat grace,　　　f. 287,
　　And boþe ȝe scholle martrid be, at on tyme in on place."
　　þe aunge[l] went wit þat word, he nyste wher he be com.
85 þe two þingus eyþer of oþer gret ioyȝe nom.
　　Tyburs com to chaumbre, to spe[k] wit his broþer þere,
　　He stood stille *and* be-held about, as he nyst wher he were.
　　" Broþer," he seyde, " howȝ goþ þis? In þis tyme of þe ȝere?
　　So swete smel smellid I neuere, as I do here.
90 þou þis hous were ful of newe rosin, *and* lylis al-so,
　　I ne myȝt sweter smelle nouȝt, me-þinkeþ, þan I do.
　　So ful I am of þis smel, *and* so moche is in my þougt,
　　þat I noot hou I am, sodeynlich, in an oþer wit I-brougt."
　　" Leue broþer," q*uod* Valerian, " garlondus we haueþ here
95 Of flourus þat þou myȝt nouȝt se, but þou were oure fere,
　　But so as þou hast þe swete smel þerfore, þorw oure bone,
　　Lif þou wolt be-leue as we do, þou myȝt hem se sone."
　　" Leue broþer," q*uod* þe oþer, " wheyþer it sooþ is,
　　Oþer I stond in meting *and* wene þat soþ it is?"
100 " In meting," q*uod* Valerian, " we haue euer be,
　　Now we be of slep awak, now we mow ferst se."
　　" Sestow nowȝ." q*uod* þe oþer, " bet þan þou hast er do?"
　　" Le," q*uod* Valerian, " wel me be-houeþ so,
　　ffor my Lordus aungel of Heuen haþ me goue lyȝt,
105 *And* for oure loue he wol þe al-so, ȝif þou wolt be-leue aryȝt."

　　I ne wilnþ noþinge on eorþe so moche. seide ualerian
　　As þat tiburs mi broþer were, wiþ me cristen man
　　Mi lord wole þis angel seide. ȝeue him þulk *grace*
　　And boþe ȝe scholle martred beo. at o tyme in on place
80 þþe angel wende forþ wiþ þis word. hi miste whar he becom
　　Moche was þe ioie of þis clene þinges : þat aiþer to¹ oþer nom　　(¹MS. co.)
　　To chamber com tiburs to speke. wiþ his broþer þere
　　Stille he stod *and* biheolde aboute. as þeiȝ he miste whar he were
　　Broþer he seide hou goþ þis. in þis time of þe ȝer
85 So swote smul ne smulde ich neuere. as me þinch ich so nou her
　　þþeiȝ þis hous were ful of newe floures. *and* white lilie also
　　Murgore miȝte hit smulle nouȝt. me þinkeþ þan ich nou do
　　So ful icham broþer of þe smul. *and* so moche hit is in mi þougt
　　þþat icham sodeinliche inot hou : in oþer witte ibrougt
90 Leue broþer seide ualerian. gerlauns we habbeþ here
　　Of rose *and* lilie þat þou ne miȝte seo. bote þou were oure fere
　　Ac as þou hast þe swote smul : þerof þorwȝ mi lone
　　Also ȝif þou wolt bileoue as we doþ. þou miȝte hem seo wel sone
　　Leue broþer seide tiburs.　Whar hit beo soþe þis
95 Oþer þat istond in metinge. *and* mete þat his so is
　　In metinge seide ualerian.　We habbeþ euere ibeo
　　Of slepe we beoþ nou furst awaked. *and* nou we mowe furst iseo
　　For oure lordes angel of heuene. haþ iȝeue me siȝt
　　And for oure loue he þe wole ȝeue also. ȝif þou wolt bileoue ariȝt

boute; L. als.; L. wher, C. ware; | 89. L. seyde; L. goþ, C. "þis is" (the þis is in a different hand); C.
þat; C. in; | 90.C. suche smel; L. smelde, C. smelled; L. I, C. ic; C. neuer; L. þinkeþ (reg.); C. now; | 91.
C. wer; L. ful, C. fulle (reg.); L. of newe roses; L. of lylie, C. of lylyen; | 92. L. myȝtteþ, C. myȝt; L.
versschere, C. swettur; L. smelle, C. smellen; L. C. now; | 93. L. C. þe; C. smelle; C. so is þer on; L.
þout; | 94. L. for-soþe, L. C. in an-oþer; L. wytte, C. wyt; L. I-brouth, C. ybroȝt; | 95. C. he sede; L.
garlandes, C. garlauns; C. habeþ; | 96. C. noȝt; L. i-se, C. se; C. but; L. C. oure; L. C. fere; | 97. L.
als, C. &; L. þane swote smel, þis smylie; L. þar-of, C. þer for; L. for, C. þorw; L. C. oure; | 98. C.
If; L. be-leue, C. lyue; L. sen, C. se; | 99. L. seyde, C. sede; C. tyburs; L. wheþur, C. ys hit soþ oþer
hit nys; L. be | 100. L. matyngge, C. metyng; C. ya; | 101. L. metyngge, C. metyng; C. sede; | 102. C.
& now; L. ben; L. ferst; L. a-waked; L. ferst, C. furst; C. se; | 103. L. sestow, C. syxte; C. bete; C.
sede tyburs; L. C. þan; C. ar; C. þis do; | 104. L. seyde; L. sone; L. be-, C. by; 105. L. flor, C. for;
L. aungel; L. I-ȝoue, C. yȝyue; L. syȝth, C. lyȝt; | 106 L. for oure: L. schal; L. wile; L. leue, C. lyue;

po sede þis holi maide "tybors leue broþer.
Wat beþ þis maumet*es* bote wrechede : þou suxt non oþer.
Ne suxtou hou it is mo*n*nes werc · Imad of old tre.
110 þing þet ne mai hi*m* sulue helpe : hou mai it helpe þe "
"Noþing nys soþer " quaþ tibors : "þen þat þou hast ised.
Wod*er* he weþer þen eny best : þat nolde do þi red*e* "
S*eyn* Cecile hi*m* custe anon : "leue tybors " heo sede
"To dai þou schalt my broþer be : vor þou wolt do bi rede.
115 þoru clene loue of good bileue : þi broþer my spouse is
þer-þoru þou schalt bicome also : my broþer wan þou art his
Myd valerian þou most go to þe biscop vrban
& be icristned & do also : as he þe rede can."
"Is þat vrban " quaþ tybours : "þat so ȝerne haþ ibe isoȝt.
120 þat ȝar*e* haþ ibe fleme & ihud : & ȝif he wer*e* uorþ ibroȝt.
Vorberne he scholde & we also : ȝif we wiþ hi*m* were
& so þe wole we heuene soȝte : vorberne we miȝte her*e*."
"& ȝif þer nere " quaþ þis maide : "soulem*en*t bote þis lif.
Fol he wer*e* þat it wolde lese : vor eny strif.
125 An wen þer is so muri lif : þat we schulleþ her-aft*er* auonge.
Fol is þat nele an wule be wo : to be In Ioie so longe."
"Leue broþer " quaþ tybours : "ic*h* biseche þe
Lede me to þulke gode mon*n*e : & haue m*er*cy of me."
þat o broþer ladde þat oþer : to þe biscop Vrban
130 & let hi*m* vorsake is fole bileue : & bicom cristene man.
Tibours þo he com aȝen : þen angel he sei anon.
þat Cecile hi*m* hadde bihote : In þe chambre wiþ hir*e* gon.

Insensibilia et muta, ita ut Tiburtius responderet ac diceret: "qui ista non credit, pecus est." Tunc
Cæcilia osculans pectus ejus dixit: "hodie te fateor meum esse cognatum, sicut enim amor Dei fratrem
tuum mihi conjugem fecit, ita te mihi cognatum contemtus faciet ydolorum. Vade igitur cum fratre
tuo, ut purificationem accipias et angelicos vultus videre valeas." Dixitque Tiburtius fratri suo:
"obsecro te, frater, ut mihi dicas, ad quem me ducturus es." Cui Valerianus: "ad Urbanum episco-
pam." Cui Tiburtius: "de illo Urbano dicis qui totiens damnatus est et adhuc in latebris commora-
tur? hic, si inventus fuerit, cremabitur; et nos in illius flammis pariter involvemur, et dum quærimus
divinitatem latentem in cœlis, incurremus furorem exurentem in terris." Cui Cæcilia: "Si hæc sola esset
vita, juste hanc perdere timeremus; est autem alia melior, quæ nunquam amittitur, quam nobis Dei filius
enarravit. Omnia enim, quæ facta sunt, filius ex patre genitus condidit, universa autem, quæ condita
sunt ex patre procedens spiritus animavit. Hic igitur filius Dei in mundum veniens verbis et
miraculis aliam vitam esse nobis monstravit." Cui Tiburtius: "certe unum Deum esse asseris, et
quomodo nunc tres esse testaris?" Respondit Cæcilia: "sicut in una hominis sapientia sunt tria,
scilicet ingenium, memoria et intellectus, sic et in una divinitatis essentia tres personæ esse possunt."
Tunc cœpit ei de adventu filii Dei et passione prædicare, et multas congruitates ipsius passionis osten-
dere. "Nam ideo," inquit, "filius Dei est tentus, ut genus humanum dimitatur peccato detentum;
benedictus maledictus, ut homo maledictus benedictionem consequatur; illudi se patitur, ut homo ab
illusione dæmonum liberetur; splueam coronam accepit in capite, ut a nobis sententiam auferat capi-
talem; fel suscipit amarum, ut sanaret hominis dulcem gustum; exspoliatur, ut parentum nostrorum
nuditatem operiat; in ligno suspenditur, ut ligni prævaricationem tollat." Tunc Tiburtius fratri suo
dixit: "miserere mei, et perduc me ad hominem Dei ut purificationem accipiam." Ductus igitur, et
purificatus, angelos Dei sæpe videbat, et omnia quæ postulabat, protinus obtinebat. Valerianus

L. a-ryȝth; | 107. L. seyde; | 108. L. what; L. ben; L. maumeites, C. maumes; C. hot; L. wreched-
hede, C. wrecches; L. sest, C. syst; C. ne; L. on hem; | 109. L. sestou; þit þese maomets, C. beþ

þo seyd þe holy mayde, "Tyburs, leue broþir,
What beþ þe maumet*us* but nouȝt, þou schal se non oþer.
þou myȝt se it is monn*us* werk ; mad of old tre ;
þing þat ne may hym-self help, how schold it helpe þe ? "
110 "Noþing is soþ," q*uod* Tybors, "as þat þou hast of sede,
Wodder*e* he wer*e* þan any best, þat nold do þy red*e*."
Seynt Sycile hym kiste anon, "Leue broþ*er*," ȝhe sede,
"To-day þou schalt my broþ*er* be, for þou wolt do by my rede.
þorw clene loue *and* good be-leue, þy broþ*er* my spouse is,
115 *And* þou schalt by-come al-so my broþ*er*, whan þou art his.
Wit Valerian þou most go to þe bysschop Vrban,
And be cristenyd *and* do as þe rede can."
"Is þat Vrban," q*uod* Tyburs, "þat so ȝerne haþ be-souȝt,
þat long haþ be flemyd *and* hid ? *And* ȝif he had be forþ brouȝt,
120 Brend he schold be, *and* we alle-so, ȝif we w*it* hym wer*e*."
"Le," q*uod* þe mayde, "ȝif it be so, we scholle to Heuin I-fer*e*."
"Lif þ*er* ner*e*," q*uod* þis mayde, "onlich but þis lyf,
Fool he wer*e*, þat it wold lese, for any man*er* strif."
"Leue broþ*er*," q*uod* Tyburs, "haue m*er*cy on me,
125 *And* leed me to þat good mon, I be-seche þe."
þat o broþer lad þat oþer to þe bysschop Vrban,   f. 287 b.
And leet him forsak his folyȝe *and* be-com cristin man.
Tyburs, þo he com a-ȝen, þe aungel he say anon,
þat Sysile hym hadde be-hote in þe chau*m*bre to gon.

100 þþo seide Cecilie þe holi maide. tiburs leue broþer   f. 157. (at top of page
What is in oure maumetes bote wrecched. þou schalt iseo non oþ*er*
Ne seostou þat hit is maumetes work. imad of old tre   "De Sa*nct*a Cecilia.")
þþinge þat mai nouȝt him sulf helpe: hou miȝte hit helpe þe
Noþinge is soþ*er* seide tiburs. þan þat þou hast ised
105 Gidiore he were þan eni best. þat nolde do þi red
Seint Cicile custe him anon. leue tiburs ȝeo sede
To dai þou schalt mi broþ*er* beo. for þou wolt don aft*er* rede
þþoruȝ clene loue *and* gode bileoue; þi broþ*er* min spouse is
þþ*er* þoruȝ þou schalt also bicome. mi broþ*er* whan þou art his
110 Wiþ ualerian þou most gon. to þe bischop vrban
And beo icristned *and* do also. as he þe rede can
Is þat vrban seide tiburs. þat so ȝurne haþ ibeo souȝte
þþat ȝare haþ ibeo fleom *and* ihudde *and* ȝif he were forþ ibrouȝte
Forbrenne he scholde *and* we also. ȝif we wiþ him were
115 And so þe while we heuene souȝte. forbarnde we scholde beon þere
Lif þat þer nere seide Cecilie. soulment þis þis lif
A fole he were þat hit wolde. lese for eni strif
Ac whan þer is as murie lif : þat we schollen her aft*er* fonge
Fole he were þat nolde a while beo wo. to beon in ioie so longe
120 Leue broþ*er* seide tiburs. haue m*er*ci on me
And lede me to þulk gode man. ic*h* biseche þe
þþe broþ*er* ladde þo þen oþ*er*. to þe bischop urban
And let him forsake his fole lawe. *and* bicom c*r*isten man.
Tiburs þo hi com aȝen. þe angel hine seiȝ anon
125 þþat Cecilie him hadde bihote. in þe chambre wiþ hire gon

hȳ of mau*m*es werke; L. ben mad, C. & ymaked; | 110. L. C. sulf; C. helpen; L. myȝte, C. scholde;
C. hȳ; | 111. L. soþere; C. sede; L. þanne, C. þan; L. i-seyd, C. ysede; | 112. L. gydiere, C. gydier; L.
C. were þan; L. any beste, C. a best; C. nold; L. don; L. red; | 113. C. swete c.; L. tiburs, C. broþer;
L. he seyde; | 114. L. to-day; L. wilt don; L. be, C. by; | 115. C. þorwe; L. C. and; C. goud; C.
spous ys; | 116. C. þer þorwe; L. when; C. b. ben ywys; | 117. L. C. mid; | 119. C. sede; L. be souȝth;
C. be soȝt; | 120. C. yflemed be; C. ȝef; L. forþ brouȝth, C. forþ broȝt; | 121. L. ffor-berne; C. for;
C. schold; C. ek; C. myd; | 122. L. while, C. wyle, L. souȝthen, C. soȝt; L. for-barnd, C. brende; L.
scholde, C. schold; L. ben here, C. ben þer; | 123. C. sede cecile; L. onliche; C. bot; | 124. C. hit; L.
any-maner; | 125. C. omits line; L. seþe; L. schulle after a-fonge; | 126. C. omits line; L. nelle a whyle
ben; | 127. C. sede; L. þou; L. C. haue mercy of me; | 128. L. led; L. C. þat; C. goud; L. C. man; L.
Ich be-; C. i*c* byseche; | 129. C. þe; C. lad þe o.; L. bisschop, C. byschop; | 130. L. þar he for-sok, C.
To forsake; L. C. his foule lawe; L. becam, C. bycome; C. cristen; | 131. C. come; L. þan, C. þe; L.

Cecile, vor heo wo*m*man was ; atom heo moste abide.
Ac þis breþeren þ*a*t wer*e* me*n* : aboute wende wide.
135 & wen me martred cr*i*stenme*n* : þud*er* hi wolde gon.   f. 187b.
& stele to wen hi mi3te best : & burie he*m* anon.   [don.
bi-uore þe Iustice hi wer*e* ibro3t : me lefte he*m* wat hi wolde
Ho made he*m* so hardi : to ben þe emp*er*ours fon.
As hi burede twei gode me*n* : þ*a*t Imartred wer*e*.
140 Come þe emp*er*ours me*n* : & nome he*m* ri3t þ*er*e.
þe misbileued tr*e*chours : þ*a*t wer*e* a3en our lawe.
þ*a*t wiþ ri3t Iugeme*n*t of londe : wer*e* ibro3t of dawe.
"Sir*e*, we wolde," queþe þis oþ*er* : "þ*a*t we wurþi wer*e*
Hor knaues uorte habbe ibe : þ*a*t 3e Iette quelle þ*er*e.
145 Hi bileuede þing þ*a*t no3t nas þei [*it*]' semblaunce hadde
& toke þ*a*t was aworþ : & no semblance nadde.   (1 MS. omits.)
Vor þei worldes wele habbe semblance · uor soþe no3t it nys.
& þei þe blisse of heuene þench*e* Iute : uor soþe much*e* it is."
"Belamys," þe Iustices seden : "3e me þencþ wode.
150 Wurþe he i[r'] to habbe wo : hose kepeþ no3t of gode." (1MS. it.)
"In wynt*er*," quaþ valerian : "idelme*n* sitteþ & drinkeþ.
To busemar hi Ii3eþ erþetilien : þ*a*t aboute gode swynkeþ.
In heruest wen hi mowe : vair corn repe.   [gr*e*pe
In meseise hi mowe go vp & doun : vor hi nabbeþ neu*er* a
155 & we scholleþ uor our tr*a*uail : þi blisse repe atenende.
Wen 3e schulleþ uor our Ioie : wepynge to helle wende"
"Eke we," quaþ þe Iustice : "þ*a*t Iordes scholde be.
Beþ Iasse worþ þen such*e* wreches : þ*a*t nelleþ neu*er* iþe."

igitur et Tiburtius elemosinis insistebant; et sanctorum corpora, quos Almachius præfectus occidebat, sepulturæ tradebant. Quos Almachius ad se vocans, cur pro suis sceleribus damnatos sepelirent, inquisivit. Cui Tiburtius: "utinam illorum servi essemus, quos tu damnatos appellas! Qui contemserunt illud, quod videtur esse et non est, et invenerunt illud, quod non videtur esse et est." Cui præfectus: "quidnam est illud?" Et Tiburtius: "quod videtur esse et non est, est omne, quod in hoc mundo est, quod hominem ad non esse perducit; quod vero non videtur esse et est, est vita justorum et pœna malorum." Cui præfectus: "non puto, quod mente tua loquaris." Tunc jubet adstare Valerianum dicens ei : "quoniam non est sani capitis frater tuus; tu saltem poteris sapienter dare responsum; constat plurimum vos errare, qui gaudia respuitis et omnia inimica gaudiis affectatis." Tunc Valerianus "se vidisse ait glaciali tempore otiosos jocantes, et operarios agricolas deridentes, sed æstivo tempore, dum advenisset gloriosi fructus laborum, gaudentibus illis, qui putabantur vani, cœperunt flere, qui videbantur urbani. Sic et nos nunc quidem sustinemus ignominiam et laborem, in futuro autem recipiemus gloriam et æternam mercedem. Vos autem nunc transitorium habetis gaudium, in futuro autem invenietis æternum luctum." Cui præfectus: "ergo nos invictissimi principes æternum habebimus luctum, et vos personæ vilissimæ perpetuum possidebitis gaudium?" Cui Valerianus: "homuntiones estis, non principes, tempore nostro nati, citius morituri et Deo rationem plus omnibus reddituri." Dixit autem præfectus:

C. sey; | 132. C. byhete; | 133. L. 3e; L. wyfman, C. wy*m*man; L. at hom, C. a com; C. most; | 134. L. at þese; C. þe broþeren; L. whane, C. wan; L. martyreden; L. cr*i*stenemen; L. þider; L. ho wolden, C. hy wold; | 136. L. to whan, C. to wan; L. he my3tte, C. hy my3t; C. beste; L. burien, C. bured; C. be a.; | 137. *ll.* 139, 140 tr. 137, 138 in L. and C.; L. to-fore, C. to; L. C. iustise, L. he weren, C. hy were; L. i-brouth; L. þei askede, C. me eschete; L. C. hem anon; | 138. L. who, C. wo; L. C. 3ou; L. burie, C. bury; L. C. emperoures; L. foon; | 139. L. þei C. hy; L. burleden, C. bured; L. y-martired; | 140. C. comen; L. C. -es; L. C. nomen; C. anon þer; | 141. L. trichours, C. traytoures; C.

130 Sysile, for ȝhe woman was, at hom moste abyde,
But þe twey breþerin þat were men, about wente wyde,
And whaᵣᵣne þey martrid Cristin men, þedir þey wende,
And stele to whan þey myȝte best, to bery heyᵣᵣ at þᵉ ende.
As þey beriid twey men þat I-martrid were,
135 Com þe emperourᵤₛ men, *and* nom hem anon þere.
To-fore þe ioustise þey were brouȝt ; me askid hem anon,
" Who made hem so hardy þe emperourᵤₛ foon,
Mys-be-leuid traytourᵤₛ, bery, þat were aȝen here lawe,
þat wᵢᵗ ryȝt iugement of lond were brouȝt of dawe ? "
140 " Syre, we wold," quod þe oþer, " þat we worþy wer
Here cnauis to be, þat were quellid þer."
" þey be-leuid þou it semblaunt made,
And tok to þing þat was good þou it semblauᵣᵣt nade,
For þe worldis ioy þat haþ semblauᵣᵣt, nouȝt worþ it nys,
145 *And* þou þe blisse of Heuin þink lyte, moche *and* good it is."
" Belamys," þe iustise seyd, " me-þinkeþ ȝou wode,
Wreþe it is worþy þat he haue wo, þat kepiþ nouȝt of gode."
" In winter," quod Valerian, " men sitteþ *and* drinkeþ,
To scorn þey lauȝe erþe tyliers, þat about here mete swinkeþ,
150 In heruest, whan þe tilyer may feyr corn *and* good repe,
In myȝeyse þey gon vp *and* doun, *and* haue neuer a grepe.
As we scholle for oure trauayl in blisse repe, at þe ende,
Whan ȝe scholle, for ȝoure ioyȝe, to pyne of helle wende."
þan seyd þe iustise, " scholle þey þat lordᵤₛ be
155 Lasse worþ þan soch wrecches ? " þat nelle neuer þe !"

Cecilie for ȝeo womman was at hom ȝeo most abide
Ac þis tweie breþeren þat were men. aboute hi wende wide
Euere whan me martred cristen men. þider hi wolde gon
And stele to whan hi miȝte best *and* binime hem anon
130 As hi bureden tweie holi men. þat martred were
Com þe amperoures men anon. *and* nom hem riȝt þere
To fore þe iustise hi weren ibrouȝte. he asked hem anon
Who mad hem so hardi to burie : þe emperoures fon
þþis misbileouede trichours. þat weren aȝen her lawe
135 þþat wiþ inggement of þe lond. were ibrouȝt of dawe
Sire seide þis godmen. icholde þat we worþi were.
Her knaues forto habbe ibeo. þat þou letest quelle þere
Hi forsoke þinge þat nouȝt nas. þeiȝ hit semblaunte hadde
And toke þinge þat worþi was. *and* non semblaunte nadde
140 Bel amys þe iustise seide. ȝou me þencheþ wod .... f. 157 b
Worþi he is sorwe to habbe. Whoso kepeþ nouȝt of god
Valerian seide in winter ofte. idel men sitteþ *and* drinkeþ
To busmare hi liȝeþ eorþe tilien. þat aboute sowinge swinkeþ
In haruest whan gode swinkares mowe. gode corn inouȝ ripe
145 þþan sitteþ hi at hom. *and* nabbeþ of corn a gripe
As we scholle for oure trauaille. in blisse ripe attan ende
Whan ȝe scholle for ȝoure ioie nou. wepinge to helle wende
þþan we seide þe iustise þat louerdes scholde beo
Beoþ villore þan ȝe wrecche cheitiues. þat neuere nolleþ iþeo

aȝens; L. C. oure; | 142. L. ryȝth; C. Iuggement; L. of þe lond; L. I-brout; | 143. C. wolde god sede
þes oþer, L. oþere seyde; L. worþi, C. ȝo; | 144. L. C. here; L. forto; C. knaues . . . þat; L. þou
let; C. ȝe aquelden; L. þare; | 145. L. he, C. hȝ; L. C. leften; L. nawt, C. naȝt; L. þei it;
C. þey hit; C. semblant; | 146. L. good þing, C. to þe þyng; C. semblant; | 147. L. þe worldes ioye
þat haþ semblant; L. so nawt, C. wors þan n. ys; | 148. L. and, C. ac þe Ioie; L. heuen; L. þinke, C.
semeþ; L. lite, C. luyte; L. mechul *and* swete it is, C. ac much hit ys ywys; | 149. L. beaus, C. bens;
L. a, . . . me, C. sede þis iustice; L. þat ȝe ben; L. þynkþ, C. þyncheþ; | 150. L. worþe, C. worþ; L.
who-so, C. þat; L. keput; L. nat; C. no goude; | 151. C. sede; L. sitten; C. stille; L. drynkun; | 152.
L. bismere, C. a scorn; L. leyen; L. here; C. in þe felde, L. sowynge; | 153. L. whan, C. wan; L. C.
þe swynkeres; L. moweþ, C. rypeþ; L. fair schef, C. corne; L. *and* good *and* rype, C. goud *and*
rype; | 154. L. ȝe mowen gon, C. þe drynkeres goþ; L. he, C. *and*; L. neuere agripe, C. a gripe; | 155.
L. als, C. so; L. C. schulle; L. C. oure; C. trauaile; L. C. rype; L. atte ende, C. at nende; | 156. L.

"Certes" quaþ ualerian "þou art lasse itold
160 þen a beggare aȝen god ! ne be þou ne so bold "
"Belamy," quaþ þe Iustice : " I ne kepe noȝt of þi Ianglinge.
Doþ ȝoure sacrifice anon ! oþer me schal ȝou to depe bringe"
"Certes" quepe þis gode men ! "þou ne bringest ous noȝt perto."
þe Iustice hem let anon ! In strong prison do !
165 Maxime þe gailer het ! þat hem In warde nom.
So þat he & alle his ! þoru hem cristene bicom
Seyn Cecile com bi þe prison : loude heo gan grede.
"Wat doþ ȝe, stalwarde knyȝtes ! cuþeþ ȝoure stalward hede.
Fiȝteþ nou stalwardliche : to bileue þis derkhede.
170 þat ȝe were In þe weie ibroȝt ! þat to cler liȝt ȝou wole lede"
Amorwe to þe maumet þis gode men were ibroȝt.
þe Iustice hem het do sacrifice ! ac þo hi nolde noȝt.
Hor heden he het boþe of smyte : & maxime isei
War angles hor soulen nome ! & to heuene bere an hei.
175 To þe Iustice he eode anon ! "cristene icham" he sede
"Ich isei þe gode menne soulen ! angles to heuene lede."
þe Iustice him let nyme anon : naked he let him bete.
Wiþ stronge scourgen vaste ibounde ! vorte he gan þat lif lete.
þat bodi hi caste wiþ-þoute toun ! þo gon Cecile uorþ gon. f. 18b
180 þis þre holi martirs : to-gadere heo burede anon.
Heo was sone Inome & ilad ! byuore þe Iustice þo.
"Wat" he sede "hou geþ þis ! beþ þer ȝut screwen mo.
Artou valerianes wif ! bi þe fei ich owe mahon.

"quid verborum circuitu immoramur ? offerte Diis libamina et illaesi abscedite." Sancti responderunt:
"nos Deo vero quotidie sacrificium exhibemus." Quibus praefectus: "quod est nomen ejus?" Cui
Valerianus: "nomen ejus invenire non potiris, etiamsi pennis volaveris." Praefectus dixit: "ergo
Jupiter nomen Dei non est?" Cui Valerianus: "nomen homicidae et stupratoris est." Ad quem
Almachius: "ergo totus mundus errat! et tu cum fratre tuo verum Deum nosti?" Valerianus respondit: "nos soli non sumus, sed innumerabilis multitudo hanc sanctitatem recepit." Traduntur igitur
sancti in custodiam Maximi. Quibus ille ait: "o juventutis flos purpureus, o germanus fraternitatis
affectus quomodo ad mortem quasi ad epulas festinatis?" Cui Valerianus ait, quod, si crediturum se
promitteret, gloriam animarum eorum post mortem videret. Et Maximus: "fulminibus ignis consumar,
si non illum solum Deum confitear, quem adoratis, si contingat, quod dicitis." Ipso igitur Maximus, et
omnis ejus familia, et universi carnifices crediderunt; et ab Urbano, qui illuc occulte venit, baptisma
susceperunt. Igitur dum aurora nocti finem daret, Caecilia exclamavit dicens: "eia milites Christi,
abjicite opera tenebrarum, et induimini arma lucis." Quarto igitur milliario ab urbe sancti ad statuam
Jovis ducuntur et dum sacrificare nollent, pariter decollantur. Tunc Maximus eum jurejurando asseruit,
se in hora passionis eorum angelos vidisse fulgentes et animas eorum quasi virgines de thalamo exeuntes,
quas in gremio suo in coelum angeli detulerunt. Almachius vero audiens Maximum christianum effectum,
eum plumbatis tamdiu caedi fecit, quousque spiritum excussit. Cujus corpus sancta Caecilia juxta Valerianum et Tiburtium sepelivit. Tunc Almachius facultates amborum coepit inquirere, et Caeciliam tam-
quam Valeriani conjugem coram se fecit adstare, jussitque, ut ydolis immolaret, aut sententiam mortis
incurreret. Cum autem ad hoc ab apparitoribus urgeretur, et illi vehementer flerent, eo quod puella tam

whanne, C. wan; L. C. schulle; L. for ȝoure; L. wepynde, C. to pyne of h.; | 157. L. ek he, C. ek we; L.
seyde, C. sede; C. schold lordis; | 158. L. C. þan; L. swiche; C. drynkeres; L. nolde neuere þe, C.
ȝþe; | 159. C. sede; C.ert; C. af tolde; | 160. L. þan is a saly beggere; C. aȝens; C. goud; L. neuere,
C. neuer, C. bolde; | 161. C. sede; L. yne, C iþ ne; L. nat, C. no; L. ianglyngge; | 162. C. oure godes;
L. sacrefise; | L. bringge; | 163. L. quaþ þis godeman, C. hþ sede; C. þo; L. ne bringgest me neuere,
C. bringest hit noȝt; | 164. C. stronge; L. prisone; C. to do; | 165. L. ieylere hete; C. in ward nome; |
166. C. al; L. þoru, C. þorwe; C. fongen; C. cristendom; L. come; L. ȝe; C. to g.; | 168. L. what;
L. C. do; L. C. godes; L. knytes; L. knþeþ; C. kepeþ; L. ȝour; L. stalewort, C. Stalward; | 169. C.

"Sertis," quod Valerian, "þou art lasse I-told
þan a begger þat nouȝt haþ, be þou neuer so bold."
"Belamy" quod þe iustise, "I kep nouȝt of þy iangling ;
Doþ ȝoure sacrefyse anon, or me schal to deþe ȝowȝ bring."
160 "Sertis," quod þis good mon, "þou bringist vs neuer þer-two."
þe iustise hem bad anon in strong preson do.
Maxime, þe iayler, heet þat hem in ward nom,
So þat he and alle his, þorw hem, tok Cristindom.
Seint Sysile com be þe preson; loud ȝhe gan to grede,
165 "What do ȝe goddus knyȝtus kep ȝoure monhede ! "
" ffyȝtiþ now strongliche to be-leue þis derk hede
þat ȝe were in þe wey brouȝt, þat schal ȝou to lyȝt lede ! "
On morw, to þe maumetus, þese good men were brouȝt.
þe iustise had hem do sacrefys, but þey nold nouȝt ;
170 Here heuedis he leet of smyte, and Maxime þo seyȝ
Wher aungelus here soulus nome, and ber to Heuin on hyȝ.
To þe iustise he went anon, " Cristin I am," he sede,
"I say aungelus to þe ioyȝe þe good mennus soulus lede."
þe iustise heet hym neme anon, and nakid hym bete
175 Wit strong scorgus fast I-bound, til he þe lyf lete.
þe body þey casste wit-oute þe toun, Secile gan þer forþ goon ;
þe þre holy marteris to-gedir ȝhe berid anon.
ȝhe was sone I-nome and lad to þe iustise þo.
"What ! " he seyde, " how gooþ þis ; be ȝit schrewis mo ? "
180 "Artow Valerianus wif ? By þe fey I owe Mahoun

f. 288.

150 Certes seide ualerian. þou art lasse itolde.
þþan a selý beggar aȝen god. ne beo þou neuere so bolde
Bel amý seide þe iustise. ý ne kepe nouȝt of þin ianglinge
Ac doþ to oure godes sacrefize. oþer me schal ȝou to deþ bringe
Certes seide þis god men. þou ne bringest hit neuere þer to
155 Anon þe iustise for wraþþe het. in to stronge prisoun hem do
Maxime het þe gailler. þat hem in warde nom
So þat he and alle his men. þoru hem cristen bicom
Seint Cecilie com bi þe prisoun. and loude gan to grede
What do ȝe ȝeo seide godes kniȝtes. cuþeþ ȝoure staleworþhede
160 Beoþ hardi and fiȝteþ staleworþliche. to bileue þis derkhede
þþat ȝe were in liȝt weý ibrouȝt. þat to cler liȝt wole ȝou lede
Amorwe to þis maumetes. þis gode men weren ibrouȝt
þþe iustise hem het don sacrefize. ac þo hi nolde nouȝt
He het her heuedes to smiten of ! and Maxime þo iseiȝ
165 Whar angles nome her soulen boþe. and bere to heuene an heiȝ
Maxime wende to þe iustise forþ :cristen icham he sede
Ich seiȝe þis tweie godmen soules ! angles to heuene lede
þþe iustise him let nime anon. and naked he let him bete
Wiþ scourges stronge. faste ibounde. forte he þat lif gan lete
170 þþe bodi hi caste wiþoute þe toun. and þo gan Cecilie forþ gon
þþis þreo swete martires, ȝeo burede hire sulf anon
Son ȝeo was inome. and iladde. to fore þe iustise þo
What he seide hou goþ þis. beoþ þer ȝut schrewen mo
Artou he seide valerianes wif ! bi þe trewþe ich owe Mahoun

---

wyteþ ȝoure strongnesse, L. staleworþliche;C. now in; | 170. L. i-brouth; | 171. L. opon þe morue;
L. maumets, C. þis maunes; C. þe goud; L. brouth; | 172. C. hete; L. don; L. þei ne wolde nat, hý
nold; | 173. L. C. here; L. heued, C. heuedes; L. let, C. lete; L. it I-sey, C. anon sey; | 174. L. whare
aungles here soules, C. foure angles here saule nyme; L. baren; | 175. L. ȝede, C. wende aȝen; | 176.
L. godemannes soule, C. sey angles now here saules; | 177. C. lete²; L. C. nymen; | 178. L. skourgen;
L. faste, C. fast; C. bounden; L. forto, C. fort; C. his l.; | 179. L. C. þe; L. þei, C. hý; L. C. casten;
L. wiþoute, C. wíthþoute; L. þet.; C. toune; L. gan, C. com; L. C. forþ; | 180. L. þese, C. þo; L.
C. martires; L. ȝe.; L. bured; L. to-gydere, C. togadre; | 181. L. omits; C. nome; ladde; to; | 182. L.
what; C. how; L. C. goþ; L. ȝet; L. C. schrewen; | 183. C. þou; L. Vallerianus; C. fay; L. mahoun,

Bote þou oþ*er* do, þi wite heu ⋮ worþ sone ibroȝt adon
185 Of wat kun artou icome ⋮ þat so folliche þe doþ ler*e*."
"Of bet*ere* ku*n*ne" quaþ þis maide "þen þou eu*er* wer*e*
In wuch man*er* lif quaþ þis oþ*er* ⋮ þencstou þi lif lyue.   [ȝiue
þou axst as a fol quaþ þis maide ⋮ & such vnsuere me schal þe
Vor al þi poer þou schalt ise ⋮ wen þou wost þen ende.
190 þat þou ne schalt fr*a*m ih*e*su cr*i*st ⋮ enes myn herte wende."
"Hou com it to þe" quaþ þis oþ*er* ⋮ "to be so hardi her.
To clepe me fol þat am þi maist*er* ⋮ ne suxstou my poer."
"þi poer wrech*e*" quaþ þis maide⋮ "worþ sone ibroȝt bi-hinde
Vor it nys bote as a bleddore ⋮ iblowe uol of wynde
195 þat be ipriked wiþ a pricke ⋮ awei it scrynkeþ al.
Also wiþ a lute sekenesse ⋮ þi wreche caroine schal.
þi poer þat þou ȝelpest of ⋮ worþ þe*n*ne suyþe lute."
"Hou geþ þis" quaþ þe Iustice ⋮ "dame, we*n*ne comeþ þi pr*u*te.
Ne mai ic*h* þe ȝeue deþ & lif ⋮ ne suxtou wiþ þi*n* eie"
200 "Certes sir*e*" quaþ þis maide ⋮ "þou luxt þ*er* of wel heie.
A wrech*e* caroine þou miȝte ȝeue deþ ⋮ þat wel schort is.
Ac of lyue þou miȝte noþi*n*g ȝeue ⋮ þi sulue noȝt iwis.
Wen þou miȝt deþ ȝeue ⋮ me þencþ bi pur riȝt.
þat þou art deþes sergant ⋮ & of lif nastou no miȝt
205 & we*n* þou deþes sergau*n*t art ⋮ deþ þi lord is.
& In deþ wiþþoute ende ⋮ þou wolt be iwis."

decora et nobilis ultro se morti traderet, dixit ad eos: "hoc, boni juvenes, non est juventutum perdere, sed mutuare, dare lutum et accipere aurum, dare vile habitaculum et accipere pretiosum, dare brevem angulum et accipere forum pellucidum. Si quis pro nummo solidos daret, nonne velocius festinaretis? Deus autem, quod accepit simplum, reddet centuplum. Creditis his, quæ dico?" Et illi: "credimus, Christum verum esse Deum, qui talem possidet famulam." Vocato igitur Urbano episcopo, CCCC et amplius baptizati sunt. Tunc Almachius sanctam Cæciliam ad se vocans ait: "cujus conditionis es?" Et illa: "ingenua sum et nobilis." Cui Almachius: "ego te de religione interrogo." Cui Cæcilia: "interrogatio tua stultum sumit initium, quæ duas responsiones una putat inquisitione concludi." Cui Almachius: "unde tibi tanta præsumtio respondendi?" At illa: "de conscientia bona, et fide non ficta?" Cui Almachius: "ignoras, cujus potestatis sim?" Et illa: "potestas vestra est quasi uter vento repletus, quem si acus pupugerit, omnis protinus rigor pallascit et quidquid in se rigidum habere cernitur, incurvatur." Cui Almachius: "ab injuriis cæpisti, et in injuriis perseveras." Cæcilia respondit: "injuria non dicitur nisi quod verbis fallentibus irrogatur; unde aut injuriam doce, si falsa locuta sum, aut te ipsum corripe calumniam inferentem, sed nos scientes sanctum Dei nomen omnino negare non possumus, melius est enim feliciter mori, quam infeliciter vivere." Cui Almachius: "ad quid cum; tanta superbia loqueris?" Et illa: "non est superbia, sed constantia." Cui Almachius: "infelix, ignoras, quia vivificandi et mortificandi mihi tradita est potestas?" Et illa: "contra veritatem publi- cam probo te nunc esse mentitum, vitam enim viventibus tollere potes, mortuis autem dare non potes

C. to M.; | 184. C. an oþer; L. wyth, C. þy whyte hewe; L. I-brouth, C. broȝt; L. -doun, C. adoune; | 185. L. what; L. kynne, C. kunde; C. þou comen; L. þus foleliche wilt, C. þe wole þus; | 186. C. beter kunde; L. quaþ C., C. sede C.; L. C. þan; L. euere; | 187. L. wich, C. wuche l.; C. sede þe l.; L. C. þenkest; L. tou, C. þou; L. to lyue; | 188. L. ffor-soþe; L. axest, C. eschete; C. heo sede; C. foule; L. swich, C. suche; L. ansuere; L. schul; | 189. C. power*e*; C. se; L. C. by þat þou; C. þe; | 190.

But þou oþer-wey torne þy wit, þou schalt sone be brouȝt a-doun."
"Of what kin art þou come, þat þus follich wolt þe leer?"
"Of beter kin," quod þe mayd, "þan þou euer wer."
"In what maner," quod þe oþer, "þenkistou þy lyf leue?"
185 "þou askist," ȝhe seyd, "as a fool, and so me schal þe answer ȝeue."
"ffor al þy pouer þou schalt se by þat þou wost þe ende,
þat þou ne schalt fro Ihesu Crist onis myn herte wende."
"How com it þe," quod þe iustise, "to be so hardy heer
To clepe me fool, and am þy mayster : ne sestou my power?"
190 þy pouer, wrecce," quod þe mayd, "worþ sone brouȝt be-hinde,
For it is but a bleddere bloue fúl of winde,
Þat be it prekid wit a prikke, awey it sinkeþ, al ;
Also wit alyte syknes þy wrecche careyne schal.
þy pouer þat þou ȝelpist of, þanne worþ wel lyte."
195 "How goþ þis?" quod þe iustise, "Dame, whennus comyþ þy pryte?"
"May I nouȝt ȝeue þe deþ and lyf, ne sestow nouȝt wit þin yȝe?"
"Sertis, Syre," quod þis mayde, "þou lyx þerof wel hyȝe."
"A wrecche careyne þou myȝt ȝeue deþ, þat wel schort is ;
Of lyf ne myȝt þou nouȝt ȝeue þy-self, I-wis.
200 Whan þou ne myȝt ȝeue deþ, ne lyf, me-pinkeþ be ryȝt
Þou art deþus seruaunt, for of lyf hastou no myȝt ;
And whan þou deþus seruaunt art, deþ þy lord is,
And in deþ wit-outen ende þou schalt be, I-wis."

175 Bote þou oþer do. þin white hew. worþ son ibrouȝt adoun
Of what kinne he seide artou icome : þat þus folliche þe wolde lere
Of noblere men ȝeo seide icham icome. þan þou euere were ;
In whuche manere lif seide þe iustise. þenkestou forto liue
þþou askest ȝeo seide as a fole. and soche answere me schal þe ȝeue.
180 For al þin power þou schalt iseo. bi þat þou wost þen ende
þþat þou ne schalt fram mi lord crist. enes min hert wende   f. 158.
Hou bicomeþ hit þe. þe iustise seide : to beo so hardi her ("De Sancta Cecilia.")
To clupe me fole þat am þi maister. ne seostou mi power
þþin power wrecche þis maide seide. worþ son ibrouȝte bi hinde
185 For hit nis bote as a bladdore. iblowe folle of winde
þþat be he ipriked wiþ a lutel pricke. a weý he schrinkeþ al
As god wiþ a lutel sikenesse. þin wrecche caroýn schal
þþin power þat þou ȝelpelst of. þan worþ wel lute
Hou geþ þis þe iustise seide. fram whannan comeþ þin prute
190 Ne mai ich þe ȝeue deþ and lif. ne seostou wiþ þin eýe
Certes sire þis maide seide. þer of þou luxt wel heýe
A wrecche caroýn þou miȝte ȝeue : deþ þat schort is
Ac of liue þou miȝte noþinge ȝeue : þi sulf nouȝt iwis
Whan þou miȝte ȝeue deþ and no lif : me þencheþ bi pure riȝte.
195 þþat þou deþes sergaunt art : for of lif nastou no miȝte.
And whan þou deþes seriaunt art : deþ þin lord is
And in deþ wiþouten ende. þou wolt beon iwis

L. ones, C. enys; C. my þoȝt; | 191. L. comeþ, C. how come þou; L. seyde, C. sede; L. C. þe iustise;
| C. to ben; C. here; | 192. C. clype; C. foul and; L. ne sixte nower my per, C. ne syxt þou my
powere; | 193. L. per, C. powere; C. wrecche; C. sede heo; L. i-brouȝth, C. broȝt; C. þe; L. be-, C.
by-; | 194. C. hit; C. bot; L. bladre, C. bladere; C. yblowen; C. ful, L. fol of a wreche w.; | 195. L. be
it, C. be hit; C. priked myd; L. a litel prikke, C. a prike; C. hit; C. schrynkeþ; | 196. L. als þi cariogne
wiþ siknesse, wreche, a-dwyne schal, C. with a lyte sykenesse þy wrecche careyn schal; | 197. C,
powere; L. boþe is þenne & lite, C. swyþe lyte; | 198. L. goþ; C. how is; L. sey
de, C. sede; L. whenne, C. wannes; L.al þis, C. þy prite; | 199. L. I may
þe ȝiue, C. ȝyue; L. as þou sixt myd, C. syxt þou myd þy neye; | 200. L. þo; C.
sede; L. lixt, C. lyxt; | 201. C. a body; L. myȝth, C. myȝt, L. ȝiue; C. ȝyue (reg); L. and; | 202. L.
ak; L. C. lyf; L. myȝtte, C. myȝt; L. nat, C. ywys (reg.); | 203. L. seþe, C. wan; L. myȝth; L. &
no lif; C. þinkþ, C. þinkeþ; L. ryȝte; | 204. C. ert; L. seriant, C. seriaunt; L. for; L. hasto, C. ne
hast þou; L. myȝtte, C. wyȝt myȝt; 205. L. ffor whan, C. & wan; L. sergeant, C. seriant; C. ert; L.
louerd; | 206. L. wiþ-outen, C. with oute; L.wilt,C. schalt ben; | 207. C. sede þis i.; L. gydihede, C. wod-

"Dame" quaþ þe Iustice : "of þi godhede ne kepe ich noȝt.
Do sacrifice to oure godes : oþer þou worst to deþe ibroȝt "
"þou seist þat ich gidi am " : Seyn Cecili sede.
210 " Ac þou art gidi & eke blynd : I sene on þi rede.
Scholde ich honoure þine godes : þat beþ of ston & tre
I lef ȝif ich segge soþ : ȝif þou miȝt noȝt ise.
Bote þou be blynd þou miȝt ise : þat þis þing soþ is.
Ȝif þou it suxst & leuest it noȝt : gidi þou art iwis.
215 Vor gidi he is þat nele ileue : þat he sucþ myd eie.
& as gidi mon & blynd þou schalt : In helle pyne deie."
þo verde þe screwe as he were wod : & het þis maide take.
& lede hire to an out hous : & a gret fur make.
& þer ouer a led uol of water : & al amidde hire caste
220 & seþe hire þe wule þer wole : a lym of hire ilaste.
þo þis Iugement was iȝeue : & me hire uorþ ladde
Wimmen & men þat it iseie : loude hi wope & gradde.
"Alas" hi sede "a þis¹ ȝong þing : & a þis¹ vair creature.
Schal nou ȝeue hire ȝonge lif : & deie þour fure."   (¹MS. þo)
225 "Beþ stille" quaþ þis holi maide : "uor me ne wepe ȝe noȝt.
Mi ȝonge lif ne lese ich noȝt : ac to lyue ich worþe ibroȝt
A scorte deþ ich schal auonge : & lif wiþþouten ende.
Fol were þat nolde so : god him me sende "
Me caste hire In þe seþende water : þer-Inne al nyȝt heo seþ
230 þe lengore þer-Inne heo was : þe verrore heo was hire deþ
Wiþ þe walmes heo sat & pleide : & þrechede of godes grace.
Mo þen four hondred men : bicome þer cristene In þe place.
þe Iustice isei þat me ne miȝte : In such deþ q[e]ulle¹ hire noȝt
He let smyte of hire heued : þat heo were to deþe ibroȝt.
235 þe quellare hire smot wiþ is mayn : þre siþe in hire suere. (¹MS. qulle.)

es igitur minister mortis, non vitæ." Cui Almachius: "jam depone amentiam et sacrificia Diis." Cui
Cæcilia: " nescio, ubi oculos amiseris; nam quos tu Deos dicis, omnes nos saxa esse videmus; mitte
igitur manum et tangendo disce, quod oculis non vales videre." Tunc iratus Almachius jussit eam ad
domum suam reduci, ibique tota nocta et die jussit eam in bulliente balneo concremari. Quæ quasi in
loco frigido mansit, nec modicum saltem sudoris persensit. Quod cum audivisset Almachius, jussit
eam in ipso balneo decollari. Quam spiculator tribus ictibus in collo percussit, sed tamen caput ejus
amputare non potuit, et quia decretum erat, ne quartam percussionem decollandus acciperet, eam

hed; C. kep; L. ryȝth nowth; | 208. C. þy; C. schalt be; C. deþ; L. i-brouth, C. broȝt; | 209. C. wode;
C. & ysene is on þy rede; | 210. L. i-sene; C. forto lete to do wel : & suyþe to do quede; | 211. C.
schoulde; L. honure, C. honour; C. þyn; L. ymad; | 212. L. I nelle it do, for-soþe, C. welle þat ic sede
þe souþ; L. for, C. þat; L. nat; | 213. C. bot; L. þat art h., C. blynde; C. souþ; | 214. L. sixt, C. syxt;
C. lyneat; C. hit; L. naut; C. woud; | 215. C. wode; L. nelle; L. C. seþ; C. wiþ; L. C. eye; | 216. L.
gydi & blind; C. as wode & blynde; C. by þat skyle; | 217. L. ferde; L. schrewe; C. þe iustise was for
wraþ wod; C. lete; | 218. L. leden; L. C. into; L. greth; C. fuyre; C. þer; | 219. C. & sete; L. led-ful;
C. lede ful; | 220. C. seþ; L. while, C. þe wyle; L. any Lime hol, C. lyme hole; L. on h. ;C. laste; | 221.
L. C. Inggement; | 222. L. wifmen; C. hire sey; C. loud; L. þe wopen, C. hy wepe; C. gurdde; | 223. L.

"Dame," seyd þe iustise, "of þy chydinge kep I nouȝt :
205 Do sacrefyse to oure godus, or to deþe þou schalt be brouȝt."
" þou seydist þat I gedy am," Seint Sycile sede,
" þou art gedy and wood, sene it is on þy dede ;
Schold I honoure þy godus þat beþ ston and tre
Fool ȝif ich segge sooþ þou ne myȝt se.
215 But þou be blind, þou myȝt se þat þis þing soþ is.
Lif þou it sest and leuist it nouȝt, þou art wood, I-wis,
ffor wood he is, þat nel leue þat he seþ wit his yȝe,
And wood mon and blind In þe pyne of hewe þou schalt dyȝe."
þo ferde ferd þe schreue as he were wood ; he het þe mayde take
220 And leed here in-to an hous. and gret fer about here make,
And þer-ouer sette a leed wit water, and amydde here caste,
And seþ here whyl þer wold any lyf in here laste.   f. 283 b
þo þis iugement was I-ȝoue, and me here forþ ladde,
Men and women þat here syȝe, loude wep and gradde,
225 " Allas ! " þey seyde, " þis ȝong þing, so feyr a creature,
Schal now lese here lyf, and deyȝe þorw þe fure ! "
" Beþ stille ! " quod þe holy mayd, " for me wep ȝe nouȝt,
My lyf I schal nouȝt lese, but I worþ to ioy brouȝt.
A schort deþ I schal fong, and lyf wit-outin ende,
230 Fool he were þat so nold god it me sone sende."
Me cast here in seþinge water, al nyȝt þer-inne ȝhe seth,
þe lenger ȝhe þer-inne was, þe forþer ȝhe was here deþ.
Wit þe bolmus ȝhe sat and pleyde ; ȝhe þonkid goddus grace,
Mo þan foure hondrid be-com Cristin in þe plas.
235 þe iustise say þat he ne myȝt wit soch deþ quelle here nouȝt,
He heet smyt of here heed, þat ȝhe to deþe were brouȝt.
þe quellere here smoot wit al his myȝt þryis in þe swyre,

Dame seide þe iustise. of þin gidihede kepe ich nouȝt
Do here sacrifize to oure godes. oþer þou worþest to deþ ibrouȝt
200 Seistou þat ich gidie am. þis holi maide seide
Ac þou art gidie and ek blinde. and þat isene is on þin rede.
Scholde ich honouri þin godes ! þat beoþ of ston and treo
þþat noþinge worþi her power nis. ȝif þou miȝte iseo
Lif þou seost and ileouest hit nouȝt. gidie þou art iwis
205 Bote þou be blinde iseo þou miȝte. þat þis þinge soþe is
For gidie he is þat nele ileoue. þat iseoþ wiþ his eye
And as gidie man and blinde. þou schalt in helle deȝe
þþis iustise was for wraþþe wod. he het þis maide take
And led hire into an oute hous ! and grete fure þerinne make
210 And sette þer on a led ful of watere. and al amidde hire caste
And seþe hire while þer wolde alime. ihol of hire ilaste
þþo þis iuggement was iȝeue. and me hire forþ ladde
Men and wimmen þat hire seȝe. loude hi wope and gradde
Alas hi seide of þis ȝonge þinge and þis faire creature
215 þþat schal lese hire swete lif. and deȝe þoruȝ þe fure
Beoþ stille seide þis holi maide. for me ne wepe ȝe nouȝt
Min ȝonge lif schal ich nouȝt lese. ac to liue ich worþe ibrouȝt
In þe seþinge watere geo was icaste. and þerinne al niȝt ȝeo seþ
þþe lengore þat ȝeo þerinne was. þe ferþer ȝeo was þen deþ.
220 Wiþ þe walmes ȝeo sate and pleide. and prechede godes grace   f. 158 b
þþat mo þan foure hondred men þer bicom. cristen in þe place
þþo þe iustise iseiȝ þat he ne miȝte. in soche deþ quelle hire nouȝt
He het þat me scholde hire heued of smite. þat ȝeo were to deþ ibrogt
þþe quellar smot wiþ al his maýn. þreo siþe on þe swere

allas; L. þei seyde, C. hÿ seden; L. þat þis gongge, C. þat þus ȝonge a þyng; L. þus fair, C. so faire; | 224. L. lese, C. lete; C. now; L. ȝongge, C. ȝong; L. þoru þe f., C. scal dy now in þe f.; | 225. C. sede; L. C. for; L. wepeþ nout; | 226. L. gongge, C. ȝong; C. schal; L. nowth; L. Icham I-brouth, to lyf hit worþ; | 227. L. ane schorte, C. an schort; C. wole; L. a-vonge, C. a fonge; C. to habbe; L. wiþ-outen, C. wíþá þouten; | 228. L. C. he; C. nold so; L. god he me sone hynes., C. sone; | 229. L. men casten, C.

He ne smot it noȝt uolliche of : þe deþ was iboȝt dere.
No quellare ne moste bi þulke daie : smyte ouer þrie.
Half slawe hi bileuede hire so : hamward he gan hie.
Nou an vuel stude god it wolde : vor he was a screwe.
240 Wo dude he þe holi maide : gulteles so hire to hewe.
& beleue hire so half alyue : welle wo him be.
Vor ho [n]uste' of no deol þer me miȝte ise.   (1 MS. muste.)
þis holi maide eode aboute : hire heued half of ismyte.
þat was half quic & half ded : þat reuþe it was to wite.
245 & pouere men muche of hire good : delede wiþ hire honde.
Hit was a uair grace of god : þat heo miȝte enes stonde.
Heo prechede & to ihesu crist : mony good mon wende.
& alle to Seyn Vrban þe biscop : to baptise heo sende.
& bed him þat he schulde hire hous : þat heo wonede Inne.
250 Halwy In our lordes name : & a chirche þer bygynne.
& burie þer hire suete bodi : & þat our lordes seruice
Vpe is poer þer-Inne were ido : In alle wise
þe þridde day after hire martirdom : þis maide adoun lay.
& prechede cristene men : & bed hem habbe good day.
255 & sede "nou ichabbe ido : al þat my wille is to.
Wende ichulle to ihesu crist : & ȝe schulle also "
þis was two hondred ȝer : & þre & twenti riȝt.
After þat our lord was In is moder aliȝt
Nou bidde we our suete lord : uor hire holi martirdom.
260 To bringe ous to þulke Ioie : þat hire soule to com.

semivivam cruentus carnifex dereliquit. Per triduum autem supervivens, omnia quæ habebat, pauperibus tradidit, et omnes quos ad fidem converterat, Urbano episcopo commendavit dicens: "triduanas
mihi inducias postulavi, ut nos tuæ beatitudini commendarem, et hanc domum meam in ecclesiam
consecrares." Sanctus autem Urbanus corpus ejus inter episcopos sepellivit, et domum suam in ecclesiam, ut rogaverat, consecravit. Passa est autem circa annos domini CC et XXIII tempore Alexandri
imperatoris. Alibi autem legitur, quod passa sit tempore Marci Aurelii, qui imperavit circa annos
domini CCXX.

heo was ycaste; L. seþing; L. þar-, C. þer in; C. a lyte; L. ȝe seeþ; | 230. L. lengere, C. lengur þat; C.
in; L. ȝe sat; L. ferþere, C. ferre; L. ȝe; L. deeþ; | 231. C. wiþ; L. C. weimes; L. ȝe; C. sate; C.
preched; | 232. C. more; L. C. þan; C. foure CCCC; C. cristy ne; L. þat; | 233. C. þo þe; L. sey, C.
say; L. he ne myȝtte, C. myȝt; L. swich; C.so; L. naut; | 234. L. het, C. hote; C. þat me schold; L.
ȝe; C. deþ; | 235. L. C. quellere (reg.); C. myd; L. C. al his; C. syþ; L. C. in þe swere; | 236. L. nat
C. myȝt fal smyt; L. hired; L. bouth to dere, C. he boȝt . . . weld; | 237. C. most; C. day; L. oftere
C. after; L. C. þan þrie; | 238. L. leuede, C. bylefte; L. C. a-weyward; | 239. C. omits 4 ll; L. yuel
stede gon he mote; schrewe; | 240. L. dede; þat; | 241. L. bi-lefte; | 242. L. ffor who-so nuste; doel; men
myȝtte it se; | 243. L. ȝede; | 244. C. omits; L. & was; quik; rewþe; | 245. C. poure; L. mechel, C. þat
heo myȝt of wyte; L. ȝe delde, C. heo deled; C. honden; | 246. C. omits; L. It; wel fair; ȝe aut
myȝtte; | 247. L. ȝe; C. preched; C. so þat; L. C. many a; L. god, C. goud; | 248. C. al; L. baptiȝe
ȝe; C. baptiȝe; | 249. L. bad, C. bade; C. þat þe bischop seint vrban; L. scholde; C. stede; L. ȝe
hadde woned; C. woned; | 250. L. halewen; L. oure louerdes (reg.); C. scholde a godes n.; L. C.

He smot it nouȝt folleche of ; þat deþ was bouȝt ful dere.
No quellere, by þat day, most smyt ofter þan þryȝe.
240 Half slawe he lefte here, *and* so aweyward gan hyȝe,
To a leber stede, god it woot, for he was a schrewe,
He dede þe mayde wo, giltles, here so to hewe,
And beleued here alyue half ; wel wo hym be,
For who so nyste of no del, þere he myȝte se.
245 þe holy mayde went about, þe heed hing half of smyte,
And was half quik *and* half ded, þat ruþe it was to wite.
And pore men, moche of here good, delid myd here hond.
It was a fayr grace of God þat ȝhe myȝt onus stond.
Lhe prechid, *and* to Ihesu Crist mony men tornde,
250 *And* alle to Seint Orban, þe bysschop, to baptise ȝhe sende,
And bad hym þat he scholde, þe hous þat ȝhe wonyd inne,
Halw in oure Lordus name, *and* a chirche þer be-ginne,
And bery þer here oune body, *and* þat oure Lordus seruise,
Vp his pouer were þer-inne do, in alle wyse.
255 þe þridde day after here marterdom, þe mayde adoun lay
And prechid Cristin men, *and* bade hem haue good day,
And seyde, " Nowȝ I haue don al þat my wille is two,
Wende I wil to Ihesu Crist, *and* ȝe scholle also."
þis was two hondrid ȝer *and* þre *and* twenty, ryȝt,
260 After þat oure Lord was in his modir alyȝt.
Now bidde we oure swete Lord, for here strong marterdom,
Bring oure soulus to þe ioyȝe þat here-to com.   Amen.

225 He ne miȝte for noþinge smiten hit of. ȝeo bouȝte þen deþ ful dere
Non quellar moste bi þulk dai. smiten oftere þan þrie
Half aslawe he bileuede hire so. a weýward he gan hýe
þþis holi wimmon wende aboute. hire heued half of ismite
Wiþ hire honden ȝeo delede pore men. hire gode. þat ȝeo miȝte of wite
230 Leo prechede *and* to oure louerd crist. mani men ȝeo sende
And alle to þe bischop seint Vrban. to baptisy ȝeo wende
And bad þat seint urban. hire hous þat ȝeo wonede inne
Halewy scholde in godes name. *and* a churche þer biginne
þþe þridde dai after hire marterdom. þis maide a doun lai
235 And prechede wel cristen men. *and* bad hem habbe gode dai
And seide þat ȝeo hadde ido. alle þat hire wille was to
Wende ȝeo wolde to oure louerd crist. *and* hi scholden after also
Hit nas bote two hondred ȝer. *and* þreo *and* twenti also
After þat oure louerd ibore was. þat þis dede was ido
Nou louerd for þulc marterdom. þat seint Cecilie hadde
Graunte ous to þulk ioie come. þer þat angles hire to ladde. Amen.

---

churche ; | 251. L. burien þere ; C. & þat he bured ; L. swete body ; C. oure ; | 252. C. vp ; L. C. his ; C. powere ; C. in ; idon ; L. on alle-kynne ; | 253. C. marterdom ; C. adoune ; | 254. C. prechod wel þe cristen, L. to þe c.; L. bad, C. bade ; L. god, C. goud ; | 255. L. seyde now ; C. þo heo hadde ; C. alle þat hire was to do ; | 256. L. I wile, C. heo wolde to oure lord c. & hÿ schold after also ; | 257. L. hundred ; C. hit nas bot ce ȝere ; L. ryȝth, C. also ; | 258. L. oure louerd ; L. his ; L. a-lyȝth ; C. after oure lord ybore was þat þis dede was do ; | 259, 260. L. oure swete louerd for ; L. bringge vs to þat i.; C. lord for þe marterdom þat seint [Cecili was [.] e, graunt ous þulke Ioie : þat hire saule ys Inne.   (Some letters are here illegible owing to a smudge on the parchment.)

MS. COTT. TIB. E VII. [*fol.* 271 a—274 b.]

Jhesus Crist, ful of pete,
To mankind es of mercy fre
And schewes his pouste & his might
Of(t)-sithes here unto su*m* men sight,
5 So þat we may his mightes ken,
Als wele i*n* wemen als i*n* men,
And all-þermost i*n* maydens ᵹing
þat will be boun to his biding.
þat may men by ensaumple se
10 Of saint Cecill, þe mayden fre,   (¹MS. Harl. mede.)
þat born was of ful gentill blode
And euer was haly & milde of mode,¹
And i*n* hir hert ful wele scho knew
All þe lare of oure lord Jhesu.
15 Vnto him was scho prayand eu*er*,
Night and day, and sesid neuer.
Of pape Urban scho was baptist
And trewly trowed i*n* Jh*es*u Crist.
With hir frendes scho was ful dere
20 And with all oþer folk in-fere,
Bycaus scho was both fayre & gude
And untill all folk milde of mode.
Hir frendes maried hir till a man
þat named was Valirian;
25 Long he was and faire of skin
And komen of ful nobill kyn,
Bot hathin he was & unbaptist
And knew no-thing þe law of Crist.
Cisill durst none oþer do
30 Bot alſ hir frendes tald hir to.

þe day was sett: þai suld be wed.
In clathes of (g)old¹ þai both war cled;
Bot Cicill had þar-of no pride— (¹MS. cold.)
Ful hard clething was next hir hid;
35 Outward scho was richely arrayd,
So alls hir frendes had puruayd.
þus on þis wise when þai war wed,
Ful fele folk þaire fre*n*des fed.
When þe bridal was broght till ende,
40 þat ilka man þaire wai gan wende,
Cicill es þan to chamber went,
Calland to Crist with gude entent.
þai herd grete noyis, þat war hir nere,
Of angels sang and organs clere;
45 Scho made hir melody omang
And al þus said scho i*n* hir sang:
    Fiat cor meum et corpus meum im-
        maculatum, ut non confundar:
þat es on þis maner to mene:
"Lord, þou mak my hert all clene
And saue my body unfiled within,
50 So þat I be noght schent with syn!"
When scho had tald all hir talent
þus unto god with gude entent,
With hir husband scho went to bed,
Als þe law wald, for scho was wed.
55 Bot i*n* hert ful wele scho thoght
To kepe hir clene, if þat scho moght.
So by hir lord when scho was layd,
Vntill him al þus scho sayd,
Scho sayd: "sir, if it war ᵹowre will,

MS. Camb. Univ. Lib. Gg. II. 6. [*fol.* 364 a—358 b.]

To say sume thing*e* is myne entent
Of sanct Cecile, þe far*e* & gent,
þat cu*m*yne wes of þe best kine
þat Rome þane ner*e* wes withine;
5 & scho folouyt wele þar*e* trace,
For bath wyſe & u*er*tuſe scho wes,
Far*e* of fasone for to se,
Enhornyt of al bewte ;
& foster*it* ves in C*r*istis fay,
10 & Crist*es* ewa*n*gele scho had ay
Hyd in hir*e* brest & þar*e*-on*e* thoc*h*t,
Na nyc*h*t na day cesit noc*h*t¹.   (¹Here a couplet is missing? H.)
Mekly to god, þat kepe vald he
Clenly hir virginite.
15 & scho eftir þe custume þane
Ves handfast w*ith* a ᵹu*n*gmane,   f. 354 b.
& callit ves Valaryane,
þat in maryag*e* vald hir*e* haf tan*e*.
þe day ves cu*m*yne þat þai twa

20 þat band of mariag*e* suld ma;
Next hir*e* flesch, þat wes far*e*,
Scho had al tyme þe harsk har*e*
& *ves*¹ owt*e*wart to þe sicht   (¹MS. wiþ.)
Cled in gold schenand bryc*h*t.
25 & quhen*e* al maſt mery
Mad w*ith* mouth & me*n*stra(l)ſy,
þane wald scho in hart² god p*ra*y
Be hir-ane & til hyme say: (²MS. hirt.)
"God, grant þat my hart ma I
30 Vnue*m*myt kepe & my body,
Sa þat I thole na varldis scha*m*e
Bot ay be thankful to þi name ;"
& for þa*t*⁸ fasting*e* & prayer*e*
Scho mad to god tymis ser*e*.   (³MS. þast.)
35 Bot quhene þa suld to bed ga
& nane wes þar bot þai twa,
Scho tuk hyme by þe hand in hy
& til hyme sad deuotely: (⁴MS. cowit.)
"My maste ſwet & lo*w*it⁵ thing*e*,

60 A cownsail haue I ȝow untill,
   þat bus be said now, with ȝowre leue —
   And, gude syr, luke ȝe ȝow noght
             greue!
   Ane angell, syr, of heuyn ful bright
   Es my speciall both day and night,
65 A seruand unto god es he —
   I luf him wele, so dose he me.
   And if he wit with any gin
   þat þow my body file with syn
   Or onclene lufing to me bede,
70 He will be wrath for swilk in dede
   And vengance will he on ȝow take,
   þat ȝe sall all solace forsake   [hede.
   And lose þe flowre of ȝowre 'ȝowth-
   Swilk grewance, sir, es gude to drede."
75 Valirian þan wex all wrathe,
   For drede he durst do hir no schathe;
   Of hir wordes he was noght payde
   And all þus unto hir he sayde:
   " Woman, if þou will þat I trow
80 þir wordes þat þou sais me now,
   Bitwix vs twa here lat me se
   Him þat þou sais so lufes þe!
   So þat I may my-self assay
   Whether he [be] angell uerray, (¹H. he be.)
85 Seruand unto god of heuyn —
   þan sall I do þi counsaill euyn.
   And if þou luf ane oþer man,
   Ful sare þou sall þe bargan ban;
   Nowþer sall skape with-owten scath,

90 Bot I my-self sall sla ȝow bath,
   With mikell schame I sall ȝow
             schende."
   þan answered scho with wordes hende:
   " Gude sir," scho said, " greue noght þe
   If þou may noght goddes angel se!
95 For here may no-man se angell,
   Bot if he trow, als I sall tell,
   In a god þat made all thing,
   þat was with-outen bygining
   And es and euer-more sall be,
100 Mast of might and of mercy fre,
   And als in his sun Jhesu Criste.
   If þou will trow & be baptiste,
   þan say I, syr, þat þou sall se,
   þe angell — þat I tell to þe.
105 And, sir, if þou will þis aff[a]y,¹ (¹H. assy.)
   Till bisschop Urban tak þi way
   And tell him all þir wordes balde,
   Right als I haue to þe talde;
   And tell him all þi life till end,
110 So þat he may þi mis amend!
   þan sall he, when þi trowth es trew,
   Cleth þe all in clething new: [þe.
   Whitte clathes and clene sal he gif
   þan sall þou in my chamber se
115 þe bright angell of god of heuyn
   þat lufes me, als I gan þe neuyn,
   And of him þan saltou haue
   What thing so þou will efter craue."

40 I wald tel þe a priwe thinge
   Sa þat I mycht sekire be
   þu suld neuire discouer me,
   For gud na Il na for mede."
   " Tel one þarfor & haf na dred! "
45 Scho sad: "goddis angel haf I,
   þat kepis me ay Ithandly
   & lufis me sa wele, þat he
   Wil thole na warldly mene haf me;
   þe quhilk gif he persawe þi wil
50 þat þu with lust nicht me til,
   He sal þe sla, ore euire he fyne,
   & þu þi fare ȝuthed sal tyne;
   Bot he þat be þi wil cane prowe
   þat¹ þu me lufit of clene lufe, (¹MS. Gyf.)
55 In gret daynte he sal haf þe
   & luf þe als wele as me
   & al his Joy (sal) saw þe til."
   Valaryane þane, thru godis wil
   Chastyit, sad: "gif þu wil I
60 Trow þi wordis parfytly,
   Schaw me þe angel, þat I may

   Se þat þi wordis are verray:
   & I sal do al þi bydynge;
   Bot gif I ma haf persawynge   f. 355 a.
65 þat þu luffis ony warldis mane,
   I sal sla þe & hyme rycht þane."
   Quod scho þane: "gyf þat þu
   Wil prowe it suth I sa now,
   þu sal trew in god hicht me,
70 & in his name baptifte be:
   & þu sal se þe suth rycht þane
   þat he is angel & na mane.
   þarfor ga fra þe cyte ewine
   Thre myle in name of god of hewine,
75 & in a rew, callit "via apia",
   Syndry poure mene þu sal ourta,
   & to þame sal þu sa but gyle
   þat "me til ȝu has send Cecile,
   To sanct Vrbane¹ to kene me (¹MS. barbane.)
80 To tel hyme hire priwete."
   & quhene þu fyndis hyme, þu ma
   Tel hyme þire wordis þat I say.
   & quhene he has hofine þe,
   þane godis angel þu sal se."

þan thurgh grace of þe haly gaste
120 Vp he rase and went in haste
Vntill þe gude bisschop Urban,
And halely talde he to him þan,
With him and his wife how it ferd.
And when Urban his tale had herd,
125 He heuyd[1] his handes to heuyn on
hight (¹H. heuyn.)
And said þus to god moste of might:
"Lord Jhesu Criste, loued mot þou be
þat sawes þe sede of chastite
And gifes unto men cha[s]te cown-
saylle
130 þat to þaire sawl m[a]ly mekill availe!
þou tak þe fruit now als þine awin
Of þe sede þou has in Cicill sawn —
For it waxes and multiplise,
Als men may se on þis wise.
135 A spows scho toke, with hir to dwell,
þat als a lion was fers and fell
And rebell both by night and day
Ogains þe lessons of þi lay:
Now meke to þe has scho made him
140 Als a lamb, in sawl and lym — (²H. moke.)
For war he noght unto þe meke,²
Saluyng of me wald he none seke.
And, sen he has to saluyng soght,
Lord, saue him and forsake him
noght!"
145 þis when he had his praier end,

Byfor þam sone þai saw descend
Ane ald man and stode þam bitwene,
All cled in lynnen cloth ful clene,
And in his hand he had a boke
150 All of gold letters, on to luke.
Valirian, [when] he saw þis sight,
Might noght luke ogains þat light:
For drede he fell doun in þat stede
And still he lay als he war ded.
155 þe ald man þan his right hand toke
And lifted him up, and bad him loke
What thing was wretyn in þat bill
þat he had þare broght him till.
Valirian þan þe letter tase
160 And þus wretyn in þat place:
Unus dominus. vna fides. vnum
baptisma.
þat es on þis maner to mene:
"A god es euer all-bydene,
And als a faith all folk sall haue,
And a baptym, all sawles to saue."
165 When Valirian had red þis bill,
þan said þe ald man þus him till:
"Trowes þou þis als þou may rede,
Or dwelles git þi hert in drede?" (¹H. answer.)
þan answerd[1] þus Valirian: [man —
170 "What thingh might be till erthli
To rede or els with mowth to neuyn —
More forto trow vnder þe heuyn?
In my wit I trow ful wele
þat here es writen euer-ilkadele."

85 Valaryane þane but abad
Passit furth þe gat scho hyme bad,
& be þe taknys, he had tane,
Fand þe bischope sanct Vrbane
Lurkand, ymange pure mene mekly,
90 Quhare mony marteris cane ly.
& quhene þat he þame tald had
His erand as Cecile hyme bad,
þe ald his handis but (ony) mare
Vphewit to þe hewine rycht þare
95 & gretand sad: "lord Jhesu,
þat chast consal wele chewis nov,
Of þat sede froit nov þu tak
þat in Cecil þu cane mak!
For Cecil as (a) besy be
100 Ententifly feruit has þe;
For hyme, þat scho als fellone
Til spouse (tuk) as a woud lyone,
Mek as a lame scho has þe send,
þi treucht til ek & til amend."
105 & as þe bischope þis & mare
had sad, þane apperit þare
A gung mane, þat nane cuth knaw,

Cled in quhytare thinge þane snaw,
& in his hand (he) bare a buke,
110 þe quhilk rycht fare ves one to luke,
Vith goldine letteris wrytine brad.
Quhame quhene Valeryane sene had,
He fel for rednes in þat[1] sted   f. 255 b.
As a mane þat had bene ded.   (²MS. þast.)
115 Bot rath þe gung mane raisit hyme
& bad hyme rede þe buk with-ine,
& he red: & fand (wrytin) þare:
"þar is a god, forout mare,
& bot a treucht, & a baptyme,
120 þat sal al leilemene saf fra pyne,
A fadir, a makare of al,
A-beoufe althinge & euir be sal."
& as he had red þis wryt,
þe bischope sais: "trewis þu It
125 Or art þu get of dout
Of It þu come here about?"
Valaryane þane loud cane cry
& sad: "na thinge sa weile trev I
Vndir hewine as I trew It
130 þat I saw wrytine in gone wryt."

175 Whils Valirian þir wordes gan say,
þe ald man was sone o way —
And how he went, no-thing þai wist.
þan þe bisschop Valirian baptist
& bad him trow with conciens clene
180 Als he þare had herd and sene. (¹H. grantes.)
Valirian granted¹ with gude will *fol. 192.*
All his bidinges to fulfill.
þan hame ogain he bad him ga
Vnto Cicill, þat he come fra, (²H. confert.)
185 And confort³ hir with all his mayne.
þus to his wife he went ogayne.
To Cisill chamber sone he went,
To thank hir þat him so had sent
To get saluing of all his sin
190 And gude lifing so to bygyn.
Kneeland in praiers he hir fand,
And sone bifor hir saw he stand
Godes angel, schineand so bright,
þat all þe hows lemid of light;
195 Twa corons in his hand he broght —
So worthi neuer in werld war
            wroght:
Vnto Ciscill he toke þe tane,
þat oþer unto Valariane,
Opon þaire heuides he set þam rathe,
200 And all þus said he to þam bathe:
" Kepes þir corons ȝow bitwene
With chast bodys and hertis clene!
Fro paradis I haue þam broght —
For in þat ilk place war þai wroght;
205 To ȝow mi lord has þam puruayd."
þan to Ualirian þus he said:
" For þat þow wald assentand be
Vnto counsail of chastite,

Mi lord Jhesu, of mercy fre,
210 Sendes þe þus bodword by me:
What thing of him so þou will craue,
Ask: and sone þou sal it haue,
What thing so euer þou will of mele —
So þat it be to þi sawl hele."
215 Valirian þan made his asking
And said: " I ȝern none oþer thing
Ne no-thing es to me so swete
Als es, my broþer bale to bete.
Wald my lord, dere Jhesus,
220 Help my broþer Tyburcius
In his law forto be fre
And cristen man, als he mad me,
þat we might both parfitely lif
And both oure gastes unto him gif!"
225 When þe angell þir wordes herd,
To Valirian þus he answerd
And said: " þi will it sall be done,
For-whi þou askes in þi bone
þat mi lord likes forto haue
230 Better, þan þe likes it to craue.
þarfore, als my lord has won þe
Thurgh Ciscill, his seruand fre,
So thurgh þe now sall he win
þi broþer out of bandes of sin.
235 And þou and he sall samyn cum
Vntill þe mede of marterdome."
When þis was said, he went up euyn
Wit grete brightnes to blis of heuyn.
And Valirian þan with his¹ wife (¹H. wisth.)
240 Ful halily ay led þaire life.
And efter þis, right als god walde,
Tyburcyus, þat I of talde,
þat broþer was to Valiriane,

þe ȝung mane þane wanyst away.
& Valeryane but delay
Of sancte Vrbane tuk baptyme,
& hame to Cecile went syne
135 & fand hire one hire bed stanand,
& ane angel, þat in his hand
Had twa cronis mad wynly
Of spanyst rose & quhyt lely;
Of þame to Cecile he gef ane,
140 & ane to Valaryane,
& sad: " þir cronys I brocht now
Of paradyse, to gif til ȝow;
þe quhilkis gif ȝe kepe clenly
With hart wnuemmyt & body,
145 þai sal neuir falow, na tyne
þe odour þat ȝe think sa fyne,
Na ȝet na vthire sal þame se

Bot gif he kepe chastyte.
&, Valeryane, sene þat þu
150 Has trewit heilesume consel now,
Ask at me quhat-euir þu wil,
& I þi ȝarnyng sal fulfil."
Sad he: " gif sa þat it sal be,
þar is na thinge sa suet, think me,
155 As my nane brothire; þare-for I
Ask þat he (als) knaw in hy
þe suthfastnes þat nov I kene."
þe angel sad til hyme þane:
" For þine askyne is rychtwyse f. 356 a.
160 & to god plesand mony-vise,
þu & þi bruthire, bath
Cronit to god, sal cume rath,
Of martirdome þe fare crone (¹MS. as.)
To bruk in hewine at¹ ȝoure wardone."

Opon a day come him-allane
245 To luke how þat his broþer ferd,
For halines he of him herd.
And als he entred in þaire hows,
He kissed him, and als his spows,
He kissed Ciscell and said þus:
250 "Gude sauore es here omanges vs —
Of rose and lilyes me think it like —
Sen I was born,¹ felde I neuer slike,
So swete sauore feld neuer man." (¹H. lorn.)

þan spak his broþer Ualirian:
255 "Broþer, sen god vowches saue
þat þou þis swete sauore may haue,
Hardily now hete I þe: (¹H. stedifast.)
If þow in trowth will stedfast¹ be
And luf oure lord Jhesus allane,
260 Vnto whas lare we haue us tane:
þan sall tou se and here þe steuyn
Of þe angeli of god in heuyn
And so be saued, for certayne."

165 Tyburcyane syne enterit þare
Quhar Cecile & his bruthire ware,
& feld þe odoure in til hy
Of þe rose & þe lely,
& sad: "bruthir, hou hapnis here
170 þis swet sawoure þis tyme of gere,
Of Nouember in þe moneth,
Quhene flouris haldine ar vndirneth?
For betyre odire I cane neuir fele.
þare-for til gou twa I grant wele
175 þat I ame chengit¹ sudendly." (¹MS. clengit.)
Valaryane sad: "na ferly;
For fare cronis & fresch haf we,
þat pine ene get ma nocht se,
Of rose & lyle wynly mad,
180 þat neuir-mare fal falou na fad.
Bot as þu nov be my prayere
Has feld wele þis odore here,
Sa sal þu, gif þu trewis me,   (¹MS. tybur-
It þat þou felis clerly se."   cium.)
185 Tyburcius² cane hyme ansuere:
"Gif þis in slepe be at I here
Or it be in to suthfastnes
þou me tellis mar & les?"
þane sad til hyme Valaryane:
190 "Ve haf slepit al our tyme gane,
Bot in suthfastnes now we duel."
Tyburcius sad: "þu me tel
Hou þis ma be?" þane one-ane
Til hyme sad Valaryane:
195 "Godis angele it tacht to me;
þe quhilkis gif þu garnis to se,
Tak baptyme & renunce til al
Fals ydolis þat ge godis cal!"
þane Cecile prechit hyme in by
200 & schewit it hyme al opynly
þat ydolis ma fele na thinge
Bot are dume & defe, but smelling
Na nocht ma grape na get se,
"Bot ar mad ne ma helpe þe, (²Metc., hekn.)
205 & þu ma breke² paime as þu wil; [til?]"
Quhy suld þu þane gif suth þaime
& as fcho had hire sermone done, f. 356 b.
Tyburcius sad til hire sone:
"Quha trewis nocht þis, mast & leste,
210 In fawte of wit is bot a beste."
Cecile þane hyme in armys hynt
& kissit his briste, or scho stynt,

& sad til him¹: "I grant þis day   (¹MS. hir.)
þat þu art my mach verray;
215 For, richt as luf of god has mad
þi bruthire my husband, but bad,
Richt sa sal godis luf mak þe
My mache, gif þu wil treu me,
Gif þu al ydol(is) wil forsake
220 & treu in god & baptyme tak;
& sa sal god grace gif to þe
His angel in-to face to se.
For-þi se þu na lettynge ma
Bot with þi bruthire sone þu ga!"
225 Til his bruthire Tyburcyane
Sad: "tel me, Valaryane,
To quhat is it þu sal me led
To mak ful endyng of þis ded?"
Sad he: "to bischope Vrbane."
230 þane sad Tyburcius one-ane:
"Is þat Vrbane þat to þe dede
Has bene condampnyt in þis sted
(&) In til hydlis ay syne duellis?
For, be he fundine, as mene tellis,
235 He will be brynt for-out mare,
& we with hyme mone fal þare,
& sa, til we are sekande
Diuinite in hewine schenand,
Ve sal be wappyt in til yre
240 Percace in erde in brynnand fyre."
Quod Cecile til hyme: "gif ware nane
Life bot in þis warld alane,
Ferly var na mene wald dout
To tyne it, war þai neuir sa stout;
245 Bot þar is a fere bettyre lyf,
þat ma (nocht) tynt be for þis strife,
þat godis sone (h)as til ws tald,
þat mad al think, as his fadir wald;
þis godis sone command fra hewyne
250 Til lar², tacht ws with his stewyne (²Metc. omits
þat (vthir) lyf is þat lestis ay,   Til lar.)
In hewine, but obir tene or tray
þat he has grathit til al his,   f. 357 a.
Til bruk in euire lestaud blis."
255 Tyburcyane sad: "tel me þis:²   (²MS. þus.)
Sene þu sais bot a god is,
Quhy is þat þu tellis me
þat þai are nov godis thre?"
& Cecile sad, þat ves war;
260 "As in a mane thre thingis ar,

Tyburcius said to him ogayne:

265 "And I might godes angell se,—
A verrayer takin might noght be:
þan will I turn vntill his lay."
When Ciscell herd him sogat say,
Down scho fell and kissed his fete,
270 And þan scho said þir wordes swete:
"Now will I grante, whore so I wende,
þou es my kosyn & my dere frende.
For als þe luf of Jhesu fre
Has made þi broþer assent to me,
275 So sall he turn þe forto take
His might & maumetry forsake.
And, sir, sen þou es redy now
To tak his trowth & trewly trow,
With þi broþer saltou ga
280 Vntill þe bisschop þat we come fra,
And be bowsom what he will bid "
Als scho has demid right so þai did.
Of þe bisschop was he baptist þan
And bycome a ful haly man.
285 So þat god gaf him slike grace,
þat he[1] might see in ilk a place   (1H. be.)
Angels of god ay at his will
And all his likeing[2] tell þam till,   (2H. liking.)
And of þam might he ask and haue
290 What thing so he wald efter craue.
þus þir breþer bot[h][3] in-fere   (3H. bot.)

And Ciscill. þat was to þam dere,
Lifed in luf and charite
And honored god in all degre.—
Passio sanctorum Tyburcii et Valeriani.
295 Tiburcius and Valiriane,
Fro-time þat þai had baptime tane,
To serue god ay war þai boune,
And fast þai prechid in feld & toun
Ogains þaire mawmettes more & min
300 þat þai bifore affied þam in.
To tell þaire life, it war ful lang,
Or meruayles þat war þam omang;
Bot in þis tretice will I tell
What ferlis in þaire ded byfell
305 And what wonders god for þam wrogt.
Yn time þat þai to ded war broght.
þare wond a prince þare in þat land
Whare þir two breþer war precheand
þar lifed all on maumettry:
310 Vnto þam had he grete enuy
And said. with dole þai suld be dede
Bot if þai tite wald turn þaire rede.
Sone he has efter þam sent.
And when þai come in his present,
315 þai prechid so of Cristes lay:
þe prince had no power to say
Ne forto do na harm þam till,

Wit frist, memor þe todire thinge,
& þe thred vndirstandinge:
Richt swa in þe mycht of godhed
Thre personis are but ony dred:
265 þe fadire, þe sone, þe[1] haly gast,   (1MS. he.)
& nocht ane of þire are in waste."
þane tald scho hyme mare & les
Quhy god in warld come & in fles,
& how hyme lykit for to tak
270 Passione of ded for mannis sak,
& tald hyme syne congruiyte
Quhy his passione suld nedful be:
"& first he tholit hyme-self ta,
Al as mane suld be lattine ga
275 þat had bene haldine lang (in)[2] syne; (2MS. langsum.)
& to be myssad lykit hyme,
Sa mane, þat ves in malysone,
Mycht þar chese lestand benysone;
& he tholit scornyt to be,
280 To mak mene of fendis scorne fre;
& he tholit a crone of thorne
One his heid be put for scorne,
For þat þe heid[3]-fenffes suld be   (3MS. he had.)
Fra mankind tane þat first gef he;
285 & gal he tastit, for to bet

It þat mane tynt tastand þe swet;
& nakit one þe croice he wes,
Til hele Adamys nakitnes;
& hangit one þe croice ves he,
290 Of first trespas to mak ws fre."
Tyburcyus þane but delay
Til his bruthire þis cane[1] say: (1MS. þan.)
"Gud bruthire, haf in þe mercy,
I pray þe, & me led in hy
295 To godis mane, þat I ma be
Clene mad, þe angel to se!"
His bruthire þane hyme has tane
Be þe hand & led til Vrbane;   f. 357 b.
þat, baptiste þane, he
300 þe angel clerly mycht se,
þat vald gif hyme his askin[g]e
Debonarly but gruchinge.   (2MS. beste.)
Tyburcius þane, or he fane,
& his bruthire Valaryane
305 þare faculte. til þ mycht leste,[2]
Til poure folk disponyt faste,
& of þe marteris þe bodyis
Sa slane for godis seruice
þai enterit ful prywely.

Bot sone he granted to wirk þaire
To Cristes law so turned he;   [will,
320 So did all halely his menȝe,
& all þo men war turned ilkane

þat suld haue bene þe breþer bane.
And sone when saint Ciscill herd tell
Of all þis fare how it bifell,
325 Vnto þam ful sone scho soght;

310 Almacius þane in (til) hy
Gert þai brethire til hyme bringe
& sad to þame, as in hethinge:
"Quharfor haf ȝe sa mykil cure
& besynes and laboure
315 To grawe þame þat for trespas,
As resone mad, condampnit ves?"
Tyburcius þane but delay
To þe prefet sadly cane say:
"Vald god we war seruandis al
320 To þame (þat) ȝe dampnyt cal!
þat has dispysit with clere thocht
It þat aperis' & is nocht . . ."
þe prefet sad: "þu tel me   (¹MS. aperis.)
Quhat manere þat may be?"
325 Quod he: "þat semys & is nocht
Is al þat in þis warld is wrocht
& ledis mane to vanyte
& til it þat nocht sal be;
Bot² it þat semys nocht to be   (²MS. for.)
330 & is, gif þu ma clerly se,
Is of richtwise mene þe lyfe,
& of Il mene þe payne but strife."
þe prefet sad: "I trew nocht þis
þu sais; of þi-self al is."
335 & bad þane þat Valaryane
Befor hyme suld be brocht one-ane,
& sad hyme: "þo þi bruthire be
Nocht of parfyt wit, as think me,
I consal þe for-out mare
340 þat þu to me mak gud ansuare;
For it war lyk þai ware wod
þat refusis bath Joy & gud
Bot folely þat maste ȝarnis
þat is maste fay to Joy & blis.   (³MS. lele.)
345 For-þi is gud ȝe wyse ȝu weile,
Or ȝe tyne al varldis fele⁴."   f. 358 a.
Valaryane sad til hyme þane:
In froiſt þat he saw Idil mene
Playand þame, makand gud chere,
350 & scorne þame þat wirkand were,
Bot in tyme of het, quhene þai
Froyt of þare travale bar away,
& gret Joy & mery mad,
þane þai þat Idil bene had,
355 Mad anoy & ewil chere;
"Richt sa til ws has hapnyt but were:
For we thole nov cald & het,
Quhile t(þ)rifte, quhyle hungire gret,
Bot sal resawe (syne) til oure med
360 Ay-lestand Joy, þat is na dred;
Bot ȝe, þat waridis glore has now,
In tyme to cume ful sare sal grew
& for a schort tyme lestand blis
In ȝour foly are lyk to mys."
365 þane þe prefet ansuert hyme but mare

& sad: "be þe pryncis, are
Vndisconfit of þis varld hale,
Sal thole, as ȝe say, lestand bale,
& ȝe, þat are content wrechis here,
370 Sic lestand blis sal bruk but were?"
Valaryane sad til hyme þane:
"Le ar na princys, bot smal mene,
Borne in our tyme, & de sal sone
& ȝeld resone hou ȝe haf done."
375 þe prefet sad, þat wes fel:
"In sic spek ganys nocht to duel.
Mak sacryfice for-out delay
&, quhar þu lykis, pas þi way!"
þai brethire þane vnerely
380 Sad to þe prefet opynly:
"Lele sacrifice to god we gife,
& sal do, til we may lif."
Quod þe prefet to þame one-ane:
"Of youre god tel me þe name!"
385 Valaryane til hyme þane cane say:
"Certis, his name fynd þu na ma,
þo þu had wengis for to fle."
þe prefet sad: "ȝet thinkis me
þat Jubiter is nocht þe name
390 Of god þat suld be I(n) mast fame?"
Valaryane sad: "Jubitere
Ves þe name of a murtherere
& of a kyd houlloure,   [oure."
þat racht noþire of mensk na hon-
395 þane ansuert hyme Almachius
& sad: "gif suth þe þu sais ws,
Al þis warld erris bot þu ane
& þi bruthire, þat has ȝow¹ tane
To trew in a god verraly?"   (¹MS. ȝone.)
400 Valaryane þane sad in hy:
"It is nocht anerly we twa
þat a god al-ane cane ta,
Bot þai are sa feile ma þane we,
þat þai ma nocht nomeryt be,
405 þat resawit þis halynes,
& ay sal eke & be na les."
þane gert þe prefet tak þaime bath
& put þame in til preſſoune rath,
In ȝemsale of Maxymy,
410 þat sad til þame ful felloun(t)y:
"Le, þat are ȝunge & fals alsa,
& bruthire-lufe betwene ȝu twa,
Me think ȝe haste ȝu to ded nov
As til a feste men callit ȝow!"
415 Valaryane sad: "gif þat þu
Wil hicht til ws þat þu sal treu,
þe Joy þu sal se in þis sted
Of oure sawlis, as we are ded."
þane Maxymyne sad: "fyre me bryne,
420 Gyf I þat god þane trou nocht ine
þat ȝe treu, gyf þat I se

And prestes þedir with hir scho
             broght,
þat baptist þam biliue ilkane,
To lif in Cristes law allane.   (¹H. price.)
When þis ilk pri[n]ce¹ Maximius
330 And his menȝe war baptist þus
Saint Ciscill confort þam ful wele
And bad þam forsake ilka dele
þaire mawmetri þat þai on trow,
And unto Jhesu baynly bow; [night
335 Scho bad þam leue þe werkes of
And cleth þam in armurs of light.
Scho said: "ȝowre cours ȝe haue ful-
             fild
Ful worthily, als Jhesus wild¹; (¹H. willd.)
A grete bataile ouer-cumen haue ȝe:
340 And þarfore sall ȝe corond be
With corons þat Criste sall ȝow gif,
In lastand blis ay forto lif.
þarfore bese noght abaist, to take
Marterdom for Cristes sake!"
345 þai granted all to do his will
And his biding forto fulfill;
Almachius þan, þe cursed king,
When he herd of þis tiþing,
He cumand þat þai suld ilkane
350 Mak sacrafise or els be slane.
And for þai wald noght wirk his will,
Ful hard paines he put þam till,

And at þe last with-outen lite (¹H. heuides.)
All þaire heuiddes¹ he gert of smite.
355 And when þaire bodis so war schent,
þaire sawles sone to heuyn went,
þat men might se with-owten mis
How angels led þam unto blis.
And mani folk for þat ilk sight
360 Turned to Crist and trowed right.
Maximius, þat gude conuers,
Omang þam gan þir wordes reherce,
He said: "I se þaire sawles ilkane
With angels vnto heuyn be tane
365 In þaire wenges, þat þai noght fall,
And like clene uirgins er þai all."
Almachius þe king herd tell
Of all þis fare how it bifell,
And how Maximius had said,
370 And how his folk war all affraid:
He cumand smertly on þe morn fol. 193.
To bring Maximius him byforn,
And grefe turmentes to him he
             wroght,
Vntill he vnto ded was broght.
375 His saul was hastly hent to heuyn,
With more solace þan men may
             neuyn.
Almachius, þat wikked king,
When he had done þus al þis thing
And saw þus þat Ualiraine

þe thinge suth ȝe sa to me."
þare Maximyne but ony mare,
& al þat euire with hyme ware,
25 & þe fel tormentouris alsua,
Of pape Vrbane cane baptyme ta,
þat in hydlis come þame til
& þare request (did) with gud wil.
& in þe dawinge of þe day
30 In hye voice cane to þame say:
"Le, þat are Cristis knychttis mad,
Puttis fra ȝou nov but abad
Vorkis of myrknes, & clethis ȝu
In armys of licht ine hast nov!"
35 Almachius þe prefet herd
How þat þer cristine knychttis ferd;
þane gert he tak þaime rycht fone,
& syne eftire for-out hone
He gert leid þame of þe tone
40 Four myle, one þat condicione:
Gyf þai to Jubitere rycht þare
Vald sacryfy but ony mare,
þai suld ga fre at þare wil,
& al þar gudis tacht þame til; f. 359
45 & gif þai gruchit to do sa,

þare nekis suld þai strik ine twa.
þane ware þe brethire one led,
Til þai come til þe lymmytstede;
& for þai wald nocht sacryfy,
450 þane Maximyne, þat þare was
Quhene þat ves done in þe place,
Sad: he saw angelis cume done
In þe tyme of þare passione,
455 & þare fawlis vpe in hewine bare
Vith þame in to wynly fayre.
Sone eftire as þis ves done,
To þe prefet ves tald sone
þat Maximyne cristine ves mad.
460 þe quhilk þane but (mar) abad
Gert mene with lumpis of led
Dynge hyme, til he ves ded.
þane Cecile tuk þe bodys thre
& in a grawe gert þaime lad be,
465 Vith sic honoure as scho cuth do
& as þe tyme askyt to.
Almacius þane wes besy
To get þe gudis gredely
Of þe forsad Valaryane

380 And all þir oþer saintes war slane,
þarfore he thinkes in his mode
At geder to him al þaire gude.
To Valiriane hows first þai haste,
For he was man of reches maste.
385 þai come unto Ciscill, his wife,
Stoutly and with ful grete strife

And bad hir lay furth þe reches
þat war hir maysters, more & les,
"For als traitur to dede he zode (¹H. omits.
390 And þel king sall haue all his gude."
Saint Ciscil gan grete mornig mak;
And so unto þa men scho spak
þat all þai turned þam unto Crist.

470 þat til his spouse Cecile had tane,
& of Tyburcius his bruthire,
& lewit nocht ane for vthire,
& sowne wes fundyne þat Cecile
þar gud(is) had to kepe a quhyle.
475 For-þi hir gert he brynge hyme til,
To grype þe gudis in-to wil,
& as scho brocht ves hyme befor,
He sad til hire with sturt & schore:
"Til ydolis þu mak sacryfice
480 & þame honoure in al wyse,"
Ore ellis for to thole gret payne
& fynaly þare-for be slane.
þane turmentoris, þo þai vald fenze,
Word of ned hire til distrenze,
485 Gret rycht sare, for sa fare a thinge,
Sa vyse, sa fare ,& sa zynge
Vald ta þe ded sa wilfully.
þane sad scho til þame in hy:
"It is nocht, zungmene, as ze thocht;
490 For my zouthed here tyne I nocht,
Bot gifis filth & takis zold fyne,
& giffis a lacht place of duellinge
& takis a place of bewte,   f. 359 b.
Sic as ma nocht comprisit be,
495 & giffis bot a lytil wra,
A vyd merkat þare-for I ta.
Richt as mane suld gif zow (¹MS. 1.)
Tene shillings¹ for a penny now,
I trew þat ze suld haste zu þene
500 To gife a penny & take tene;
Sa to god gif we gife ocht
Of waridly thinge þat he has wrocht,
He sal gif ws þarefor in med
Ane hundre tyme sa fele, but dred."
505 Sad scho þane: "trew ze þis?"
La, sad þai, sa hafe we blis,
Ve trew þat Criste is god verray
þat sic a seruand has þis day."
þay of a wil eurilkane
510 Gert brynge þe bischope ald Vrbane:
Of quhame richt þane baptyme cane ta
Four hundre personis & ma.
Almachius gert hire til hyme bring
& sad hire, as with symlynge,
515 He sad: " of quhat condicione is þu ?"
Scho sad: "gentil-womane, I trew."
Almacius sad (hir) syne tyte: (² MS. þat.)
"I spere, womane, of þi° ryte."
Cecile sad hyme: "þine askin(g)e
520 Of foly takis begynnynge, (³MS. ansgere.)
Venand I suld answer(is)³ twa

Vndir a demand þe to ma."
Almacius sad til hire bone:
" Quhene has þu sic presumpcione
525 Of redy ansuere til a mane ?"
& Cecile sad til hyme þane:
" Of conscience gud & clere
&¹ fath vnfenzet, but were." (¹MS. A.)
Almacius sad hire one hicht: [mycht."
530 " Me think þu knawis nocht my
Scho sad: " zis, I cane wele fynd
þi poweste lik a bose, of wynd
þat fillit ware & with a prene
Mocht out be latine for-out wene (² Mete.,
535 & feige (?)³ and to-giddire fal   The word
& tyne þe vowsty⁶ blawing al."   legible in
Almacius cane til hire say: MS.)
" Vith iniure⁴ þu begynnis ay (⁴MS. in
& in It syne perseueris;
540 Quhat is he þat þe þis leris ?"
Quod scho: " iniure is it nocht   f. 360
Bot fraud in word be thocht;
þar-for, gif I do wrang, me teche,
Or with fals wordis I þe fleche,
545 Or⁵ blame þi-selfe þat me blamys (⁵MS.
& of fraud me defamys.
Bot we, þe haly name þat wat
Of god, ma nyt it na-gat,
& bettire is de happely
550 Na for to lif here⁶ wrechitly." (⁶MS. de
Almacius sad in þat tyde:
" Quhy spekis þu with sic pryde ?"
" Na, quod scho, pryd is It nocht,
Bot It is stedfastnes of thocht."
555 Almacius þane til hire cane say:
" þu wreche, wat þu nocht I may,
Gif⁷ me lykis, now fa þe,   (⁷MS. gif
Or, gif me lykis, lat þe be?
For sic poweste is tacht me til
560 þat I ma do quhat-say I wil."
þane sad scho: " I ma prewe wele
þat þu has leyt Ilke deile
Agane opyne suthfastnes;
For, þo þu of poware wes
565 þe lyf to tak⁸ of ony mane,   (⁸MS. ma
Of powere wes þu neuir zet þane
To quhykine mane þat ded had bene;
For-þi is þu seruand but wene
Of doulful ded & nocht of lyfe,
570 & nocht of quyet bot of stryfe."
Almacius cane til hire say:
" þat wedand wodnes do away
& sacryfy oure godis til,

And in his name þai war baptist,
395 þai forsoke all þaire maumetry
And trowed in Jhesu almighty;
Him þai wirschipt als þe wise
And lifed and died in his seruise.
400 Bot when Almachius herd of yit[1], (¹H. þit?)
Wode he was, out of his wit.
He bad þat Ciscill suld be soght
And hastili[2] bifor him broght; (²H. hastily.)
And al hir howsing cumand he
þat it with fire all brint suld be.
405 Bot first he frained with eger mode,
Whare was all Valirian gude.
And scho said þat scho gan it take
Vnto pouer men for goddes sake.
At þa wordes was he full tene
410 And bad all suld be brint bidene
Hows and catell, more and min,
And als hir-self he bad þam brin.
And sone, to fulfill his desire,
Al hir place þai set in fire;
415 Hir-self in mides gert þai stand,
And all obout þe fire brinand.
Bot all þat [f]here[3] to hir was sene (³H. here.)
Als scho in ane erber had bene
Clene and faire with flores bright.
420 So stode scho a day and night,
Prayand to god wit hert ful hale.
And when Almachius herd þis tale,

He biddes þam þat broght þe tiþandes
Smite hir hede of, þar scho standes.
425 His slaghter-man to Ciscill went
Whare scho stode in gude entent;
To god hir prayers gan scho make
And bed hir nec furth till þe strake.
þe custum was in þat cuntre
430 þat none suld strike bot strakes thre.
And when he had thre strakes hit,
Lit was hir hals noght sunder kit, (¹H. sun.)
Hale war sum[1] of sins and uaines.
And so he left hir in grete paines —
435 For þe lau was, als I said are,
He suld gif thre strakes & nomare.
So opon hir knese scho sat,
Lifand thre daies efter þat.
And maidens þat had with hir bene
440 Come unto hir albidene,
And al þa daise scho sesed noght
To confurt þam so als scho moght.
Efter þe pape Urban scho sent
And tald unto him hir entent:
445 "Sir, scho said, god has gifen me
In þis liue þir daies thre,
Als I him praied, and by þis scill:
þat I might tell to þe my will.
All my maidens to þe I gif,
450 To ʒeme þam wele, ay whils þ[a]i[2] lif, (²H. þi.)
And teche þam wiseli forto wirk;

Gyf to luf langere, be þi wil!"
475 Sad Cecile þane, or scho stynt:
"It semys þu has þine eyne tynt;
For, þat þu godis cane cal,
Ar bot stanis & stokis al,
As þu ma with þi handis taste,
480 þo þu ma nocht se a laste."
þane ves Almacius rycht wa
þat scho sic ansuere cane til hyme ma,
& gert mene til hire ine[1] hire led, (¹MS. me.)
For he wald (þat) scho war dede;
485 & al a day & al þe nycht
He gert leid meelte in menis sycht,
& band hire faste fut & hand
& kest hir in þe led brynnande. f. 360 b.
Bot of het scho feld nomare
490 þane scho in a bath set þane vare,
For ocht þat scho cane se or here
Na changit contenance na chere,
Bot ves blyth, as scho had bene
In maste mycht þat euir wes sene.
495 And as Almacius þat herde,
As out of wit[2] nere he ferde; (²MS. wet.)

Ine-to þat leid, þat brynnyt swa,
He bad strik hire nek ine twa. (¹MS. he.)
& þo þe[1] basar strak hire thrise,
600 He mocht vnhied hire na-wyse;
&, for þe law bad, þat, quha
Suld haf þe hed strikine hyme fra,
þe ferd strak suld haf na-way,
For-þi þe basare ʒed his way
605 & lefyt hire lyand in þat sted,
Thre days fullely, as nere ded.
& in þe meyne-tyme nocht-for-thy
Scho delt hire gudis vysly
Ymange powre folk þat had ned,
610 & til vntrowand godis sede
Sew & to god wysly wane
Thru hire prechinge mony mane,
& þame þat scho conuertit swa,
Fra Wrbane scho gert baptyme ta,
615 & sad hyme þat scho had mad purchas
To god þat scho mycht luf þe space
þat scho mycht þaime til hyme com-
þat to be baptist scho hyme send, [mend
& of hire house of lyme & stane

And in mi name þou mak a kirk ([1]H. eyuyn.)
þat mi maidens may dwell in euyn[1]
And serue god with will and steuyn."
455 When þis was said, ful sone in haste
Vnto god scho gaf þe gaste.
And þe bischop, when scho was dede,

Beried hir in þat same stede
And made a kirk of ful grete spens
460 In wirschip and in grete reuerence
Of Jhesu Crist, oure sawiowre[1]
Vnto wham be euer honore! ([1]H. sawiow
Amen.   Amen.   Amen.

620 Gert mak a kirk, of sancte Vrbane
Halouyt, & eftire lad hire þare [are.
Quhare nov fele bischopis grawyne
& þis, þat I tel here, done wes
Eftire þat Criste had tane flesch
625 Twa hundre thre & thretty gere;
& þane wes emperoure but were
Marcyus, þat Arelyane

Had þane til his surname.—
Now, sancte Cecile, þat had sic grace
630 þat, quhat þu wald, þu mycht purches
Fra Jhesu, þat þu lufit swa:
Purches ws, ore we hyne ga,
Of þis varld þat we ma twyne
But schame, det or dedly syne

VII

NOTES.

1. Chaucer's well-known Life of St. Cecilia (The Second Nonnes Tale), begins with a Prologue of twelve stanzas, the first four stanzas of which are taken from Jehan de Vignay's Introduction to his translation of Jacobus a Voragine's Legenda Aurea. Caxton's English version of De Vignay has this prologue in free translation. Bokenam enlarges this to 75 lines.

11. *sauter:* The book of Psalms, frequently found in distinct volumes prepared for the devotional use of both Jewish and Christian churches.

10. *stilliche song:* Chaucer's lines at this point are:

> ' And whyl the organs maden melodye,
> To god alone in herte thus sang she; 135.

De Vignay says: 'et quant les instrumens chantoient elle chantoit a nostre seigneur en son cueur.'

Caxton: 'and she heeryng the organes making melodye she sang in hir herte onelye tu god.'

Ælfric: ' þa betwux þam sangum, and þam singalum dreamum
        sang cecilia symle þus gode . . . .
        and sang smyle swa;' 27.

Bokenam: ' Whyl þe orgons sunge in her melodyous guyse,
        Cycyle to god song in thys wyse:' 98.

The M. H. G. version, (Fürstenburg Bibl. f. 47-96), *ed.* Schönbach:

> ' ir vasten vnde ir weinon
> vor gotte so grose kraft hatte
> daz si die engel steteklich zv ir latte.
> ir gebet in gottes oren drang
> alse ein suzes orgenen sanch.'

12. Psalm CXIX. 80.

37. *þre mile henne;* Here were the catacombs of Calixtus and Prætextatus on the Appian way, used by the early Christians as meeting places for worship. These became also their hiding places in times of oppression. Chaucer has mistranslated this,

> 'Goth forth to Via Apia. . . . .
> That fro this toun ne stant but myles three.' 173.

47. *as me cristene men þreu:* This was *outside* the city wall.

48. *ware me eny ikneu:* ' Wherever they (the emperor's servants,) knew of any (Christian men);' *ikneu:* pt. sg. from OE. *gecnéow.*

52. ' Is this the cruel tyrant, Valerian, who calls me!'

55. *old mon:* Bokenam says; 'A man . . . fer runnyn in age,' 231. Barbour: ' a ȝungman,' 107.

61-2. Eph. IV. 5-6.

85. Tib. 237-8, *he went up euyn:* cf. the modern expression ' with equal wing'; nicely poised, well balanced.

89. *þis tyme of þe ȝere:* The scribe is perhaps thinking of Cecilia's birthday, Nov. 22, for Barbour goes farther to say:

> ' of Nouember in þe moneth
> quhene flouris haldine ar vndirneth.' 172.

120-21. *fleme & ihud:* This is the common impression about Urban. Ælfric: ' Se is geutlagod and lið him on digelan for his cristen-dome.' 132.

De Vignay: 'Dis tu de celuy vrbain qui tant de fois a este condamne, & demeure encore en vng lieu secret.' The Chaucerian ring is in the following: 2nd N. T. 309·13.

> . . . 'Urban
> That is so ofte dampned to be deed,
> And woneth in halkes alwey to and fro,
> And dar nat ones putte forth his heed;
> Men sholde him brennen in a fyr so reed
> If he were found, or that men might him spye;'

137. *þe Iustice:* The Southern versions generally, do not mention the name of this justice or governor. Alfred and Ælfric mention him as Alma-theus or Almachius, Bokenam and Chaucer as Almache. DeVignay and Cax-ton give him the title of prevost, while Tib. refers to him as ' þe cursed *king'* 347, 367, 377.

145-8. 'They (the Christians) rejected the thing that was naught although it had a fair appearance, and accepted that which was cast out, and had no fair appearance. For, though the world's happiness has a fair exterior, in truth it is (worth) naught, and though the joy of Heaven seems little, it is, in truth, much.' cf. MS. Gg. II. 6. 325-332.

149. *þe Justices seden:* Plural; otherwise the text refers to one Justice.

151-154. 'In winter, said Valerian, loafers sit and drink and laugh to scorn the tillers of the soil who busy themselves about future store; in harvest, when they (the toilers) may gather fair grain, they (the loafers) are obliged to go up and down in discomfort, for they have not even a furrow (of grain).' cf. MS. Gg. II. 6. 347-356.

163. *queþe þis gode men: þis* appears here and in *l. 171* as the plural de-monstrative.

165. *Maxime, þe gailer:* Chaucer calls him 'corniculere,' which term he derived from the *'cubiculario'* of Surius, Vita S. Cæciliæ, XIX. (See Kölbing, *Eng. Stud.* I. 215). Bokenam also says 'cornyculer' 614. The early legends call him simply 'jailer' except Tib. which says 'þis ilk prince Maximus', 329.

169-70. Tib. 335-6, *armurs of light:* Rom. XIII. 12.

171. *maumet:* Chaucer, Bokenam, and Barbour, Caxton, and De Vignay, specify that it is Jupiter who is the object of Almachius' idolatry.

184. *þi wite heu:* 'thy white countenance,' referring probably to her beauty and gentle breeding, not to palor occasioned by fear.

194. *bleddore:* This is a favorite metaphor at this point from Ælfric to Chaucer. The former says:

> ' Ælces mannes miht þe on modignysse færð.
> is soðlice þam gelíc swílce man siwige
> ane bytte, and blawe hí fulle windes
> and wyrce siððan an þyrl þonne heo to-þunden bið
> on hire greatnysse þonne togæð seo miht.' 319.

Chaucer, 2nd N. T: *ll.* 337-341.

> 'Your might' quod she, 'ful litel is to drede;
> For every mortal mannes power nis
> But lyk a bladdre, ful of wind, y-wis.
> For with a nedles poynt, whan it is blowe
> May al the boost of it be leyd ful lowe.'

The M. H. D. version gives it as follows: *ll.* 1589-96.

> ' da ist din gewalt anders niht getan
> Wan als ein blater, du vast ist ʒeblan:
> vnde als shiere ir kraft zerbrichet,
> so mat mit einer kleiner nadelon dar in stichet,
> als shiere ist och din gewalt ʒergan gen
> den dv von dinen herren hest enphangen.'

223. *a þis ʒong þing:* 'that this young thing!' *a* s written *þat* in Laud and Cmb. R. 3. 25. See Mætzner, *Eng. Sprachpr.*, *at*, (rel.)

239-245. These lines are omitted in MS. Cmb. R. 3. 25.

242. The MS. form *m*uste and the impersonal *me* make this the most ambiguous line of the text. The meaning is most apparent in the Bodleian version: 'for whoso knew (by observation or experience,) of no suffering, there might see it.'

247. *mony good mon:* Laud 108, avoids this expression by the use of '*many a.*'

252. *Vpe is poer:* 'over her (body), his power should be done,' *i. e.* masses should be said.

257. Ælfric does not mention the year of St. Cecilia's death. Caxton says: 'She suffred hir passyon about the yere of our lord two hundred and xxiii in the tyme of Alexaunder the emperour and it is redde in another place that she suffred in the tyme of marcii aurelii which reygned aboute the yere of our lord two hondred and twenty.' Jehan De Vignay says: ' Et elle souffrit mort enuiron l'an de nostre seigneur deux cens XXIII au temps de Alexandre empereur. Et on lit ailleurs qu'elle souffrit au temps de marc aurelien qui fut empereur enuiron l'an de nostre seigneur *Sept cens et vingt.*' Legenda Aurea mentions the date c. A. D. CCXX. Chaucer omits the allusion altogether, while Osbern Bokenam writes,

'I say þat martyred was Cycyle þe holy uirgyne
The yere of grace, treuly to ternyne,
Two hundyrd twenty & eek three—
Legenda aurea thus techyth me—
The tende kalende euene of Decembre;
Wych tym regnyth, as he doth remembre,
Alexaundyr of Rome þe emperour.—'

Skeat, *Notes to Cant. Tales,* p. 414, suggests that because Alexander's full name was Marcus Aurelius Alexander Severus, the reason for confusion of this name with that of the earlier Marcus Aurelius becomes apparent.

VIII.

GLOSSARIES.

[The character þ follows t; u and v are only discriminated as vowel and consonant. Semicolons are used to separate different groups of meanings, and among the word-citations to separate different case and tense groups. When the designations of mood and tense are omitted, 'ind. pres.' is to be understood; when of mood only, supply 'ind.' if no other has immediately preceded, otherwise the latter. The numbers refer to the line in the version under consideration. The asterisk before a verb indicates a suppositional infinitive which is constructed according to analogous forms found in the version. Letters which are variable in their occurrence in a word are included in parentheses, letters inserted or changed by emendation are italicized and enclosed by brackets. Parallel or related forms in early and modern languages are set off by brackets.]

MS. ASHMOLE 43.

A

a, indef. art., a: 5, 16, 54, 55, 56, 154, 160, 188, 194, 195, 196, 201, 218, 219, 220, 227, 239, 246, 250.

abide, sv., intrans., *wait, stay, remain:* inf. 133.

aboute, adv., *around, on every side:* 88, 134, 152, 243.

ac, conj., *but:* 25, 37, 75, 97, 134, 172, 202, 210, 226.

adoun, adv., *down:* 49, 57, 253; adon, 184.

after, prep. w. dat., *according to; following in the succession of time:* 30, 48, 65, 253, 258.

agen, adv., *again:* 67, 131.

agen, prep. w. dat., *against:* 24, 141, 160.

al, adj., *all that is possible; everything; every one:* ns. alle, 166; ds. al, 89, 229, alle, 252; as. al, 24; used absolutely, ds. alle, 62; as. al, 30, 255. ap. alle, 248.

al, adv., *wholly, entirely:* 195, 219.

alas, interj., *alas:* 223.

*aliȝt(e), wv., intrans., *come down, descend:* pt. 3 sg. aliȝte, 55; pp. aliȝt, 258.

also, adv., *likewise, in addition:* 20, 91, 116, 118, 121, 196, 256.

alyue, adj., *alive, in the living state:* as. alyue, 241.

amidde, adv., *into the middle of:* 219.

among, prep. w. dat., *surrounded by:* 47.

*awak(e), wv., trans., *awake:* pp. 102.

amorwe, adv., *on the morrow:* 171.

an, indef. art., *an:* 20, 31, 46, 69, 126, 174, 219, 239.

an, conj., *and:* 125; &, (101 times).

an, prep. w. dat., *in:* 70.

angel, sb., *angel, divine messenger:* ns. 20, 69, 83, 85, 105; as. angel, 28, 33, 42, 131; np. angles, 174, 176.

anon, adv., *soon, forthwith:* 37, 43, 45, 49, 66, 113, 131, 136, 162, 164, 175, 177, 180.

anyȝt, adv., *in the night time, by night:* 13.

apie, pr. n., Appia: gs. 37.

ariȝt, adv., *in a right way, justly:* 106.

*arys(e), sv., intrans., *arise:* pt. 3 sg. aros, 43.

as, adv., *in such wise; in the manner as, like; when;* w. adv. of place. *where* 3, 13, 17, 26, 43. 46, 47. 54, 72, 82, 88. 90, 97. 98, 118, 139. 188, 194. 216, 217.

at, prep. w. dat., *at, expressing time and place:* 1, 84.

atenende, contr. form; prep. w. dat. sb., *at the end, at last:* 155. [OE. æt ðām ende].

atom, contr. form; prep. w. dat. sb., *at home:* 133.

awei, adv., *away:* 195.

aworþ, ppl. adj., *cast away, degraded:* as. 146.

auonge, sv., trans., *receive:* inf. 125, 227.

B

baptise, wv. trans., *baptise:* inf. 41, 248; pp. baptise, 3.

baptisinge, sb., *baptism:* ns. 61.

be, sv., intrans., *be, exist:* 1 sg. am, 192, 209, contr. form, icham, 19, 93, 94. 175; 2 sg., art, 116, 204, 205, contr. form, artou, 183, 185; 3 sg. be, 64, is, 20, 52, 61, 62, 77. 93, 99, 100, 109, 115, 119, 125, 126, 148, 150, 201, 205, 213, 215, 255; contr. form, nys. = ne+is, 64, 111, 194. 1 pl., beþ, 158; 3 pl. beþ 62, 76, 108, 182, 211; pt. 3 sg., was, 11, 53, 133, 145, 230², 236, 239, 244, 246, 257, 258, nas, 145, opt. pt. 3 sg., were 82, 88, 91, 120, 124, 217, 228, 234, nere, 123; 2 sg. were, 96; 1 pl., were, 121, 143; 3 pl., were, 134, 141; imp. 2 sg. beþ, 225; opt. pr. 2 sg., be, 160, 213; 3 sg. be, 241. aux, be, 12⁵, 34, 51, 114, 118; art, 159; beþ, 102; were, 48, 137, 139, 142, 170, 171, 186, 252; was, 1, 5, 13, 181, 221; inf., be, 126¹, 138, 157, 191, 206; pp. ibe, 67, 101, 119, 120, 144.

bedde, sb., *bed:* ds. bedde, 13.

beggare, sb., *beggar:* ns. 160.

belamy, sb., *bel ami, conventional form of address:* vs. belamy, 161; vp. belamys, 149.

beleue, wv., trans., *leave:* inf. 241.

best, sb., *beast, ferocious animal:* ns. 112.

*ber(e), sv., trans., *to bear, carry, bring into being:* pt. 3 sg. ber, 56; 3 pl., bere, 174; pp. ibore, 1.

bi, prep. m. dat., *beside of; in accordance with; to; in:* 69, 114, 167, 183, 203, 237; by, 21.

bicom(e), sv., trans., *come to be,* used with reference to the locality of a person *to go, become of:* pt. 3 sg. bicom, 65, 85; 3 pl. bicom, 166, 232; inf. bicome, 116, bicom, 130.

*bid(de), sv., trans., *pray, entreat; say, utter, express; command:* 2 sg. bist, 80; 1 pl. bidde, 259; pt. 3 sg., bed., 4, 59. 249, 254; bad, 44.

*bihald, sv., trans., *behold, look:* pt. 3 sg., bihuld, 65, 88.

bi-hinde, adv., *behind:* 193.

*bihot(e), sv., trans., *command:* 1 sg. bihote, 18; pp. bihote, 132.

*bi-hou(e), wv., trans., *behove, befit, is due to:* 3 sg. bi-houeþ, 104.

bileue, sb., *belief, faith:* ns. 61; ds. bileue, 115; as. bileue 130.

bileue, wv., trans., *believe:* pt. 3 sg. bileuede, 235; 3 pl. bileuede, 145; inf., 32, 34, 98, 106.

bileue, wv., trans., *lighten, fill with light:* inf. 169

*bind(e), sv. trans., *bind, fasten, tie up:* pp. ibounde, 178.

biscop, sb., *bishop:* ds. biscop, 117, 129, 248.

*bisech(e), sv., *ask; entreat:* 1 sg. biseche, 127; pp. bisoзt, 14.

bi-uore, prep. w. dat., *in the presence of:* 137; byuore, 181.

bleddore, sb., *bladder:* ns. 194.

blisse, sb., *perfect joy, blessedness:* ns. 148; ds. blisse, 155.

*blow(e), wv. trans., *blow, fill:* pp. iblowe, 194.

blynd, adj. *blind* (spiritually): ns. 210, 213, 216.

bodi, sb., *body, the material frame:* ds. bodi, 73; as. bodi, 179, 251.

boke, sb., *book:* ds. boke, 72.

bold, adj. *confident, daring, strong:* ns. 160.

bone, sb., *prayer, petition:* ds. bone, 97; as. bone, 80.

bote, conj., *but, except, unless:* 96, 108, 123, 184, 194, 213.

boþe, adj., standing in attributive relation to a plural pron., *both:* np. boþe 84; ap. both, 173; ap. boþe, 42.

briȝtore, adj., comp. of briȝt; *brighter:* ns. 70.

bringe, sv., trans. *bring:* 2 sg. bringest, 163; inf. 162, 260; pp. ibroȝt, 13, 74, 94, 120, 137, 142, 170, 171, 184, 193, 208, 222, 234, 236.

broþer, sb., *brother:* ns. 82, 114, 115, 116, 129; ds. 87; vs. 89, 95, 99, 107, 127; np. breþeren, 134.

burie, wv., trans., *bury, inter:* pt. 3 sg. burede, 180; 3 pl., burede, 139; inf., 136, 251.

burles, sb., *place of burial, tomb:* dp. burles, 47.

busemar, sb., *mockery, contumely:* ds. busemar, 152.

bygynne, sv., trans., *begin:* inf. 250.

by-nyme, sv., trans., *take, rob:* pt. 2 sg. by-nome, 22; inf. 23.

C

*can, pot. aux., *can:* 118.

caste, wv. trans., *cast, throw:* pt. 3 pl. caste, 179, 229; inf. 76, 219.

caroine, sb., *carrion, carcase:* ns. 196, 201.

Cecile, pr. n., *Cecilia:* ns. 132, 133, 179, cicile, 50, 53; cecili, 209; ds. cicile, 71; as. cecile, 69; cecilie, 79; Seyn Cecile, ns. 1, 113, 167, 209; ds. 67.

certes, adv., *certainly:* 158, 162, 200.

chambre, sb., *chamber, apartment:* ds. chambre, 87, 132; as. chambre, 68.

chast, adj., *pure, undefiled:* ds. 73.

chirche, sb., *church:* as. chirche, 250.

clannesse, sb., *cleanness:* ds. clannesse, 30.

clene, adj., *undefiled, chaste:* ds. clene, 25, 73, 115; np. clene, 86.

clepe, wv. trans., *call, designate:* 3 sg. clepeþ, 52. inf. 192.

cler, adj., *full, bright:* ds. 170.

cloþes, pl. sb., *clothes:* ap. 7.

*com, sv., intrans., *come:* 3 sg. come, 2; com, 191; comeþ, 198; pt. 3 sg. com. 46, 49, 55, 87, 131, 167, 260: 3 pl. come, 140. pp. icome, 185.

conseil, sb., *counsel:* ns. 17; as. conseil, 41.

corn, sb., *corn, grain:* as. (coll.) corn, 153.

cradel, sb., *cradle, the symbol of infancy:* ds. cradel. 2.

creature, sb., *creature:* ns. 223.

crie, wv., trans., *cry, call:* inf. 38.

crist, sb. *Christ:* (see *þesu crist* and *lord.*)

cristendom, sb., *Christianity:* as. cristendom, 50, 66.

cristene, sb., *a believer in Christ:* ns. 175; np. cristene, 166, 232. (used without the article).

cristene, adj., *Christian:* ns. 130; np. cristene, 47; dp. cristene, 254.

cristeneman, sb., *Christian:* ns. 82, ap. cristenmen, 135.

*confound, wv., trans., *confound, discomfit:* pp. confounded, 12.

*cuss(e), wv., trans., *kiss:* pt. 3 sg. custe, 113.

*cuþ(e) wv. trans., *make known, show:* 2 pl. cuþeþ. 168.

D

dame, sb., *a form of address applied to a woman of rank:* vs. dame, 198, 207.

day, sb., *day,* (period of 24 hours); in compo. ibroȝt of dawe, *deprived of life, slain:* ds. day, 253; daie, 237; dp. dawe, 142; as. (in adv. phr. good day), 254.

ded, ppl. adj., *dead:* ns. 244.

deie, wv., intrans., *die:* inf. 78, 216, 224.

*del(e), wv., trans., *divide, share:* pt. 3 sg. delede, 245.

deol, sb., *grief, mourning:* ds. deol, 242.

dere, adv., *dearly, at great cost:* 236.

derkhede, sb., *darkness:* as. derkhede, 169.

deþ, sb., *death:* ns. 205, 230, 236; gs.
deþes, 204, 205: ds. deþ, 206, 233,
deþe, 162, 208, 234; as. deþ, 199, 201,
203.

do, sv., trans., *do; make, perform:* 1
pl. doþ, 98; 2 pl. doþ, 168; pt. 3 sg.
dude, 240; opt. pr. 2 sg. do, 184; imp.
2 sg. do, 208; doþ, 162; aux., do, 90,
92; dest, 63, 79, 184; doþ, 25, 74,
184; inf. 30, 112, 114, 118, 164, 172,
don, 137; pp. i-do, 19, 103, 252, 255.

doun, adv., *down:* 154.

drede, sb., *mortal fear, awe:* ds.
drede, 57.

*drink, sv., trans., *drink, imbibe:* 3
pl. drinkeþ, 151.

E

eche, ind. pron., *each:* ds. eche, 62.
as. ech, 26.

eie, sb., *eye:* ds. eie, 199, 215.

eiþer, pron., *either, each:* ns. 86.

eke, adv., *also:* 157, 210.

emperour, sb., *emperor:* gs. emperours, 138, 140.

ende, sb., *termination, conclusion;
mode of death, fate:* ds. ende, 206,
227; as. ende, 189. ds. (contr. form),
atenende, 155.

enes, adv., *once:* 190, 246.

eny, adj., *any:* ns. 54, 70, 112; ds.
eny, 124.

er, adv., *before, formerly:* 53, 103; ar,
2.

erþetilie, sb., *tiller of the soil:* ap.
erþetilien, 152.

esce, wv., trans., *ask, seek:* 2 sg.
axst, 188; inf. 50.

euer, adv., *ever:* 75, 101, 186.

F

fader, sb., *father:* ns. 62.

fei, sb., *faith:* ds. fei, 183.

fiȝte, sv., trans., *fight:* imp. 2 pl.
fiȝteþ, 169; inf. 24.

*find(e), sv., trans., *find:* 1 pl. fi[n]d-
eþ, 3, 72. pt. 3 sg. vond, 68, uond,
69; inf. vynde, 38.

*flem(e), wv., trans., *put to flight:* pp.
fleme, 120.

floure, sb., *flower:* np. floures, 76; dp.
floures, 96.

fo, sb., *foe:* ap. fon, 138.

fol, sb., *fool;* ns. 124, 126, 188, 228;
as. fol. 192.

fole, adj., *foolish:* ns. 14; as. fole,
130.

folie, sb., *folly:* ds. folie, 14, 31.

folliche, adv., *foolishly:* 185.

fot, sb., *foot:* dp. fet. 49.

four, card. num., *four:* np. four, 232.

fram, prep. w. dat., *from:* 2, 26, 35,
55, 190.

frende, sb., *friend:* gp. frendes, 5.

fur, sb., *fire:* ds. fure, 224; as. fur,
218.

G

gailer, sb., *jailer:* ns. 165.

ȝare, adv., *long ago:* 120.

ȝe, adv., *yea, yes:* 104.

*ȝelp, sv., trans., *boast:* 2 sg. ȝelpest,
197.

ȝe[m]e, wv., trans., *take care of,
guard, protect:* inf. 26.

ȝer, sb., *year:* ns. 257; ds. ȝere, 89.

gerlan, sb., *garland, wreath:* ap.
gerlans, 8, 70, 95.

ȝerne, adv., *willingly, eagerly:* 4,
119.

ȝeue, sv., trans., *give:* pt. 3 sg. ȝaf,
66, ȝef, 43; inf. 83, 199, 201, 202, 203,
224; ȝiue, 188; pp. iȝeue, 105, 221.

gidi, adj., *giddy, foolish:* ns. 209, 210,
214, 215, 216.

ȝif, conj., *if:* 21, 25, 27, 29, 31, 33, 35,
98, 106, 120, 121, 123, 212², 214.

*gin, aux. sv., *begin; used as a pret-
erit intensive:* gan, 58, 167, 178, 238;
gon, 179.

go(n), sv., intrans., *go;* in comp.,
"hou geþ þis?" *what means this:*
3 sg. geþ, 89, 182, 198; pt. 3 sg.,
eode, 175, 243; inf. go, 37, 55, 117,
154, gon, 40, 132, 135, 179. [Mn. Ger.,
wie geht es?]

god, pr. n., *God, the supreme being;
god, idol:* ns. 62, 228, 239; gs. godes,
231; ds. god, 10, 160, 246; dp. godes,
208; ap. godes, 211.

godhede, sb., *deity:* ds. godhede, 207.

golde, sb., *gold:* ds. golde, 8.

ʒong, adj., *young:* ns. ʒong, 223, ʒonge, 226; as. ʒonge, 224.

good, sb., *property, possessions:* dp. good, 245.

good, adj., *good:* ds. good, 25, 115, gode, 128; as. gode, 69; np. gode, 163, 171; gp. gode, 176; ap. gode, 139, good, 247; compar. *better:* ns. bet, 64; ds. betere, 186.

grace, sb., *the love and favor of God:* ns. 246; ds. grace, 231; as. grace, 83.

grante, wv., trans., *grant, permit, bestow:* opt. 2 sg. grante, 16; inf. 80.

grede, sv., intrans., *cry out:* pt. 3 sg. gradde, 222; inf. 167.

grepe, sb., *furrow:* as. grepe, 154.

gret, adj., *great, large in amount:* ds. gret, 6; as. gret, 36, 218.

gulteles, adj., *guiltless, innocent:* as. gulteles, 240.

ʒut, adv., *yet, still:* 182.

H

habbe, wv., trans., *have:* 1 sg. ichabbe, 255; 2 sg. hast, 15, 24, 97, nastou, 204; 3 sg. habbe, 147; 1 pl. habbeþ, 95; 3 pl. nabbeþ, 154; pt. 3 sg. hadde, 145, nadde, 146; imp. 2 sg. haue, 128; aux., 1 sg. habbe, 74; 2 sg. hast, 29, 103, 111; 3 sg. habbe, 53, haþ, 105, 119, 120; 1 pl. habbeþ, 101; pt. 3 sg hadde, 14, 67, 132; inf. 144, 150, 254.

*hald(e), wv., trans., *hold one's own, keep up, avail:* pt. 2 sg. halt, 24.

half, adv., *half:* 238, 241, 243, 244².

halwe, sb., *holy one:* ns. 59.

halwy, wv., trans., *hallow:* inf. 250.

hamward, adv., *homeward:* 238.

harde, adv., *hard, severely, sorely:* 23.

hardi, adj., *bold, daring in a bad sense:* ns. 191; ap. hardi, 138.

he, per. pron., *he:* ns. (56 times); gs. his, 69, 116, 166, is, 49, 87, 130, 235,

252, 258; ds. him, 24, 40, 41, 43, 49, 59, 66, 83, 121, 228, 241; as. him, 28, 32, 45, 50, 53, 57, 58², 59, 66, 110, 113, 130, 132, 177², 249; np. hi, 39, 48, 75, 135, 137³, 139, 145, 152, 153, 154², 172, 179, 222, 223, 238; gp. hor, 9⁴, 76, 86, 144, 173, 174; dp. hem, 166, þem, 97; ap. hem (12 times).

hede, sb.,*-hood:* as. hede, 168.

hei, adj. used as sb., *a high place:* ds. hei, 174.

heie, adv., *to a high degree, greatly:* 200.

helle, sb., *hell:* gs. helle, 216; ds. helle, 35, 156.

helpe, wv. trans., *help:* inf. 110.

henne, adv., *hence:* 37.

heo, per. pron., f., *she:* ns. (22 times), ds. hire, 69, 132; as. hire, 3, 14, 218, 219, 220, 221, 229, 233, 235, 238, 240, 241; gs. hire, 4, 5, 8, 11, 13, 68, 224, 230, 234, 235, 243, 245², 251, 253, 249, 259, 260. For plural, see *he.*

her-after, adv., *hereafter:* 125.

here, adv., *here:* 90, 95, 122, 191; her, 21, 63.

here, sb., *hair, a hair garment:* ns. 8.

herte, sb., *heart, the seat of moral affections:* ns. 12; as. herte, 190.

heruest, sb., *harvest:* ds. heruest, 153.

heu, sb., *hue, color:* ns. 184, as. heu, 76.

heued, sb., *head:* ns. 243; as. heued, 233; ap. heden, 173.

heuene, sb., *heaven:* ds. heuene, 55, 59, 105, 148, 174, 176; as. heuene, 122.

hewe, wv., trans., *cut, strike with a sword:* inf. 240.

hie, wv., intrans., *go in haste:* inf. 238.

ho, rel. and interr. pron., *who, whoso:* ns. 138, 242, hose, 150; as. (to) wen, 136.

*hold(e), sv., trans., *hold, have:* pt. 3 sg. huld, 70.

holi, adj., *holy, righteous, saintly:* ns. 107, 225, 243; ds. holi, 240, 259; ap. holi, 180.

honde, sb., *hand:* ds. honde, 245.

hondred, card. num., *hundred:* np. hondred, 232, 257.

honoure, wv., trans., *honor, worship:* inf. 211.

hor, adj., *hoary:* ns. 56.

*hot(e), sv., trans., *command:* pt. 3 sg. het, 6, 165, 172, 173, 217. See *bihote.

hou, inter. and rel. adv., *how, that:* 89, 94, 109, 110, 182, 191, 198.

hous, sb., *house:* ns. 91; ds. hous, 218; as. hous, 249.

I (vowel).

I, per. pron., *I:* ns. 32², 81, 92, 94, 161, 212; ich, 16, 17, 18, 27, 28, 29, 31, 39, 90³, 92; 74, 100, 127, 176, 183, 199 ,207, 209, 211, 212, 226², 227, contr. Ine, 12; ichabbe 265, gs. my, 20², 22, 80, 82, 83, 93, 105, 114, 115, 116, 192, 255, myn 12, 190, mi, 226; ds. me, 15, 21, 28, 31, 105, 128, 225, as. me, 17, 25, 26, 192, 228; as. (impersonal) 85, 90, 92, 104, 149, 188, 203; np. we, (16 times); gp. our, (13 times), oure, 208; ap. ous, 35, 42, 163, 260.

ibore, ppl. adj., *born:* ns. 1.

icristened, ppl. adj., *made Christian, baptised;* ns. 34, 118.

idelman, sb., *idler, loiterer:* np. idelmen, 151.

*i-full(e), wv., trans., *baptise:* pp. i-fulle, 67.

ihered, ppl. adj., *glorified, honored:* ns. 51.

ihud, ppl. adj., *hidden:* as. ihud, 120.

*iknou(e), sv., trans., *know, recognize:* pl. 3 pl. ikneu, 48.

ilast(e), wv., intrans., *last, remain in existence:* inf. 75; pp. ilaste, 220.

ileue, wv., trans., *believe:* inf. 215; 2 sg. contr. ileuestou, 63; opt. 1 sg. ileue, 27.   (see *bi-leue,* and *leue*.)

in, prep. w. dat., *in, with; within; into; at,* (time or place): 11, 13, 19, 25, 30, 31, 46, 62, 72, 73, 84, 93, 94, 100, 101, 126, 132, 151, 153, 154, 164, 165, 170, 187, 206, 216, 229, 232, 233, 235, 250, 252, 258; inne, 249.

inou, adj., *enough:* ds. inou, 86.

ise, sv., trans., *see:* cond. 1 sg. ise, 31; pt. 1 sg. isei, 176; 3 sg. isei, 57, 173, 233: 3 pl. iseie, 222; inf. 28, 29, 33, 35, 42, 63, 96, 98, 102, 189, 212, 213, 242.

it, per. pron.. *it:* ns. (11 times), hit, 246; as. it, (6 times). For pl. see *he.*

itold, ppl. adj., *esteemed:* ns. 159.

iþe., sv., intrans., *thrive, prosper:* inf. 158.

iuere, sb., *companion, associate, fellow:* ns. 96.

iwis, adv., *indeed, truly, certainly:* 28, 202, 206, 214.

*iwrit(e), sv., trans., *write:* pp. iwrite, 3.

I (consonant).

ianglinge, sb., *jangling, prating:* ds. Ianglinge, 161.

ihesu crist, pr. n., *Jesus Christ:* ds. ihesu crist, 4, 34, 38, 190, 247, 256.

ioie, sb., *joy; heavenly felicity:* ds. Ioie, 86, 126, 156, 260; as. Ioie, 36.

iugement, sb., *process of law; verdict:* ns. 221; ds. Iugement, 142.

iustice, sb., *justice, provost:* ns. 157, 161, 164, 172, 177, 198, 207, 230; ds. Iustice, 137, 175, 181; np. Iustices, 149.

K

kepe, wv., trans., *keep; take, receive:* 1 sg. kepe, 207; 3 sg. kepeþ, 150; inf. 161.

knaue, sb., *knave, servant:* np. knaues, 144.

knyȝte, sb., *knight:* vp. knyȝtes, 168.

kunne, sb., *race, family:* ds. kunne, 1, 186, kun, 185.

L

lasse, adv., *less:* 158, 159.

lawe, sb., *law:* ds. lawe, 141.

led, sb., *a leaden vessel:* as. led, 219.

lede, sv., trans., *lead:* pt. 3 sg. ladde, 129; 3 pl. ladde, 221; inf. 58, 128, 170, 176, 218; pp. ilad, 181.

*lef(e), wv., intrans., *give leave, allow, permit, give hearing:* pt. 3 sg. lefte, 137.

lefmon, sb. *dear one, beloved:* ns. 20; vs. lefmon, 27.

leue, adj., *dear:* vs. leue, 95, 99, 107, 113, 127.

lene, wv., trans., *lend, grant:* inf. 74.

leome, sb., *light, brightness:* ns. 70.

lere, wv., trans., *teach, speak:* inf. 185.

lese, sv., trans., *lose:* 1 sg. lese, 226; inf. 124.

lete, wv., trans., *delay, detain:* pt. 3 sg. let, 164; inf. 22.

lete, sv., trans., *cause, permit, leave, let go:* pt. 3 sg. lette, 3; aux. let, 12, 130, 177², 234; lette, 144; inf. lete, 178. [Mn. Eng. to *let* blood].

leue, wv., trans., *believe:* 1 sg. lef, 212; 2 sg. leuest, 214; inf. 64.

liche, sb., *body:* ds. liche, 8.

lif, sb., *life:* ns. 125, 226; ds. lif, 25, 187, 204; ds. lynue, 202, 226; as. lif, 178, 187, 199, 224, 227.

*liʒ(e), sv., trans., *laugh, deride:* 3 pl. liʒeþ, 152.

*liʒ(e), sv., trans., *lie:* pt. 3 sg. lay, 253.

*liʒ(e), sv., intrans., *lie, tell a false-hood:* pt. 2 sg. luxt, 200.

liʒt, sb., *light, intellectual clear-ness:* ds. liʒt, 170.

liʒt, adj., *light, bright:* ns. 68.

lilie, sb., *lily:* ns. 77; dp. lilion, 91, lylion, 71.

lomb, sb., *lamb:* ns. 54.

loude, adv., *loudly:* 167, 222.

londe, sb., *land, nation:* ds. londe, 142.

loue, sb., *love:* ds. loue, 36, 73, 106, 115; as. loue, 15.

*lou(e), wv., trans., *love:* 2 sg. louest, 25, 31; pt. 3 sg. louede, 2.

longe, adv., *long:* 126; comp. len-gore, 230.

lord, sb., *Lord; an earthly master, husband:* ns. 43, 61, 74, 83, 205, 258; gs. lordes, 105, 250, 251; ds. lord, 13, 80, 259; vs. lord, 12, Louerd, 51; as. lord (crist) 2.

lute, adj., *little, small:* ns. 148, 197; ds. lute, 166; as. lute, 16.

luþer, adj., *evil, bad:* ns. 52.

lym, sb., *limb, any part of the body:* ns. 220.

lyue, wv., trans., *live:* inf. 187.

M

mahon, pr. n., *Mahomet:* ds. 183.

*mai, mod. aux., *may:* pt. *might:* mai, 29, 36, 110², 199; pt. miʒte, 92, 122, 201, 202, 233, 242, 246; miʒt, 18, 35, 96, 98, 203, 212, 213.

maide, sb., *maid, young woman:* ns. 7, 10, 15, 19, 33, 44, 107, 123, 186, 188, 193, 198, 199, 217, 225, 243, 253; ds. maide, 240.

maidenhod, sb., *maidenhood, virgin-ity:* as. maidenhod, 4, 22, 77.

maister, sb., *master, sovereign:* ns. 192.

make, wv., trans., *make:* pt. 3 sg. made, 138; inf. 218; pp. imad, 53, 109.

maner, sb., *manner, sort:* ds. maner, 187; np. maner, 76.

(seynte) marie, pr. n. *Mary, the mother of Christ:* ds. 10.

martir, sb., *martyr:* ap. martirs, 180.

martirdom, sb., *martyrdom:* ds. mar-tirdom, 253, 259; as. martirdom, 78.

*martre, wv., trans., *martyr, kill:* pt. 3 sg. martred, 135; pp. Imartred, 48, 139.

maumet, sb., *mawmet, idol:* ds. Mau-met, 171; np. maumetes, 108.

maxime, pr. n. *Maximius:* ns. 165, 173.

mayn, sb., *power, strength:* ds. mayn, 235.

me, for man, *one,* impersonally: ns. 47, 48, 52, 85, 135, 137, 221, 229, 233, 242.

menstrale, sb., *minstrel:* np. men-strales, 9.

menstrasie, sb., *minstrelsy:* ds. men-strasie, 9.

mercy, sb., *mercy, compassion:* as. mercy, 128.

meseise, sb., *lack of ease:* ds. mes-eise, 154.

*met(e), wv., trans., *dream:* 1 sg. mete, 100.

metynge, sb., *dreaming:* ds. metynge, 100, 161.

miȝte, sb., *power, might:* ns. 51; as. miȝte, 231, miȝt, 204.

milde, adj., *mild, meek:* ns. 54.

mile, sb., *mile:* dp. mile, 37.

misbileued, adj., *unbelieving, infidel:* ap. misbileued, 141.

moder, sb., *mother:* ds. moder, 258.

mon, sb., *man, a human being:* ns. 14, 55, 216, 247, men, 163 (= man), man, 46, 130; gs. monnes, 109; ds. mon, 40, 45; monne, 128, man, 5; as. mon, 65; np. men, 45, 47, 134, 140, 171, 222, 232, 245, gp. menne, 176; dp. men, 254; ap. men, 38, 139.

mony, adj., *many; many a;* compar. *more:* ap. mony, 247; compar. np. mo, 182, 232.

*mot(e), mod. aux., *may, must:* sg. mote, 16, 17, 78; pl. mowe, 102, 153, 154; pt. most, 28, 34, 37, 40, 117, moste, 133, 237.

muche, sb., *a large quantity, a great deal:* ns. 148; as. muche, 245.

muche, adv., *much, to a great degree:* muche, 81, 93; compar. more, 54; superl. mest, 11.

muri, adj., *joyous:* ns. 125.

myd, prep. w. dat., *with:* 115, 117.

N

naked, adj., *unclothed:* as. naked, 177.

name, sb., *name, character:* ds. name, 250.

ne, adv., *not, used as a negative intensive:* 24, 36, 46, 75, 81, 90, 92, 96, 109, 110, 160², 161, 163, 190, 192, 199², 207, 225, 226, 233, 236, 237, -ny, 81.

neuer, adv., *never:* 75, 76, 154, 158, neuere, 90.

next, adv., *next:* 8.

no, adj., *no, not any:* ns. 36, 46, 237; ds. no, 242; as. no, 146, 204, non, 108.

noble, adj., *noble, royal:* ds. noble, 1.

nobleie, sb., *nobility:* ds. nobleie, 6.

noȝt, ind. pron., *naught, nothing:* ns. 145, 147; as. noȝt, 161, 207.

noȝt, adv., *not:* 12, 24, 150, 163, 202, 212, 214, 225, 226, 233, 236.

nou, adv., *now:* 92, 102², 103, 169, 224, 239, 255, 259.

noþer, ind. pron., *other, another:* as. noþer, 31.

noþing, ind. pron., nothing: ns. 64, 111; ds. noþing, 22, 32; as. noþing, 81, 202.

nyȝt, sb., *night:* ds. nyȝt, 229.

nyme, sv., trans., *take, seize:* pt. 3 sg. nom, 58, 66, 86, 165; 3 pl. nome, 140, 174; inf. nyme, 177; pp. inome, 181.

O

of, prep. w. dat. and gen., *with; from; over; concerning; of, denoting possession:* w. dat. 1, 6, 7, 8, 9, 10, 11, 14, 36, 59, 62, 71², 80, 89, 91², 93, 96, 102, 105, 109, 115, 128, 142², 148, 150, 161, 185, 186, 194, 197, 202, 204, 207, 211, 220, 231, 242, 245, 246; w. gen. 37.

off, adv., *off, away:* 173, 234, 236.

old, adj., *old:* ns. 55; ds. old, 46, 109, olde, 40, 45; np. olde, 75; dp. olde, 47.

o(n), card. num., *one:* ns. 61², o, 61, 62, 129; ds. one, 84², as. on, 71.

on, prep. w. dat., *upon, in:* 34, 38, 210.

oþer, ind. pron., *other:* ns. 18, 64, 99, 103, 143, 187, 191; as. oþer, 72, 108, 129; ds. 86.

oþer, adj., *other:* ds. oþer, 94.

oþer, adv., *otherwise:* 184.

oþer, conj., *otherwise; or:* 100, 162, 208.

out, adj., *outside:* ds. out, 218.

ouer, adv., *more than:* 237.

ouer, prep. w. dat., 62, 219.

*owe, wv., trans., *owe, be under obligation:* 1 sg. owe, 183.

P

pal, sb., *pallium, a costly sort of cloth:* ds. pal. 7.

place, sb., *place:* ds, place, 84, 232.

*play, wv., intrans., *play:* pt. 3 sg.
    pleide, 231.
poer, sb., *power:* ns. 193, 197, 252; ds.
    poer, 189; as. poer, 192; np. pouere,
    45, 245; ap. pouere, 38.
*preche, wv., trans., *preach:* pt. 3 sg.
    prechede, 231, 247, 254.
prick, sb., *a pointed instrument, a
    pin:* ds. prick, 195.
*prik(e), wv., trans., *prick, puncture:*
    pp. ipriked, 195.
prison, sb., *prison:* ds. prison, 164,
    167.
priue, adj., *private, secret:* ds.
    priue, 17; as. priue, 41.
priuete, sb., *matter of privacy:* as.
    priuete, 16.
prute, sb., *pride:* ns. 198.
pur, adj., *pure, simple:* ds. pur, 203.
putt, sb., *pit:* dp. puttes, 47.
pyne, sb., *pain, torments:* ds. pyne,
    216.

Q

quellare, sb., *executioner, torturer:*
    ns. 235, 237.
quelle, wv., trans., *kill, torture:* inf.
    144, qu[e]lle, 233.
*que(e), sv., trans., *say, speak:* pt.
    3 sg. quaþ, 15, 18, 19, 33, 63, 64, 83,
    95, 99, 103, 111, 119, 123, 127, 151,
    157, 159, 161, 186, 187, 188, 191,
    193, 198, 199, 207, 225; pr. 3 sg.
    queþe, 143, 163.
quic, adj., *alive:* ns. 244.

R

rede, sb., *counsel, advice:* ds. 210,
    30; as. rede, 112.
rede, sv. trans., *read:* pt. 3 sg. radde,
    60; inf. 59.
rede, sv., trans., *counsel, advise:*
    inf. 118, red, 79.
rede, adj., *red:* dp. rede, 91.
repe, wv., trans., *reap:* inf. 153, 155.
reuþe, adj., *sad, pitiful:* ns. 244.
riche, adj., *rich:* ds. riche, 13; ap.
    riche, 7.
richesse, sb., *riches, opulence:* ds.
    richesse, 6.

riȝt, sb., *power, authority:* as. riȝt,
    203.
riȝt, adj., *just, equitable:* ds. riȝt,
    142.
riȝt, adv., *exactly, just:* 140, 257.
robe, sb., *robe:* as. robe, 7.
rome, pr. n., *Rome:* ds. rome, 1.
rose, sb., *rose:* ns. 78: dp. rosen, 71,
    91.

S

sacrifice, sb., *sacrifice, offering:* as.
    sacrifice, 162, 172, 208.
sauter, sb., *psalter:* ds. sauter, 11.
scewe, wv., trans., *show:* inf. 28.
*schal, sv., fut. and pot. aux., *shall;*
    pt. *should:* 1 and 3 sg. schal, 41, 42,
    162, 188, 196, 224, 227; 2 sg. schalt,
    38, 42, 114, 116, 189, 190, 216; contr.
    1 sg. ichulle, 30, 256; 1 pl. schulleþ,
    125, scholleþ, 155; 2 pl. scholleþ, 84,
    schulle, 256; 3 pl. schulleþ 156; pt.
    pot. aux. 1 sg. scholde, 211, 3 sg.
    scholde, 121, schulde, 249; 1 pl.
    scholde, 157.
schort, adj., *short, brief:* ns. 201; as.
    scorte, 227.
scourge, sb., *scourge:* dp., scourgen,
    178.
screwe, sb., *shrew, evil person:* ns.
    217, 239; np. screwen, 182.
*scrynk(e), wv., trans., *shrink, con-
    tract:* 3 sg. scrynkeþ, 195.
scryue, sv., trans., *shrive, confess:*
    inf. 17.
seg(e), wv., trans., *say, speak:* pt. 3 sg.
    sede, 50, 51, 60, 73, 87, 89, 103, 107,
    113, 175, 182, 209, 255; 3 pl. seden,
    149, sede, 223; opt. 1 sg. segge, 212;
    imp. 2 sg. sei, 39; pp. ised, 29, 111.
*sek(e), sv., trans., *seek:* pt. 1 pl.
    soȝte, 122; pp. isoȝt, 119.
sekenesse, sb., *sickness:* ds. seke-
    nesse, 196.
*se, sv., trans., *see:* 1 sg. sene, 210;
    2 sg. seist, 131, 209, suxst, 214, suxt,
    108; 3 sg. sei, interrog. contr., sux-
    tou, 103, 109, 199, suxstou, 192; opt. 3
    sg. seoþ, 25; pp.sg. sucþ, 215 (see ise).
semblance, sb., outward appearance,
    show: as. semblance, 145, 146, 147.

sende, wv., trans., *send:* 1 sg. sende, 39; pt. 3 sg. sende, 50, 248; inf. 228.

sergant, sb., *servant:* ns. 204, sergaunt, 205.

seruice, sb., *service:* ns. 251.

seþe, wv., trans., *seeth, boil:* pt. 3 sg. seþ 229; inf. 220.

seþende, adj., *boiling:* ds. seþende, 229.

seyn(te), sb., *saint,* used as an epithet in connection with a name, see Cecile, Marie, Vrban.

siȝt, sb. *sight, vision:* as. siȝt, 105.

***sing,** sv., trans., *sing:* pt. 3 sg. song, 10, 11; 2 pl., songe, 9.

sire, sb., *sir:* vs. 143, 200.

***sit,** sv., intrans., *sit:* 3 pl. sitteþ, 151; pt. 3 sg. sat, 231.

siþ, sb., *time:* ap. siþe, 235.

sle, sv., trans., *slay, kill:* inf. 32; pp. slawe, 238.

slepe, sb., *sleep:* ds. slepe, 102.

smul, sb., *smell, fragrance:* as. smul, 90, 97; smulle, 68.

smul, wv., trans., *smell:* pt. 1 sg. smulde, 90; inf. 92.

smyte, sv., trans., *smite, strike:* pt. 3 sg. smot, 235, 236; inf. 23, 173, 234, 237; pp. ismyte, 243.

so, adv., *so, thus:* 35, 36, 49, 53, 77, 81, 90, 93², 97, 100, 119, 122, 125, 126, 138, 160, 166, 185, 191, 228, 238, 240, 241.

sodenliche, adv., *suddenly:* 94.

sone, adv., *soon:* 14,79,98,181,184,193.

song, sb., *song:* as, song, 9.

soþ, adj., *true:* ns. 99, 213; compar. ns. soþer, 111.

soþe, st., *sooth, truth:* ds. soþe, 18, 147, 148; as. soþe 29³, soþ 212.

soule, sb., *soul:* ns. 260; ap. soulen, 174, 176.

soulement, adv., *only:* 123.

speke, sv., trans., *speak; tell:* inf. 41, 87.

spouse, sb., *wife, husband:* ns. 115; as. spouse, 69.

***spous(e),** wv., trans., *espouse, betroth:* pp. ispoused, 5.

stalward, adj., *stalwart, strong:* as. stalward, 168; vs. stalwarde, 168.

stalwardliche, adv., *stalwartly, courageously:* 160.

stele, sv. trans., *steal:* inf. 136.

stille, adj., *still, quiet:* np. 225.

stille, adv., *quietly; motionless:* 44, 88.

stilliche, adv., *quietly:* 3, 10.

ston, sb. *stone:* ds. stone, 211.

stonde, sv., intrans., *stand:* 1 sg. stonde, 100; 3 sg. stonde, 69, stont, 21; pt. 3 sg. stod, 88; inf. 246.

strengþe, sb., *strength, power:* ds. strengþe, 5.

strif, sb., *strife, struggle:* ds. strif, 124.

strong, adj., *strong:* ds. strong, 164; dp. stronge, 178.

stude, sb., *place:* ns. 239; ds. stude, 44, 46.

such, adj., *such:* ds. such, 233; as. such, 188; np. suche, 158.

suere, sb., *neck:* ds. suere, 235.

suete, adj., *fragrant; dear:* ns. suote, 68, 77; ds. suete, 259; as. suete, 251; suote, 90, 97; dp. suote, 71.

sueteheorte, sb. phr., *sweetheart:* vs. suete heorte, 15,19, swete heorte, 33.

sulue, ind. pron., *used with reflexive force, -self:* as. sulue, 110.

suyþe, adv., *very, such:* 55, 56, 197; swiþe, 7, 68.

***swynk,** sv., intrans., *labor, work:* 3 pl. swynkeþ, 152.

T

take, sv., trans., *take:* pt. 3 sg. tok, 59, toke, 71; 3 pl. toke, 146; inf. 217.

***tech(e),** sv., trans., *show:* pt. 3 pl. teiȝte, 45; opt. 3 pl. teche, 39.

telle, sv., trans., *tell, recount:* inf. 16, 36; pp. itold, 159.

tiraunt, adj., *tyrannical, cruel:* ns.54.

to, prep. w. dat., *to; unto; towards;* used as inf. sign: w. dat., 5, 15, 17, 18, 37, 40², 44, 45, 49, 67, 86, 87, 117, 128, 129, 152, 156, 162, 170, 171, 172, 174, 176, 192, 208², 218, 233, 247, 248, 256, 260; inf. sign, 4, 50, 64, 87, 126, 136, 138, 150, 169, 191, 192, 226, 240, 244, 248, 255, 260². w. as. to(wen),136.

to dai, adv. phr., *today:* 114.

to-gadere, adv., *together:* 180.

*token, wv., trans., *betoken, signify:* 3 sg. tokeneþ, 77, 78.

tonge, sb., *tongue, speech:* ns. 36.

toun, sb., *town:* ds. toun, 179.

trauail, sb., *travail, sufferings:* ds. trauail, 155.

tre, sb., *tree, wood:* ds. tre, 109, 211.

trechour, sb., *traitor:* np. trechours, 141.

tresour, sb., *jewels, adornments:* ap. tresours, 8.

trewe, adj., *true, faithful:* ds. trewe, 73.

tristiliche, adv., *trustfully, with confidence:* 18.

twenti, card. num., *twenty:* np. twenti, 257.

two, card. num., *two:* np. two, 76, 86, 257; ap. to, 70, twei, 139.

tybors, pr. n. *Tyburcius:* ns. 82, tibors, 87, 111, tybours, 119, 127, Tibours, 131; vs. tybors, 107, 113.

tyme, sb., *time, season:* ds. tyme, 84, 89.

þ

þat, rel. pron., *that:* ns. 6, 11, 52, 53, 60, 62, 64, 77, 111, 112, 119, 120, 124, 126, 129, 145, 165, 170, 185, 192, 197, 201, 215, 228, 244, þet, 110; ds. þat, 44, 260; as. þat, 24, 29², 63, 72, 125, 129, 132, 146, 178, 179, 195, 215, 255; np. þat, 62, 76, 96, 134, 141, 142, 152, 157, 158, 211, 222; ap. þat, 139, 144.

þat, dem. pron., *that:* ns. 111, 119, 129; as. 29², 71, 72, 129², 178, 179; instr. þe . . . þe, 230.

þat, conj., *to the effect that; so that; used after a prep. introd. a noun clause:* 12, 15, 16, 17, 22, 23, 25, 27, 28, 29, 31, 32, 36, 39², 48, 50, 82, 84, 94, 100, 143, 170, 190, 204, 209, 213, 233², 234, 244, 246, 249, 251, 258; a, 223², þe, def. art., *the:* (52 times); þe . . . þe, 230, (see þat, dem. pron.); as. þen, 33, 42, 131, 189.

þei, adv., *though, although:* 91, 145, 147, 148.

þen, conj., *than:* 31, 54, 70, 92, 103, 111, 112, 158, 160, 186, 232.

*þench(e), sv., trans., *think, intend, expect:* 2 sg. þenstou, 187.

*þench(e), sv., intrans., *seem; appear:* 3 sg. þencþ 90, 92, 149, 203. þenche, 148.

þenne, adv., *then, at that time:* 42, 197.

þer, adv., *there; where, an indef. grammatical subject:* 38, 46, 55², 64, 67, 76, 87, 123, 125, 140, 144, 182, 219, 220, 232, 242, 250, 251.

þer-inne, adv., *therein:* 229, 230, 252.

þer-of, adv., *thereof:* 97, þer of, 200.

þeron, adv., *thereon:* 78.

þerto, adv., *thereto:* 163.

þer-þoru, adv., *there-through, thereby:* 116.

þing, sb., *thing; individual:* ns. 110, 213, 223; ds. þinge, 62; as. þing, 145; np. þinges, 86.

þis, dem. pron., *this:* 7, 10, 14, 15, 18, 19, 33, 44, 52, 59, 64, 83, 89, 91, 99², 103, 107, 123², 143, 163, 182, 186, 187, 191, 193, 198, 200, 213, 221, 223², 225, 243, 253, 257; ds. þis, 85, 89, 93; as. þis, 11, 27, 59, 60, 65, 73, 169, 217; np þis, 45, 86, 108, 134, 171; ap. þes, 60, þis, 180.

þo, adv., *then; when:* 55, 57, 67, 107, 131, 172, 179, 181, 217, 221.

þoȝt, sb. *thoughts, mind:* ds. þoȝt, 11, 93.

þoru, prep. w. dat., *through:* 5, 97, 115, 166; þour, 224.

þou, per. pron., *you:* ns. (58 times), þe, 24, 185, gs. þi, 23, 30², 51, 80, 112, 115, 155, 161, 184, 187, 189, 192, 193, 196, 197, 198, 202, 205, 207, 210, þine, 211, þin, 199; ds. þe, 16, 17, 23, 26, 106, 127, 188, 191, 199; as. þe, 18, 26, 32, 39², 41, 110, 118; np. ȝe, 78, 84, 144, 149, 156, 168, 170, 225, 256; gp. ȝoure, 77, 78, 162, 168; dp. ȝou, 74; ap. ȝou, 162, 170.

þre, card. num., *three:* ns. 257; ds. þre, 37; ap. þre, 180, 235, þrie, 257.

þridde, ord. num., *third:* ds. þridde: 253.

*þrow(e), sv., trans., *throw, cast away:* pt. 3 pl. þreu, 47.

þuder, adv., *thither:* 50, 135.
þulke, adj., such, that: ds. þulke, 128, 237, 260; as. þulke, 83.
þus, adv., *to this extent:* 54.

U, V (vowel).

vuel, adj., *evil:* ns. 239.
vpe, adv., *over, above:* 58, 154; vpe, 252.
*vnderзet(e), sv., trans., *perceive:* opt. 3 sg. vnderзete, 21.
vnsuere, sb., *answer:* as. vnsuere, 188.
un-wemmed, adj., *unmoved, unde-filed:* ns. 12.
vrban, pr. n., *Urban:* ns. 119; Seyn Vrban, ns. 51, 58, 63, 66; ds. Seyn Vrban, 40, 45, 248, biscop Vrban, 117, 129,

U, V (consonant).

valerian, pr. n., *Valerian:* ns. 6, 43, 52, 57, 60, 95, 101, 103, 151, ualerian, 81, 159; gs valerianes, 183; ds. valerian, 117, ualerian, 72.
*val, sv., intrans., *fall:* pt. 3 sg. vel, 49, 57.
vair, adj., *fair, beautiful:* ns. 223, uair, 246; as vair, 153, uair, 56.
vaste, adv., *fast, closely, firmly:* 21, 178.
*ver(e), wv., intrans., *behave:* pt. 3 sg. verde, 217.
verisore, adj., *fresher:* compar. ap. verisore, 92.
verrore, adv., *father:* compar. verrore, 230.
vers, sb., *verse:* as. vers, 11.
verst, adv., *first, for the first time:* 102, uerst, 102.
vestemen, sb., *vestment, garments:* dp. vestemens, 56.
uol, adv., *full:* 194.
vol, adj., *full:* ns. 91, 93, as. uol, 219.
uolliche, adv., *fully:* 236.
vor, prep. w. dat., *in; for; in spite of; because of:* 24, 124, 189; uor: 15, 22, 32, 57, 147, 148, 155, 156, 225, 259.
vor, conj., *because,* 40, 75, 79, 105, 106, 114, 133, 147, 154, 194, 215, 239, 242; uor, 41, 78.

vorberne, wv., trans., *burn:* inf. 121, 122.
uor-let, ppl. adj., *forsaken:* ds. uor-let, 46.
vorsake, sv., trans., *forsake:* inf. 130.
vorte, adv., *until; forto:* 59, 144, uorto, 178.
uorþ, adv., *forth:* 44, 58, 120, 179, 221.

W

walm, sb., *bubbling water, wave:* dp. walmes, 231.
war, adv., *where:* 65, 85, 88, 174, ware, 48.
war, adj., *aware, cautious, prudent:* as. war, 53.
warde, sb., *keeping, charge:* ds. warde, 19, 165.
wardeyn, sb., *guardian:* ns. 20.
wat, inter. and rel. pron., *what:* ns. 108, 137, 168; used elliptically, 182; as relative, as. wat, 80.
water, sb., *water:* ds. water, 229.
weie, sb., *way, path:* ds. weie, 170.
wel, adv., *very; well:* 2, 44, 103, 200, 201, used elliptically, welle, 241.
wele, sb., *weal, happiness:* ns. 147.
welluwe, wv., intrans., *fade, wither:* inf. 75.
wen, adv., *when, at the time that:* 9, 135, 153, 156, 189.
wen, conj., *since, because:* 125, 203, 205; wan, 116.
wende, wv., trans., *turn; go; convert:* pt. 3 sg. wende, 44, 67, 85, 247, 3 pl. wende, 134; inf. 156, 190, 256.
wenne, adv., *whence:* 198.
*wep(e), sv., intrans., pt. 3 pl. wope, 222; imp. 2 pl. wepe, 225; pr. pp. wepynge, 156.
werc, sb., *work, contrivance:* as. werc, 109.
*wer(e), wv., trans., *wear:* pt. 3 sg. werede, 7.
werreour, sb., *warrior:* ns. 52.
weþer, adv., *nevertheless, yet, still; whether:* 99, 112.
wide, adv., *widly:* 134.
wif, sb., *wife:* ns. 183.

*will, sv., trans., *will, desire, decree:* 1 sg. wilny, 81; aux., 1 sg.
(contr). nele, 32², 2 sg. wolt, 27, 33,
35, 98, 114, 206, worst, 208; 3 sg.
wole, 26, 35, 80, 83, 106, 170, 220,
nelleþ, 158; nele, 126, 215; 3 pl.
nelleþ, 75, 76; pt. 3 sg. (contr.)
nolde, 22, 23, 112, 228, wolde, 124,
239; 3 pl. wolde, 135, 137, 143,
(contr). nolde, 172.

wille, sb., *desire, determintion:* ns.
255; as. wille, 30, 43.

wise, sb., *wise, manner:* ds. wise,
252.

wise, wv., trans., *show, guide:* inf.
42.

wite, adj., *white:* ns. 184, wit, 77;
as. wite, 65; dp. wite, 56, 91.

wite, wv., trans., *protect, guard,
save; know, perceive:* pt. 1 sg.
(contr.) not, 94, opt. 2 sg. nost, 189;
imp. 2 pl. witeþ, 73; pt. 3 sg. nuste,
65, 85, 88; inf. 4, 26, 35, 244.

wiþ, prep. w. dat., *with:* 13, 41, 56,
73, 85, 86, 87, 121, 132, 142, 178, 195,
196, 199, 231, 235, 245.

wiþþinne, adv., *within:* 68.

wiþ-þoute, adv., *beyond:* 179.

wiþþoute, prep. w. dat., *without:* 206,
wiþþouten, 227.

witte, sb., *state of mind:* ds. witte,
94.

wo, sb., *trouble, distress, evil:* ns.
241, ds. wo, 126, 240; as. wo, 150.

wod, adj., *mad, furious:* ns. 217; np.
wode, 149; compar. *woder*, ns. 112.

wolf, sb., *wolf:* ns. 54.

womman, sb., *woman:* ns. 133, np.
wimmen, 222.

*won(e), wv., intrans., *live in, inhabit:*
pt. 3 sg. wonede, 249.

word, sb., *word; saying:* ds. word,
85; ap. wordes, 60.

world, sb., *world:* gs. worldes, 147.

worþ, sb., *worth, value:* ds. worþ,
158.

*worþ(e), sv., intrans., *become, will be:*
pt. 3 sg. worþ, 36; aux. worþ, 184,
193, 197, worþe, 226.

wreche, sb., *wretched:* vs. wreche,
193; np. wreches, 158.

wreche, adj., *wretched:* ns. 196; ds.
wreche, 201.

wrechede, sb., *misery:* ns. 108.

writ, sb., *writing:* as. writ, 56, 59, 60.

wuch, interr. pron., *which:* ds. wuch,
187.

wule, sb., *while, space of time;* ds.
wule, 126, 220; wole, 122.

wurþe, aj., *worthy:* ns. wurþe, 150,
np. wurþi, 143.

wynde, sb., *wind, air:* ds. wynde, 194.

wilde, adj., *wild, violent:* ns. 53.

wynter, sb., *winter:* ds. wynter, 151.

A

a, num. adj., *one:* 162, 163, 164.

a, indef. art, *a:* 23, 60, 284, 420, 452, (see *ane*).

***abais(e),** wv., trans., *dismay:* pp. a-baist, 343.

***affray,** wv., intrans., *cause to fear, disturb:* pp. affraid, 370.

***affi(e),** wv., intrans., *trust:* pt. 3 pl. affied, 300.

all, sb., *everyone, everything:* 309, 417.

all, adj., *the entire quantity or extent of:* 14, 20, 22, 51, 72, 107, 109, 163, 164, 182, 185, 189, 288, 321, 345, 354, 380, 390, 395; al, 294, 378, 403, 406, 414, 441.

all, adj., *entirely, altogether; everywhere; very:* 48, 75, 112, 148, 150, 320, 404, 416.

allane, adv., *only, quite by oneself:* 259, 328; in compo., *himself:* him-allane, 244.

all-bydene, adv., *at once, at the same time:* 162; albidene, 440.

ald, adj., *old, aged:* ns. 155, 166, 176, as. ald, 147.

alls, adv., *as:* 36, (see *als*).

all þermost, adv., *in a signal degree, surpassingly:* 7.

all þus, adv. phr., *thus, in this manner:* 78, 200; al þus, 46, 58.

almachius, pr. n., *Almachius:* ns. 347, 367, 377, 399, 422.

almighty, adj., ds. *almighty:* 396.

als, adv., *like, to the extent or degree of, or in which:* 30, 54, 96, 108, 116, 131, 134, 136, 140, 154, 180, 218, 231, 273, 338, 389, 397, 418, 435, 447; so als, 442; *likewise:* 163; *when:* 101, 247; *then:* 248; with correlative, *as . . . as:* als, . . . als, 6; *as . . . so:* als . . . . so, 231.

amen, interj., *expression of affirmation and belief:* 463[2].

amend, wv., trans., *correct, reform:* inf., 110.

ane, indef. art., *an:* 63, 87, 147, 418,

and, conj., *and:*

angel, sb., *angel, divine messenger:* ns. angell, 63, 84; gs. angell, 262; as. angel, 94, 193; angell, 95, 115, 265; np. angels, 358; gp. angels, 44; dp. angels, 364; ap. angels, 287.

***answer,** wv., trans., *reply:* pt. 3 sg. answerd, 92, 169, 226.

any, indeter. adj., ds. *any:* 67.

are, adv., *erewhile, before:* 435. [O.E. ær.]

armur, sb., *armor:* dp. armurs, 336.

***array,** wv., trans., *attire:* pp. arrayd, 35.

ask, wv., trans., *request:* 2 sg. askes, 228; imp. 2 sg. ask, 212; inf. 289.

asking, sb., *request, prayer:* as. asking, 215.

assay, wv., trans., *put to the test:* inf. 83, 105.

assent, wv., intrans., *give concurrence to comply:* inf. 274: pr. pp. assentand, 207.

at, prep. w. dat., *at, to, according to:* 287, 353, 382.

availe, wv., trans., *afford help, profit:* inf. 130.

awin, sb., *profits, reward:* as. awin, 131.

ay, adv., *ever:* 240, 287, 297, 342, 450.

B

balde, adj., *bold:* ap. balde, 107.

bale, sb., *woe: miserable estate:* as. bale, 218.

ban, wv., trans., *curse:* inf. 88.

band, sb., *bond:* dp. bandes, 234.

bane, sb., *bane, destruction:* ns. bane, 322.

bath, (see *both*).

baptime, sb. *baptism:* as. baptym, 164, baptime, 296.

baptis(e), wv., trans., *baptise:* pt.
3sg. baptist, 178; 3 pl. baptist, 327;
pp. baptist, 102, 283, 330, 394.

bargan, sb., *bargain, transaction:*
as. bargan, 88.

bataile, sb., *battle, moral conflict:*
as. bataile, 339.

baynly, adv., *at once:* baynly, 334.

be, sv., intrans., *be, exist:* 2 sg. es,
272, 277; 3 sg. es, 2, 47, 64, 65, 74,
99, 111, 161, 162, 217, 218, 250; 3 pl.
er, 366. pt. 3 sg. was, 11, 12, 19, 21,
25, 27, 34, 98, 136, 176, 243, 384, 400,
409, 457; pt. 3 pl. war, 43, 302, 330,
370, 388, 433 (?); aux. (passive) sg.
was, 11, 15, 17, 24, 31, 35, 39, 54, 57,
77, 157, 160, 237, 252, 374, 375, 417,
432, 455; be, 31, 50, 61, 102, 263, 350,
401; bese, 343; es, 41, 174; pl. war,
32, 37, 196, 204, 297, 306, 308, 321,
330, 355, 380, 394; opt. 3 sg. be 84,
462, war, 59, 141, 154; pt. 3 sg. war,
301; inf. be, 70, 99, 127, 170, 266, 281,
311, 340, 404; pp. bene, 322, 418,
439.

bed, sb., *bed:* ds. bed, 53.

bed, sv., trans. *offer:* 2 sg. bede, 69;
inf. d, 428. cf. *bid*.
[OE. bēodan, Mn. Ger. bieten]

beri(e), wv., trans., *bury, inter:* pt.
3 pl. beried, 458.

bete, wv., trans., *remedy, heal:* inf.
218.

better, adv., comp. of *well:* 230.

betwix, prep. w. dat., *between:* 81.

bid, sv., trans., *ask pressingly, command:* 3 sg. biddes, 423; pt. 3 sg.
bad, 156, 179, 183, 332, 401, 410;
3 pl. bad, 387; inf. d, 281. [OE.
bidden]

bidene, adv., *in one body or company,
together:* 410.

biding, sb., *commands:* as. biding,
346; dp. biding, 8; ap. bidinges,
182.

bifall, sv., intrans., *befall, chance,
occur:* pt. 3 sg. bifell, 324, 368, byfell, 304.

bifore, adv., *before:* 192, 300, 402.

biliu(e), wv., trans., *believe:* pt. 3 pl.
biliue, 327.

bill, sb., *a written document:* ds. bill,
157; as. bill, 165.

bind(e), sv., trans., *bind, pledge:* pp.
boun, 8, boune, 207.

bisschop, sb., *bishop:* ns. 178; bischop,
457; ds. bisschop, 106, 121, 280, 283.
[Lat. episcopus].

bitwene, prep. w. dat., *between:* 147,
201.

blis, sb., bliss, *the perfect joy of
heaven:* ds. 238, 342, 358.

blode, sb., *lineage, parentage:* ds.
blode, 11.

bodword, sb., *message:* as. bodword,
210.

body, sb., *body, the human frame:*
as. body, 49, 68; np. bodis, 355; dp.
bodys, 202.

boke, sb., *book:* as. boke, 149.

bone, sb., *petition:* ds. bone, 228.

born, ppl. adj., *born, brought into
being:* 11, 252.

bot, conj., *but, unless:* 33, 55, 96, 303,
312, 318, 399, 405.

bot, prep., *only:* 30, 430.

both, adj., *both:* np. 32, bo[f]h, 291;
dp. bathe, 200; ap. bath, 90, both,
224.

both, conj., *both:* both . . . and, 21,
64, 137.

bow, wv., intrans., *render obedience:*
inf. 334.

bowsom, adj., *flexible, obedient:* ns.
281. [Mn. Ger. biegsam.]

bridal, sb., *wedding festival:* ns. 39.

bright, adj., *bright, shining:* ns. 63;
as. bright, 115; dp. bright, 419.

bright, adv., *brightly:* 193.

brightnes, sb., *brightness:* ds. brightnes, 238.

brin, wv., intrans., *burn:* inf. 412, pr.
pp. brinand, 416; pp. brint, 404,
410.

bring, sv., trans., *bring:* pt. 3 sg.
broght, 195, 326; 3 pl. broght, 423;
inf. 372; pp. broght, 39, 158, 203,
306, 374, 402.

broþer, sb., *brother:* ns. 245, 254, 274;
gs. broþer, 218; ds. broþer, 279; as.
broþer, 220, 234; np. breþer, 291,
308; breþer, 322.

bus, sv., trans., contracted, impersonal form 3 sg. bus, 61. *it behoves:* cf. Chaucer. R. T. 107. baes. [OE. bihofian.]

by, prep. w. dat., *by the side of; by, denoting means or agency:* 57, 210.

bycaus, adv., *because, for the reason that:* 21.

*bycum, sv., trans., *become:* pt. 3 sg. bycome, 284.

byfall, (see bifall).

byfor, prep. w. dat., *before:* 147; byforn, 373.

byginning, sb., *commencement:* ds. bygining, 98.

bygyn, sv., trans., *begin, commence:* inf. 190.

C

*call, wv., trans., *call by name, appeal to:* pr. pp. call and, 42.

catell, sb., *property, goods:* as. catell, 411.

certayne, sb., ds. in adv. phr. *assuredly:* (for) certayne, 263.

ciscill, pr. n., *Cecilia:* ns. 292, 323, 331; ciscil, 391; ciscell, 267; cisill, 29; cecill, 33, 41; gs. cisill, 187; ds. ciscill, 197, 232, 385, 425; cecill, 101, 132, 184; as. ciscill, 401; ciscell, 249.

chamber, sb., *room:* ds. 41, 114, 187.

charite, sb., *the sum of the Christian graces:* ds. charite, 293.

chast, adj., *pure, continent; morally pure:* as. chaste, 129; dp. chast, 202.

chastite, sb., *chasteness, virginity:* gs. chastite 128, 208.

clathes, sb., *clothes:* dp. clathes, 32; ap. clathes, 113.

clene, adj., *pure, undefiled, chaste:* ns. 419; ds. clene, 148, 179; as. clene, 48, 58, 113; np. clene, 366; dp. clene, 202.

clere, adj., *ringing, pure, well defined:* dp. clere, 44.

cleth, wv., trans., *clothe:* inf. 112, 336; pp. cled, 148.

clething, sb., *clothing:* ns. 34; ds. clething, 112.

9

cloth, sb., *cloth:* ds. cloth, 148.

conciens, sb., *conscience:* ds. conciens, 179.

confort, wv. trans., *comfort, hearten:* pt. 3 sg. confort, 331; inf. 185; confurt, 442.

conuers, sb., *convert, proselyte:* ns. 361.

coron, sb., *wreath, chaplet:* dp. corons, 341; ap. corons, 195, 201.

*coron, wv., trans., *crown:* pp. corond, 340.

counsail, sb., *counsel, advice; a matter of confidence or secrecy; resolution, vow:* ds. counsail, 208; as. counsaill, 86; cownsaylle, 129; cownsail, 60.

cours, sb., *course, career:* np. cours, 337.

craue, wv., trans., *to ask earnestly, beg:* inf. 118, 211, 230, 290.

Criste, pr. n., *Christ:* ns. 341, gs. Cristes, 315, 319, 344, Crist, 28; ds. Crist, 42, 393.

Cristen, adj., *Christian:* ns. 222.

cum, sv., intrans., *come, spring from:* pt. 3 sg. come, 184, 244; 1 pl. come, 280; 3 pl. come, 314, 385, 440; inf. 235; pp. komen, 26, oner-cumen, 339.

*cumand, wv; trans., *order, decree:* pt. 3 sg. cumand, 349, 371, 403.

cuntre, sb., *country, land:* ds. cuntre, 429.

cursed, ppl. adj. *cursed:* ns. 347.

custum, sb., *usage, law:* ns. 429.

D

*dar(e), sv., trans., *dare, venture boldly:* pt. 3 sg. durst, 29, 76.

day, sb., *day,* (12 hours); *day,* (24 hours); *an appointed time;* (with *night*), *constantly:* ns. 31; ds. day, 16, 64, 137, 420; dp. daies, 438; ap. daies, 446.

dede, sb. *dede:* ds. in adv. phrase, in dede, 70, *indeed, in very truth:*

*di(e), wv., intrans., *die:* pt. 3 pl. died, 368;

dede, sb., *death:* ds. ded, 304, 306, 374, dede, 389.

*ded(e), wv., trans., *kill:* pp. dede,
   311.

dede, ppl. adj., *dead:* 457; ded, 154;

dele, sb., *part:* ds. in adv. phr., *entirely, altogether:* ilka dele, 332,
   euer-ilkadele, 174.

*dem(e), wv.; trans. *deem, judge,
   think:* pp. demid, 282.

dere, adj., *dear, beloved:* ns. dere,
   19, 272, 292; vs. 219.

descend, wv., intrans., *descend:* inf.
   146.

desire, sb., *bidding, command:* as.
   desire, 413.

do, sv., trans., *do:* 3 sg. dose 66; pt.
   3 pl. did 282, 320; inf. 29, 317, 345;
   pp. done 227, 378.

dole, sb., *grievous pain:* ds. dole
   311. [Mn. E. poetic *dole.*]

down, adv., *down:* 269.

drede, sb., *dread, terror:* ds. drede,
   76, 153, 168.

drede, wv., trans., *dread, fear:* inf.
   74.

durst, (see dare).

dwell, wv, intrans., *dwell:* 2 sg.
   dwelles, 168; inf. 135, 453.

E

efter, adv., *later in time, afterward:*
   241, 438.

efter, prep., *in pursuit of, for:* 290,
   313, 443.

eger, adj., *eager, excited by ardent
   desire:* ds. eger, 405.

els, adv., *else, otherwise:* els, 171,
   350.

end, sb., *end, conclusion:* ds. ende,
   39, end, 109.

*end(e), wv., trans., *finish:* pp. end,
   145.

ensaumple, sb., *illustration:* ds. 9.

entent, sb., *desire, will; fixedness
   of purpose:* ds. entent, 42, 52, 426;
   as. entent, 444.

*enter, wv., intrans., *enter:* pt. 3 sg.
   entred, 247.

enuy, sb., *envy, hatred:* as. enuy,
   310.

er, (see *be*).

erber, sb., *arbor, garden:* ds. 418.

erthli, adj.; *earthly, carnal:* ds. 170.

euer, adv., *at all times, continually:*
   12, 15, 162, 462: euer-more, 99.

euer-ilkadele, adv., *every part, every
   bit, altogether:* 332.

euyn, adv., *exactly, without devia-
   tion;   evenly, gently,   nicely
   poised; undisturbed,   in   even,
   regular life, tranquilly:* 86, 237,
   453.
   [cog. Lat æquus. OE. efne.]

F

faire, adj., *comely; of light hue, un-
   blemished:* ns. 25, 419; fayre, 21.

faith, sb., *belief, faith:* ns. 163.

*fall, sv., intrans., *fall:* pt. 3 sg. fell,
   153, 269; opt. 3 pl. fall, 365.

fare, sb., *affair, circumstance:* ds.
   fare, 324, 368.

*far(e), sv., intrans., *fare, get on as
   to circumstances:* pt. 3 sg. ferd, 123,
   245.

fast, adv., *steadfastly:* 298.

*fed(e), wv., *fed, feasted:* pt. 3 pl. fed,
   38.

fele, adj., *many:* ap. 38. [Mn. Ger.
   viel.]

*fel(e), wv., trans., *feel, perceive:* pt.
   1 sg. felde. 252; 3 sg. feld, 253.

feld, sb., *field, country as opposed to
   town:* ds. feld. 298.

fell, adj., *cruel, bloodthirsty:* ns. fell,
   136.

ferly, sb., *miracle, wonder:* np. ferlis,
   304.   [OE. fær-lāc].

fers, adj., *fierce:* ns. fers, 136.

file, wv., trans., *defile:* opt. 2 sg. file,
   68.

*find(e), sv., trans., *find:* pt. 3 sg.
   fand, 191.

fire, sb., *fire:* ds. fire, 404; as. fire,
   416.

first, adv., *first:* 383, 405.

floure, sb., *flower, youthful vigor,
   prime:* as. floure, 73; dp. flores, 419.

folk, sb., *folk, people in general:* np.
   folk, 163, 359; ap. folk, 38, 370; dp.
   folk, 20, 22.

for, prep. w. dat., *for, on account of, because of:* 70, 153, 408.

for, conj., *because, for the reason that, since:* 54, 95, 133, 140, 204, 246, 351, 389, 435.

forsake, sv., trans., *forsake, renounce:* pt. 3 pl. forsoke, 395; inf. 72, 144, 276, 332.

forto, prep , *to:* 172, 221, 229, 275, 317, 342, 346, 451.

for-whi, conj., *for what, for that which:* 228.

fot, sb., *foot:* ap. fete, 269.

ful, adj., *full, abounding in:* ns. 1.

ful, adv., *very:* 19, 26, 34, 38, 55, 63, 88, 148, 173 284, 325, 338, 352, 421, 455, 459; full, 409.

fulfill, wv., trans., *fulfill, carry out, bring to consummation:* inf. 182, 346, 413; pp. fulfild, 337.

furth, adv , *forth, forward, out:* 387, 428.

fra, prep. w. dat., *from:* 184, 280; fro, 203.

*frain(e), wv., trans., *inquire, question, ask:* pt. 3 sg. frained, 405.

fre, adj., *beloved, favored:* ns. 2, 100, 209; gs. fre, 273; ds. fre, 10, 232; as. fre, 221.

frende, sb., *friend, relative:* ns. 272, np. frendes, 23, 30, 36, 38.

ro, (see fra).

fro tima, adv., *from the time:* 296.

fruit, sb., *fruit, outcome:* as. fruit, 131

G

ga, sv , *go:* inf. 183, 279; pt. 3 sg. ȝode, 389 (see *wende*).

gaste, sb., *ghost, spirit:* ds. gaste 119; as. gaste, 456; ap. gastes, 224.

ȝe, (see þou).

geder, wv., trans., *gather:* inf. 382

ȝeme, wv., trans., *care for:* inf. 450.

gentill, adj., *gentle, noble:* as. gentill, 11.

gere; wv., trans., *cause, make:* pt. 3 sg. gert, 354; pt. 3 pl. gert, 415.

*ȝern, wv., *yearn for, desire:* 1 sg. ȝern, 216.

get, sv., trans., *get, obtain:* inf. 189.

gif, sv., trans., *give, yield, grant, impart, commit, administer:* 1 sg. gif. 449; pt. 3 sg. gaf, 285, 456; opt. 2 sg. gifes, 129; inf. 113, 224, 341, 436; pp. gifen, 445.

gin, sb., *snare, crafty means, artifice:* as. gin, 67.

*gin, sv. intrans., *do:* (as aux.) gan, 116, 362, 391, 427.

ȝit, adv., *yet, still:* 168, 432. yit, 399.

god, pr. n., *the Supreme Being:* ns. 241, 255, 285, 305, 445; gs. god, 115, 262, 287, godes, 193, 265, goddes, 94, 408; ds. god, 52, 65, 85, 97, 126, 421, 427, 456; as. god, 293, 297.

gold, sb., *gold:* ds. [g]old, 32.

gold, adj., *golden:* dp. gold, 150.

ȝong, adj., *young:* ns. 25; dp. ȝing, 7.

ȝowth-hede, sb., *youth:* gs. ȝowth-hede, 73.

grace, sb., *grace, favor:* as. grace, 285; ds. grace, 119.

grante, wv., trans., *grant, accept, concede:* pt. 3 sg. granted, 181, 318; pt. 3 pl., granted, 345; inf. 271.

grefe, adj., *grievous:* ap. grefe. 373.

grete, adj., *great, hard:* as. grete, 43, 310, 339; ds. grete, 238, 386, 459, 460; dp. grete, 434.

*greu(e), wv., trans., *grieve, burden:* imp. 2 sg. greue, 62, 93.

grewance, sb., *grievance:* as. grewance, 74.

gude, sb., *goods, property:* ns. 406, as. gude, 382, 390.

gude, adj., *good, real, earnest, serious; worthy:* ns. 21, 74, 250, 361; ds. gude, 42, 52, 121, 181, 426; as. gude, 190; vs. gude 62.

H

hale, adj., *sound, whole, undaunted:* ds. hale, 421; np. hale, 433.

halely, adv., *wholly:* 122, 320.

halily, adv., *holily, piously:* 240.

halines, sb., *holiness, adherence to Christianity:* ds. halines, 246.

hals, sb., *throat, neck:* ns. 432.

haly, adj., *holy; perfect in religious character:* ns. 12, 284; ds. haly, 119.

hame, sb., *home;* ds. hame, 183.

hand, sb., *hand:* ds. hand, 149, 195; as. hand, 155; ap. handes, 125.

hard, adj., *harsh to the touch; severe:* ns. 34; dp. hard, 352.

hardily, adv., *boldly:* 257.

harm, sb., *harm, injury:* as. harm, 317.

haste, sb., *haste;* ds. haste 120, 455.

hastily, adv., *quickly;* hastly, 375; hastili, 402.

*****hast(e),** wv., trans., *hasten:* 3 pl. haste, 383.

*****hat(e),** sv., trans., *tell, advise;* 1 sg. hete. 257.

hathin, sb. *heathen, pagan:* ns. 27.

haue, wv., trans., *possess; hold by obtaining, acquiring:* 1 sg. haue, 60; pt. 3 sg. had, 149; pt. 3 pl. had, 33, 310; inf. haue, 117, 163, 229, 256, 289, 390.

he, per. pron., *he:* ns. he (74 times); gs. his, (24 times); ds. him, (19 times); as. him (12 times). np. þai, (30 times); þ(a)i, 450; gp. þaire, (16 times); dp. þam, 146, 147, 200, 288, 289, 292, 302, 305, 310, 313, 317, 325, 352; ap. þam, 199, 203, 205, 300, 327, 331, 332, 335, 336, 358, 393, 423, 442, 450, 451.

hede, sb., *head:* as. hede, 424; dp. heuides, 199; ap. heuiddes, 354.

-hede, suffix,-*hood:* gs. ȝowth-hede, 73.

hele, sb., *health, salvation:* ds. hele, 214.

help, wv., trans., *help, assist:* inf. 220.

hende, adj., *prompt, ready, gracious:* ap. hende, 92.

*****hent(e),** wv., trans., *take, catch up:* pp. hent, 375.

here, wv., trans., *hear:* pt. 3 sg. herd, 225, 267, 323, 348, 367, 399, 422; pt. 3 pl. herd, 43; inf. 261; pp. herd, 124, 180.

here, adv., *here, in this place:* 4, 81, 95, 174, 250.

hert, sb., *intellectual faculties; seat of moral affections:* ns. 168; ds. hert, 13, 55, 421; as. hert, 48; ap. hertis, 202.

*****heue,** wv., trans., *raise, lift:* pt. 3 sg. heuyd, 125.

heuyn, sb., *heaven:* gs. heuyn, 85, 115, 238; ds. 63, 125, 172, 262, 356, 364, 375.

hid, sb., *skin, flesh:* ds. hid, 34.

hight, sb. *high;* in compo. adverbially, *above:* ds. on hight, 125.

hir, (see scho).

hir-self, pron., *her:* as. hir-self, 412, 415.

*****hit,** wv., trans., *strike:* pp. hit, 431.

*****honer,** wv., trans., *reverence, adore, worship:* pt. 3 pl. honord, 294.

honore, sb., *honor:* ns. 462.

how, adv., *by what means; in what manner; what:* 123, 177, 245, 324, 358, 368, 369, 370.

hows, sb., *house:* ns. 194; ds. hows, 247, 383; as. hows, 411.

howsing, sb., *collection of houses, home, in general:* ns. 403.

husband, sb., *husband:* ds. husband, 53.

I

I, pron., *I:* ns. (30 times); gs. my, 48, 49, 64, 68, 173, 219, 220, 231, 272, 448; mi, 205, 209, 229, 452, 453; ds. me, 69, 80, 81, 142, 217, 274, 445; as. me, 66, 116, 251; np. we, 5, 223, 260, 280; gp. oure, 14, 224, 259, 461; dp. us, 81; vs, 81, 250; ap. us, 260, vs. my-self. 83, 90.

if, conj., *in case that; notwithstanding that:* 56, 59, 79, 87, 94, 96, 102, 105, 256, 312.

ilk, adj., *same, very same:* ns. 329, ds. ilk, 204, 286, 359.

ilka, adj., *each:* ns. 40; as. ilka, 332.

ilka dele, adv. phr., *entirely, altogether:* 332; euer-ilkadele, 174.

ilkane, pron., *each one:* np. ilkane, 321, 349; ap. ilkane, 327, 363.

in, prep., w. dat., *within:* 6⁴, 7, 13, 46, 149, 157, 160, 228, 262, 286, 298, 303, 307, 342, 365, 381, 398, 415, 418, 429, 434, 446, 453, 458; *in conformance with:* 221, 258, 293, 327, 394, 452; *upon* (belief), 18, 101, 300, 396; *with:* 294, 336, 426, 456, 460²; on (on fire), 414; *into:* 247, 314; at, (time, occasion), 304, yn, 306.

in-fere, adv., *together:* in-fere, 20, 291.

it, pron., *it:* ns. 59, 123, 133, 214, 227, 251, 301, 324, 368, 404, (10 times); ds. it, 230; yit, 399; as. it, 213, 407.

J

Jhesus, pr. n., *Jesus Christ:* ns. 219, 338; Jhesus Crist, 1; lord Jhesu, 209; ds. lord Jhesu, 14; Jhesu Criste, 18, 101, 461; as. lord Jhesus, 259; vs. Lord Jhesu Criste, 127.

K

ken, wv., trans., *show, declare, teach:* inf. 5.

kepe, wv., trans., *preserve; hold possession of:* imp. 2 pl. kepes, 201; inf. 56.

king, sb., *king:* ns. 347, 377, 390.

kirk, sb., *an edifice for religious worship; church; cloister:* as. kirk, 452, 459.

*****kiss**, wv., trans., *kiss:* pt. 3 sg. kissed, 248, 249, 269.

*****kit**, wv., trans., *cut:* pp. kit, 432.

*****knaw**, sv., trans., *know:* pt. 3 sg. knew, 13, 28.

kne, sb., *knee:* dp. knese, 437.

*****knel(e)**, wv., intrans., *kneel:* pr. pp. kneleand, 191.

komen, see cum.

kosyn, sb., *relative, kinsman:* ns. 272.

kyn, sb., *kind, race:* ds. kyn. 26.

L

lamb, sb., *lamb:* as. lamb, 40.

land, sb., *land, region:* ds. land, 307

lang, adj., *long,* ns. 301.

lare, sb., *doctrine; precept:* ds. lare, 260; as. lare, 14.

last, sb., *last:* in compo. adverbially, *finally:* (at þe) last, 353.

lastand, ppl. adj., *lasting:* ds. lastand, 342.

*****lat**, wv., intrans., *let, permit:* opt. 2 sg. lat, 81.

law, sb., *law:* ns. 54, lau, 435; ds. law, 28, 221, 319, 328.

lay, wv., trans., *lay, set forth:* inf. 387. [OE. lecgan.]

lay, sb., *law, creed, religion:* gs. lay, 138; ds. lay, 267, 315. [OF. lei, Lat. lex.]

*****led(e)**, wv., trans., *pass; lead, conduct:* pt. 3 pl. led, 240, 358.

*****lem(e)**, wv., intrans., *give light, shine:* pt. 3 sg. lemid, 194.

les, adj., *less; little, small:* ap. les, 388.

lesson, sb., *lesson, teachings:* dp. lessons, 138.

letter, sb., *letter, alphabetic character:* dp. letters, 150.

leue, wv., trans., *leave, desert:* pt. 3 sg. left, 434; inf. 335.

leue, sb., *permission:* ds. leue. 61.

*****li(e)**, sv., intrans , *lie, to rest prostrate:* pt. 3 sg. lay, 154. [OE. licgan.]

lif, wv., trans., *live:* 3 pl. lif, 450; pt. 3 pl. lifed, 293, 309, 389; inf. 223, 328, 342; pr. pp. lifand, 438.

life, sb., *life, career:* ds. life, 109, 301; liue, 446. as. life, 240.

lifing, sb., *manner of life:* ns. 190.

*****lift**, wv., trans., *lift:* pt. 3 sg. lifted, 156.

light, sb., *light:* ds. light, 152, 194, 336.

like, adj., *like, similar to:* ns. 251, 366.

*****lik(e)**, wv., trans., *take pleasure in:* 3 sg. likes, 229.

likeing, sb., *pleasure, desire:* as. likeing, 288.

lily, sb., *lily:* dp. lilyes, 251.

lion, sb., *lion:* as. lion, 136.

lite, sb., *flaw, vice, sin:* ds lite, 353.

lord, sb., *lord, earthly master; Lord:*
ns. 205, 219, 229; vs. Lord, 48, 144;
ds. lord, 57. (see *Jhesus.*)
lose, wv., trans., *lose, let slip:* inf. 73.
luf, sb., *love:* ns. 273, ds. luf, 293.
luf, wv, trans., *love:* 1 sg. luf, 66;
3 sg. lufis, 82, 116; opt. 2 sg. luf 87;
inf. 259, pp. loued, 127.
lufing, sb., *love:* as. lufing, 69.
luke, wv., intrans., *look:* imp. 2 sg.
luke, 62; inf. 150, 152, 245; loke, 156.
lym, sb., *body, physical appearance:*
ds. lym. 140.
lynnen, adj., *linen:* ds. lynnen, 148.

M

maiden, sb., *maiden, virgin:* ds.
mayden, 10; np. maidens, 439; dp.
maydens, 7; ap. maidens, 449, 453.
mak(e), wv., trans., *make:* pt. 3 sg.
made, 45, 97, 215, 459, mad, 222; opt.
3 sg. mak, 48; imp. 2 sg. mak, 452;
inf. 350, 391; make, 427; pp. made,
274.
man, sb., *a male adult; a human
being:* ns. 40, 155, 166, 176, 253, 384;
ds. man, 23, 170; as. 87, 147, 284;
np. men, 134, 321, 357, 376; gp.
men, 4; dp. men, 6, 129, 392, 408.
maner, sb., *manner, way:* ds. maner,
47, 161.
mani, adj., *many:* ns. 359.
mankind, sb., *the human race:* ds.
mankind, 2
*mari(e), wv., trans., *cause to be
married:* pt. 3 pl. maried, 23.
mast, adj., *most, greatest:* ns. 100,
gs. moste, 126; dp. maste, 384.
maumettry, sb., *idolatry:* as mawmetri, 333; as. maumetry, 276, 395;
ds. maumettry, 309.
mawmette, sb., *idol:* dp. mawmettes, 299.
Maximius, pr. n., *Maximus:* ns. 329,
361, 369; as. Maximius, 372.
may, aux. sv., intrans., defective,
may, can: 5, 9, 83, 94, 95, 110,
130, 376; pt. might, 170, 223, 265,
286, 289, 357, 448; moght, 56, 442.

mayne, sb., *strength, main:* ds.
mayne, 185.
mayster, sb., *master, husband:* gs.
maysters, 388.
mede, sb., *meed, reward, recom-
pense:* ds. mede, 236.
meke, adj., *meek, tractable:* ns. 141,
as. meke, 139.
mekill, adv., *much:* 130.
mele, sb., *payment:* ds. mele, 213.
melody, sb., *song:* as. melody,
45.
mene, wv., intrans., *mean, signify:*
inf. 47, 161.
menge, sb., *household, retainers:*
ns. 320, 330. [Chaucer, meynee;
cf. Mn. E. menials.]
mercy, sb., *compassion, forbearance:*
ds. mercy, 2, 100, 209.
meruayle, sb., *miracle:* dp. meruayles, 302.
mides, sb., *middle, midst:* ds. mides,
415.
might, sb., *mighty act, power:* ds.
might, 100, 126; as. might, 3, 276;
ap. mightes, 5.
mikell, adj., *much, great:* ds.
mikell, 91.
milde, adj., *mild, gentle:* ns. 12,
22.
min, adj., *less:* np. 411, dp. min,
299.
mis, sb., *misdeed, error; failure:* ds.
mis, 357; as. mis, 110.
mode, sb., *mind; mood, manner:* ds.
12, 22, 381, 405.
more, adj., *more:* ns. 172; ds. more,
376; np. more, 411; dp. more, 299;
ap. more, 388.
morn, sb., *morn, morning:* ds. morn,
371.
mornig, sb., *mourning, lamentation:*
as. mornig, 391.
moste, (see mast).
mowth, sb., *mouth, word of mouth:*
ds. mowth, 171.
*multipli(e), wv., trans., *multiply,
increase:* 3 sg. multiplise, 133.
my-self, refl. pron., *myself:* ns. 83,
90.

N

na, see no).

name, sb., *name:* ds. name, 394, 452.

ne, conj., *nor:* 217, 317.

nec, sb., *neck:* as. nec, 428.

nere, adv., *near, close by:* ns. 43.

neuer, adv., *never:* 16, 252, 253.

neuyn, wv., trans., *set forth, recount:* inf. 116, 171, 376.

new, adj., *new:* ds. new, 112.

next, adj., *next, against:* ns. 34.

night, sb., *night;* in compo. with day, *continually:* gs. night, 335, ds. 16, 64, 137, 420.

no, adj., *no, not any:* as. no, 33, 76, 316; na, 317.

nobill, adj., *noble, illustrious:* ds. nobill, 26.

noght, adv., *not:* 50, 62, 77, 93, 94, 141, 144, 152, 266, 343, 351, 432, 441.

no-man, ind. pron., *no one:* ns. 95.

nomare, adj., *no more:* ap. nomare, 436.

none, adj., *not any:* as. none, 29, 216.

none, pron., *not one; not any:* ns. 430; as. none, 142.

no-thing, sb., *nothing:* ns. 217; as. 28, 177.

now, adv., *now; at this time:* 61, 80, 131, 139, 233, 257, 271, 277.

nowþer, pron., *neither:* ns. 89.

noyis, sb., *sound:* ap. noyis, 43.

O

o, prep., *on, in the process of:* 176.

obout, adv., *on every side:* 416.

of, prep. w. gen., *of,* (denoting possession); w. dat., *in, from, out of, concerning:* w. gen., 28, 251², 335, 461; w. dat., 1, 2, 10, 22, 25, 33, 44, 63, 77, 100³, 115, 117, 119, 132, 142, 150, 189, 209, 211, 234, 242, 246, 287, 324, 336, 384, 399, 400, 459.

of, adv., *off:* 354, 424.

of[t]-sithes, adv., *oft-times; frequently:* 4.

ogains, prep. w. dat., *against; toward:* 138, 152, 299.

ogayne, adv., *again:* 186, 264; ogain, 183.

omang, adv., *meanwhile, at the same time:* 45.

omang, prep. w. dat., *among, surrounded by:* 302, 362.

omanges, prep. w. dat., *amongst:* 250.

on, prep. w. dat., *on, in, upon, up to, against:* 47, 71, 121, 150, 161, 309, 333, 371.

onclene, adj., *unchaste, morally impure:* as. onclene, 69.

opon, prep. w. dat., *on, upon:* 199, 244, 437.

or, conj., *or:* 69, 302.

organ, sb., *organ, a reed instrument:* dp. organs, 44.

oþer, pron., *other:* as. oþer, 198.

oþer, adj., *other:* ds. oþer, 20; as. oþer, 29, 87; np. oþer, 380.

*ouer-cum, sv., trans., *overcome, win:* pp. ouer-cumen, 339.

out, adv., *out, forth, from:* 234, 400.

outward, adv., *externally, as regards appearance:* 35.

P

paines, sb., *pain, torture:* ds. paines, 352, 434.

pape, sb., *pope, priest:* ds. pape, 17, 443.

paradis, sb., *heaven:* ds. paradis, 203.

parfitely, adv., *perfectly, acceptably:* 223.

*pay, wv., *pay, satisfy:* pp. payde, 77.

pete, sb., *pity, compassion:* ds. pete, 1.

place, sb., *place:* ds. 160, 204, 286.

pouste, sb., *power, dominion:* as. pouste, 3. [Mn. F. pousser.]

power, sb., *authority, ability:* as. power, 316.

pouer, adj., *poor, needy:* dp. pouer, 408.

*pray, wv., intrans., *pray, supplicate:* pt. 1 sg. praied, 447; pr. pp. prayand, 15, 421.

praier, sb., *prayer, supplication:* as. praier, 145; dp. praiers, 191; ap. prayers, 427.

*prech(e), wv., intrans., *to expound religious matters:* pt. 3 pl prechid, 298, 315; pr. pp. precheand, 308.

present, sb., *presence:* ds. present, 314.

preste, sb., *priest:* ap. prestes, 326.

pride, sb., *inordinate self-esteem:* as. pride, 33.

prince, sb., *prince:* ns. 307, 316, 329.

*puruay, wv., trans., *purvey, provide:* pp. puruayd, 36, 205.

*put, wv., trans., *subject:* pt. 3 sg. 352.

R

rathe, adv., *quickly, soon:* 199.

rebell, adj., *rebellious:* ns. 137.

reches, sb., *riches;* dp. reches, 384, ap. reches, 387.

rede, sb., *counsel, course of action, resolution:* as. rede, 312.

rede, wv., trans., read: inf. 167, 171; pp. red, 165.

redy, adv., *suitably disposed in mind, willing:* 277.

reherce, wv., trans., *narrate, recount:* inf. 362.

reuerence, sb., *reverence, veneration:* ds. reuerence, 460.

richely, adv., *richly:* 35.

right, adj., *right, opposed to left:* as. right, 155.

right, adv., *just, precisely, according to truth:* 108, 241, 282, 360.

*ris(e), sv., intrans., *rise:* pt. 3 sg. rase, 120.

rose, sb., *rose, a garden flower:* gs. rose, 251.

S

sacrifise, sb., *sacrifice,* as. sacrifise, 350.

saint, sb., *saint:* up. saintes, 380.

Saint Ciscill, pr. n., *Saint Cecilia:* ns. 331; saint Ciscill, 323; Saint Ciscil, 391; ds. saint Cecill, 10. (see Ciscill.)

sake, sb., *sake, cause:* ds. sake, 344, 408.

sall, aux. sv., intrans., *shall; will:* to express future tense, 1 sg. sall, 86; 2 sg. sall, 72; sal(tou), 117; sal,

212; 3 sg. sall, 111, sal, 113; to express potentiality, obligation, necessity: 1 sg. sall, 91; 2 sg. sal(tou) 279, sall, 103; 3 sg. sall, 89, 227; pt. suld, 31, 311, 401, 404, 410, 430, 436.

saluyng, sb., *saving; salvation:* ds. saluyng, 143; as. saluyng, 142, saluing, 189.

same, adj., *same, identical:* ds. same, 458.

samen, adv., together, in company: 235.

saue, wv., trans., *save:* opt. 2 sg. saue, 49; 144; inf. 164; pp. saued, 263.

saue, adj., *safe, assured:* ns. 255.

sang, sb., *song:* ds. sang, 44, 46.

sare, adv., *sore, grievously:* 88.

sauore, sb., *odor, fragrance:* ns. 250, as. sauore, 253, 256.

*saw, wv., trans., *sow:* 3 sg. sawes, 128; pp. sawn, 132.

sawiowre, n. pr., *Savior:* ds. sawiowre, 461.

sawl, sb., *soul:* ns. saul, 375; ds. sawl, 130, 140; np. sawles, 356; ap. sawles, 164, 363.

say, wv., trans., *say:* 1 sg. say, 103; 2 sg. sais, 80, 82; pt. 1 sg. said, 435; 3 sg. said, 46, 58, 78, 93, 126, 166, 200, 206, 216, 227, 249, 264, 270, 311, 337, 407, 445, 455; sayde, 78, inf. 103, 175, 267, 316; pp. said, 61, 237, 369.

scath, sb., *scathe, injury, retribution:* ds. scath, 89; as. schathe, 76.

schame, sb., *ignominy:* ds. schame, 91.

schathe, (see scath).

schende, wv., trans., *disgrace:* pp. schent, 50, 355. inf. 90.

*schew, wv., trans., *make known, manifest:* 3 sg. schewes, 3.

*schine, sv., intrans., *shine:* pr. pp. schineand, 193.

scho, per. pron., *she:* ns. (38 times); gs. hir, (16 times); ds. hir, (11 times); as. hir, (6 times). (For plural, see under *he*). as. hir-self, 412, 415.

scill, sb., *reason:* ds. scill, 447.

se, sv., trans., *see; perceive mentally:*
1 sg. se, 363; pt. 3 sg. saw, 151, 192,
379; 3 pl. saw, 146; inf. 9, 14, 81, 94,
95, 134, 261, 265, 286, 357; pp. sene,
180, 417.

sede, sb., *seed:* dp. sede, 132; ap.
sede, 128.

seke, sv., trans., *desire, or try to
obtain; go to; search for:* pt. 3 sg.
soght, 325; inf. 142; pp. soght, 143,
401.

sen, conj., *inasmuch as; from the
time when:* 143, 252, 255, 277.

*send, wv., trans., *send:* 3 sg. sendes,
210; pt. 3 sg. sent, 443; pp. sent, 188,
313.

seruand, sb., *servant; follower:* ns.
65, 88; ds. seruand, 232.

serue, wv., trans., *serve; worship:*
inf. 297, 454.

seruise, sb., *service:* ds. seruise,
398.

*sese, wv., trans., *cease:* pt. 3 sg.
sesid, 16, sesed, 441.

*set, wv., intrans., *set to; fix upon:*
pp. set 414, sett, 31.

sight, sb., *sight, consciousness; appearance:* ds. sight, 4, 359; as.
sight, 151.

sin, sb., *moral or physical trans-
gression of the law of God or the
church; injuries* (objective), *the result of sinful ideas:* ds. sin, 189,
234; syn. 50, 68; dp. sins, 433.

sir, sb., *a respectful title of address,
sir:* vs. sir, 59, 74, 93, 105, 277,
445; syr, 62, 63, 103.

*sit, sv., intrans., *sit:* pt. 3 sg. sat,
437.

skin, sb., *skin, complexion:* ds. skin,
25.

sla, wv., trans., *slay, put to death:*
inf. 90; pp. slane, 350, 380.

slaghter man, sb., *executioner:* ns.
425.

slike, adj., *such, of the like kind or
degree:* as. slike, 252, 285.

smertly, adv., *sharply, severely:*
371.

smite, wv., trans., *smite, strike:* inf.
354, 424.

so, conj., (so þat) *to the end that, in
order that; according as:* 5, 50, 83,
110, 285, 442.

so, adv., *so, thus, in this way; such;
to such an extent; in such a way;
therefore:* 36, 188, 263, 315, 355, 420;
82, 193, 217, 253, 392; 57, 275, 319,
437, so þat, *to the end that, in order
that:* 5, 50, 83, 110, 285 so . . als,
233, 282; what thing . . . so,
118, 211.

sogat, adv., *in such a manner, thus:*
267. [Scotch, gait.]

solace, sb., *relief, alleviation; joy:*
ds. solace, 376; as. solace, 72.

sone, adv., *soon:* 146, 176, 187, 192, 313,
318, 323, 356, 413.

speciall, sb., *a special companion, a
paramour:* ns. 64.

*speke, sv., intrans., *speak:* pt. 3 sg.
spak, 254, 392.

spens, sb., *expense, cost:* ds. spens,
459.

spows, sb., *spouse, husband or wife:*
as. spows, 135, 248.

stand, sv., trans. and intrans., *stand,
to maintain an upright position;
to set, to cause to stand:* pt. 3 sg.
stode, 147, 420, 426; inf. 192, 415.

stede, sb., *place:* ds. stede, 153, 458.

stedfast, adj., *resolute, constant:* ns.
258.

steuyn, sb., *voice; utterance:* ds.
steuyn, 454; as. steuyn, 261.

still, adj., *motionless, quiet:* ns. 154.

stoutly, adv., *boldly:* 386.

strake, sb., *stroke, blow:* ds. strake,
428; ap. strakes, 430, 431, 436.

strife, sb., *discord, tumult:* ds. strife,
386.

strike, sv., trans., *strike, wield:* inf.
430

swilk, adj., *such:* ds. swilk, 70; as.
swilk, 74.

sum, pron., *a certain one:* np.sum,433.

sum, adj., *some, certain:* dp. sum, 4.

sun, sb., *son:* ds. sun, 101.

sunder, adv., *asunder:* 432

swete, adj., *pleasing to the smell,
fragrant; gracious, kind:* ns. 217;
as. swete, 253, 256, 270.

T

take, sv., trans., *take, begin; receive,
accept; carry, convey; inflict:* 3 sg.
tase, 159; pt 3 sg. toke. 135 155,
197, imp. 2 sg. tak, 106, 131; inf. 71,
275, 343, 407, tak, 278; pp. tane, 260,
296, 364.

takin, sb., *token, symbolic gift:* ns.
266; as tane, 197.

tale, sb., *narrative;* as. tale, 124, 422.

talent, sb., *desire:* as. talent, 51.

***tech(e)**, sv., trans., *teach:* imp. 2 sg.
teche, 451.

tell, sv., trans., *relate; say; express;
bid:* 1 sg. tell, 104; 3 sg. tell, 323,
367; pt. 1 sg. talde, 242; pt. 3 sg.
talde, 122, tald, 444; pt 3 pl. tald, 30;
imp. 2 sg. tell, 107, 109; inf. 96, 288,
301, 303, 448; pp. tald 51; talde, 108.

tene, adj., *vexed, angry:* ns. 409.

thank, wv., trans., *thank:* inf. 188.

thing, sb., *object of thought, material object; fact:* ns. 157; thingh,170;
as. thing, 118, 216, 290, 378; ap.
thing, 97.

***think**, sv., trans., *purpose; intend:*
3 sg. thinks. 381; pt. 3 sg. thoght, 55.

***think**, sv., intrans., *seem, appear:*
3 sg. impres. (me) think, 251. [Mn.
Ger. mich dünkt, OE. mē þyneð.]

thre, num. adj., *three:* ap. 430, 431,
436, 438, 446.

thurgh, prep. w. dat., *through, by
means of:* 119, 232, 233.

till, prep. w. dat., *to:* 23,39,106,109 158,
166 170, 288,317, 352, 428. (see *untill*)

time, sb., *occasion:* ds. time, 306.

tite, adv., *quickly:* 312.

tiþande, sb., *message, tidings:* ap.
tiðandes, 423.

tiþing, sb., *event:* ds. tiþing, 348.

to, prep., *to, towards, unto; for; of:*
w. dat. 53, 104, 108, 122, 125, 126,
130, 143, 187, 188, 189, 190, 200, 217,
238, 243, 264, 274, 292, 306, 319, 356,
360, 373, 375, 382, 383, 389, 417, 421,
425, 427, 448, 449; w. inf. 30, 56, 135,
139, 171, 245, 278, 297, 301, 316, 318,
343, 345, 372, 442, 450.

tou, (see *þou*).

toun, sb., *town:* ds. toun, 298.

traitur, sb., *traitor, a person guilty
of perfidy or treachery:* ns. 389.

tretice, sb., *tale, a written composition:* ds. tretice, 303.

trew, adj., *true, faithful:* ns. 111.

trewly, adv., *faithfully, sincerely:*
18, 278.

trow, wv , trans., *believe; think, sup-
pose:* 1 sg. trow, 173; 2 sg. trowes,
167; pt. 3 sg. trowed, 18; pt. 3 pl.
trowed, 366, 396; opt. 1 sg. trow,
79; 3 sg. trow, 96; pt. 3 pl. trow,
333; inf. 102, 172, 179, 278.

trowth, sb., *belief, acceptance of the
truth:* ns. 111, ds. trowth, 258; as.
trowth, 278.

turment, sb., *torment, torture:* ap.
turmentes, 373.

turn, wv , trans., *change, with
respect to convictions or conduct:*
pt 3 sg. turned, 319; pt. 3 pl.
turned, 360, 393; inf. 267, 275, 312;
pp. turned, 321.

twa, num. adj., *two:* np. two, 308; dp.
twa, 81; ap. twa, 195.

Tyburcius, pr. n., *Tyburcius:* ns. 264,
295, Tyburcyus, 242; as. Tyburcius,
220.

Þ

þai, (see *he*).

þan, adv., *then:* 41, 75, 86, 92, 103,
111, 114, 117, 119, 122, 155 159, 166,
178, 183, 254, 261, 267, 283, 347.

þan, conj., *than:* 376.

þar-of, adv., *of it:* 33.

þare, adv., *in that place; an indef.
grammatical subject: where:* 158,
180, 307², þar, 309, 424; here, 417.

þarfore, adv., *therefore:* 231, 340, 343,
381; when . . . þarfore, 378-81.

þat, rel. pron., *who, which:* 8, 9, 11,
24, 43, 47, 61, 80, 82, 97, 98, 104 116,
128, 130, 136, 158, 161, 174, 184, 188,
242, 213, 280, 300, 302, 322, 327, 333,
388, 417, 423, 439.

þat, dem. pron , *that:* ns. 361; ds. 152,
153, 157, 160, 196, 204, 296, 306, 307,
359, 377, 438; np. þo, 321; dp. þa,
392, 409, 441.

þat, conj., *in that, because, in order that, to the effect that, so that:* 5, 40, 50, 56, 68, 72, 79, 83, 103, 110, 214, 223, 245, 256, 285, 286, 349, 365, 393, 401, 404, 407, 430, 448, 453.

þe, def. art.; *the:* 14, 39, 104, 115, 119, 121, 128, 155, 159, 166, 172, 176, 178, 194, 225, 262, 280, 283, 371, 423, 436, 456, 457, 459.

þedir, adv., *thither:* 326.

þis, dem. pron., *this,* pl. *these:* ns. 329, 455; ds. þis, 47, 446, 447; as. þis, 165, 348, 378, 422; þus, 210; np. þir, 291, 308, 380; ap. þir, 80, 107, 175, 201, 225, 270, 362, 446.

þis, adv., *for this, thus, so:* 145.

þou, per. pron., *you,* pl. *you, ye:* ns. (26 times); þow, 68, 207, 258; þe, 230; ou, 117; tou, 261; ȝe, 62, 72; gs. þi, (13 times); ȝowre, 59, 61, 73; gs. þine, 131; ds. þe, 104, 108, 113, 116, 139, 141, 233, 448, 449; ȝow, 60, 71; as. þe, 82, 93, 112, 231, 257, 275; ȝow, 62; np. ȝe, 337, 339, 340; gp. ȝowre, 337; dp. ȝow, 201, 205, 341; ap. ȝow, 90, 91.

þus, adv., *in this way, accordingly:* 37, 52, 58, 126, 160, 166, 169, 206, 249, 291, 330, 379; þis, 145.

U, V

uaine, sb., *vanity, abuse:* dp. uaines, 433.

Valirian, pr. n., *Valirian:* ns. 24, 75, 150, 159, 165, 169, 175, 181, 215, 239; Ualirian, 254, 379; Valiriane, 295; gs. Valirian, 406; Valiriane, 383; ds. Valirian, 198, 226; Ualirian, 206; Valiriane, 243; as. Valirian, 178.

vengance, sb., *vengeance:* as. vengance, 71.

uerray, adj., *real, veritable:* 84. comp. deg. ns. verrayer, 266.

uirgin, sb., *one of a class, male or female, under churchly vows of chastity:* np. uirgins, 366.

*vowch, wv., trans., *promise, guarantee:* 3 sg. vowches, 255.

vnder, prep., w. dat., *below, beneath:* 172.

unbaptist, ppl. adj., *unbaptised, unregenerate:* ns. 27.

unfiled, ppl. adj., *undefiled:* as. unfiled, 40.

vntill, conj., *until, up to the time that:* vntil, 374. (see *untill*).

untill, *prep. w. dat., to, unto:* 22, 58, 60, 121, 236, 267, 280. vntill, 236, 267, 280.

unto, prep. w. dat., *to, unto:* 4, 52, 65, 78, 85, 129, 141, 184, 197, 198, 208, 224, 260, 325, 334, 358, 364, 374, 385, 392, 393, 408, 440, 444, 456, 462; vnto, 184, 260, 374, 408, 456, 462.

up, adv., *up:* 120, 156, 237.

Urban, pr. n., *Urban:* ns. 124; ds (pape) Urban, 17, 443; (bisschop) Urban, 107, 121.

W

*wax, sv., intrans., *wax, grow:* 3 sg. waxes, 133; pt. 2 sg. wex, 75.

way, sb., *way, course:* ds. wai, 40; way, 176; as. way, 106.

wele, adv., *in full measure, greatly; determinately:* 6, 55, 66, 173, 331, 450.

*wed, wv., trans., *wed, marry:* pp. wed, 31, 37, 54.

wende, wv., intrans., *go, proceed:* pt. 3 sg. went, 53, 117, 120, 186, 237, 356, 425; inf., 40, 271; pp. went, 41.

weng, sb., *wing, pinion:* dp. wenges, 365.

werk, sb., *deed, act:* ap. werkes, 335.

werld, sb., *world:* ds. werld, 196.

wha, rel. pron., *who:* gs. whas, 260, ds. wham, 462.

whare, adv., *at which place, wherever:* 308, 406, 426; whore, 271.

what, rel. pron., *whatever, that which:* ns. 118, 157, 170; ds. 281; as. 211, 213, 290, 304, 305.

when, rel. conj., *at the time that, as soon as,* 37, 39, 51, 57, 111, 124, 145, 151, 165, 268, 314, 323, 329, 348, 355, 378, 399, 422, 431, 455, 457.

whether, interrog. adv., *whether:* 84.

whils, conj., *at the time that; as long as:* 175, 450.

whitte, adj., *white:* ap. whitte, 113.

wife, sb., *wife:* ds. wife, 123, 186, 239, 385.

wikked, adj., *wicked, cruel:* ns. 377.

will, sb., *desire, judgment, intention, decree, heart:* ns. 59, 227; ds. will, 181, 287, 454; as. will, 318, 345, 351, 448.

*will, sv., trans., *desire, decree:* 2 sg. will, 213; pt. 3 sg. wild, 338; opt. 2 sg. will, 79; pt. 3 sg. walde, 241; aux. of potentiality, pt. wald, 142, 207, 219, 312, 351.

win, sv., trans., *win, redeem:* inf. 233; pp. won, 231.

wirk, sv., trans., *do, make, work, perform:* intrans., *labor:* pt. 3 sg. wroght, 373; wrogt, 305; inf. 318, 351, 451; pp. wroght, 196.

wirschip, sb., *worship:* de wirschip, 460.

*wirschip, wv., trans., *worship, adore:* pt. 3 pl. wirschipt, 397.

wise, sb., *wise, way, manner; Wise One:* ds. (on þis) wise, 37, 134; as. wise, 397.

wiseli, adv., *wisely, prudently:* 451.

wit, sb., *mind, reason:* ds. wit, 173, 400.

*wit(e), sv., trans., *know, understand:* 3 sg. wit, 67; pt. 3 pl. wist, 177.

wit, (see with).

with-outen, prep. w. dat., *without:* 98, 353; with-owten, 89, 357.

with, prep., w. dat., *with; by; in relation to:* 19, 20, 53, 61, 68, 123, 181, 202, 238, 279, 264, 311, 376, 386, 404, 419, 439, 454; wit, 238, 421.

within, adv., *within:* 49.

wode, adj., *mad, furious:* ns. 400.

wonder, sb., *wonder, miracle:* ap. wonders, 305.

*won(e), wv., intrans., *live, dwell:* pt. 3 sg. wond, 307.

woman, sb., *woman:* vs. woman, 79; dp. wemen, 6.

word, sb., *work, saying, speech:* np. wordes, 80; dp. wordes, 77, 92; ap. wordes, 107, 175, 225, 270, 362.

worthi, adj., *noteworthy, desirable:* ap. 196.

worthily, adv., *worthily, honorably:* 338.

wrathe, adj., *wrathful, angry:* ns. 75.

*writ(e), sv., trans., *write, inscribe:* pp. writen, 174; wretyn, 157, 160.

wroght, wrogt, (see *wirk*).

IX.

GENERAL BIBLIOGRAPHY OF SAINTS' LIVES.

I. MIDDLE ENGLISH TEXTS AND TEXTS OF THE CECILIA LEGEND.

Benedict, A., *Leben d. Heil. Hierony-mus.* Leipzig (noticed in LIT. BLATT, II. 6. 233).

Bollandus, *Acta Sanctorum.*

Bradshaw, Henry, *Saint Werburge.* E. E. T. S. No. 88, 1887.

Bülbring, K. D., ANGL. XIII. pp. 301-309. *Das " Trentalle Sancti Gre-gorii" in der Edinburgher Hand-schrift.*

Cockayne, Oswald, *St. Margaret.* E. E. T. S. No. 13. 18, 1866 (from MS. Reg. 17 A. XXVII and MS. Bodl. 34).

Cockayne, T. O., and Brock, E., *St. Juliana.* E. E. T. S. No. 51, 1872 (from MSS. Royal, 17 A. XXVII, Bodl. 34, and Ashmole 43).

Einenkel, Eugen, *St. Katherine.* E. E. T. S. No. 84, 1884 (from MS. Royal 17 A. XXVII with its Latin original from Cotton. MS. Calig. A. VIII).

Einenkel, E., ANGL. XVII. pp. 110-123. *Das Altenenglische Cristoforus-Fragment.*

Furnivall, F. J., *E. E. Poems and Lives of Saints.* PHIL. SOC. TRANS. 1858 (including St. Dunstan, St. Swithin, St. Kenelm, St. James, St. Christopher, 11000 virgins, St. Ed-mund (Conf.), St. Edmund (King), St. Katherine, St. Andrew, St. Lucy, St. Edward).

Furnivall, F. J., *Political, Religious and Love Poems.* E. E. T. S. No. 15. 25, 1866 (including, p. 83) *Tren-talle Sancti Gregorii* from MS. Cott. Calig. A. II, and MS. Lamb. 306).

Furnivall, F. J., *Originals and Ana-logues of some of Chaucer's Can-terbury Tales.* Publ. of Chaucer Society, Pt. II. London, 1875, p. 189 ff. (containing four versions of the Cæcilia legend, viz: (1) The Latin of Jacobus a Voragine ab. 1290 A. D. (2) The French of Je-han de Vignay, ab. 1300 A. D. (3) The Early Eng. of Ashmole MS. 43, bef. 1300 A. D. (4) The Later English of Caxton, A. D. 1483).

Gollanz, I., *The Exeter Book.* E. E. T. S. No. 104, 1895 (including Saint Guthlac, p. 104, Saint Juliana, p. 243).

Hickes, Geo., *Thesaurus of Old Northern Languages.* 1705 (con-taining, Pt. II., Wanley Cat. of *Early Eng. Calendars,* and Life of *St. Margaret,* MS. Bodl. 34).

Horstmann, C., *Barlaam und Josa-phat.* Sagan, 166, Progr. 1877.

Horstmann, C., *Sammlung Alteng-lischer Legenden.* Heilbronn, 1878 (MS. Vernon containing the saints' lives, Paula, Ambrosius, Theodora, Bernard, Augustin, Savinia and Savina, St. Magdalena; MSS. Laud 108, and Auchin. Edinb. Adv. Lib., Marina; MS. Harl. 2253, Eufrosyne; MS. Vernon, Cristyne; MS. Arund. 168, Dorothe; MS. Harl. 5272, Eras-mus; MSS. Harl. 2382 and Bedford, Robt. of Sicily).

Horstmann, C., *Barbour's Des Schot-tischen Nationaldichters Legend-ensammlung.* Bd. I. 1881, Bd. II. 1882. Heilbronn (MS. Camb. Gg. II. 6, containing the lives of 50 saints).

Horstmann, C., *Altenglische Legenden.* Heilbronn, 1881. (1) MS. Harl 4196 and Cott. Tib. E. VII (30 legends); (2) S. Malhor aus Barbour's Leg. Samml.; (3) Einzellegenden, (18 legends from various MSS.).

Horstmann, C., *S. Editha, Sive Chronicon Vilodunense im Wiltshire Dialect.* Heilbronn, 1883 (MS. Cott. Faustina, B. III).

Horstmann, C., *Osbern Bokenam Legenden,* Alteng. Biblioth. von Eugen Kölbing. Bd. I. Heilbronn, 1883 (from MS. Arundel, 327, containing Margareta, Anna, Christina, Elizabeth, 11000 Jungfrauen. Fides, Agnes, Dorothea, Magdalena, Katherina, Cæcilia, Agatha, Lucia).

Horstmann, C., *Prose Lives of Women Saints.* MS. Stowe 949. E. E. T. S. No. 86, 1886 (including Helena, Ursula, Keyna, Brigidae, Dympna, Edburg, Eanswide, Ethelburge, Milburge, Mildrede, Ebba, Etheldred, Kinesburge, Ethelburge, Hildelitha, Cuthburge, Withburge, Inthware, Frideswide, Walburge, Wenefride, Modwen, Oswitha, Maxentia, Oswen, Elfiede, Edith, Wulfhilde, Margaret, Mectilde, Monica, Agnes, Gorgonia, Nonna, Julitta, Iberia, Macrina).

Horstmann, C., *The Early South-English Legendary or Lives of Saints.* E. E. T. S. No. 87, 1887 (containing lives of 57 saints from MS. Laud 108, Bodl. Lib.).

Horstmann, C., *St. Katherine of Alexandria.* E. E. T. S. No. 100, 1893 (from MS. Arundel, 396, and MS. Rawlinson, 118).

Horstmann, C., ANGL. I. pp. 55-102. *Die Legenden von Celestin und Susanna* (MS. Laud L. 70, fol. 118 b and MS. Vernon fol. 517).

Horstmann, C., ANGL. I. p. 390. *Celestin.*

Horstmann, C., ANGL. III. p. 293. *Prosalegenden* (S. Wenefreda, MS. Lamb. 306, fol. 188; Marienlegenden, MS. Lamb. 432, fol. 95; S.

Dorothea, MS. Lamb. 432, fol. 90; S. Hieronymus, MS. Lamb. 432, fol. 1).

Horstmann, C., ANGL. IV. p. 116. *Prosalegenden (S. Antonius.* MS. Reg. 17. C. XVII. fol. 124b).

Horstmann, C., ANGL. VIII. p. 102. *Prosalegenden des MS. Douce* 114 (S. Elizabeth of Spalbeck, S. Cristyne þe Meruelous, S. Marye of Oegines, S. Kateryn of Senis).

Horstmann, C., HER. ARCH. LII. p. 33. *St. Bernhard* (from MS. Digby 86).

Horstmann, C., HER. ARCH. LIII. p. 17. *Nachträge zu den Legenden. St. Brendan* (from MS. Ash. 43. f. 41b).

Horstmann, C., HER. ARCH. LVI. p. 391. *Nachträge zu den Legenden. Zwei Alexiuslieder* (from MS. Vernon, fol. 43, MS. Trin Col. Oxf. 57. MS. Laud, L. 70. fol. 115).

Horstmann, C., HER. ARCH. LVI. p. 223. *Nachträge zu den Legenden, Alteng. Marien legenden* (from MS. Vernon).

Horstmann, C., HER. ARCH. LIX. pp. 71-107. *Nachträge zu den Legenden, Alexiuslieder* (from MS. Laud, 622, MS. Cot. Tib. A. 26, and Caxton MS. in Brit. Mus.).

Horstmann, C., HER. ARCH. LXII. pp. 397-431. *Nachträge zu den Legenden* (Alexius, (Barbour), MS. Camb. Gg. II. 6, St. Paul. MS. Digby. 86 fol. 132 (1290), Susanna, MS. Cot. Cal. A. II. fol. 1 (1430), Erasmus, MS. Cbr. Dd. I. 1. fol. 295 (1370), Robt. of Sicily, MS. Cbr. Ji IV. 174; Cbr. Caj. Col. 174; Cbr. Ff. II. 38).

Horstmann, C., HER. ARCH. LXVIII. p. 52. *Nachträge zu den Legenden. Magdalena* (from MS. Trin. Coll. Cmb. R. 3. 25. f. 127 b. and MS. Lamb. 223).

Horstmann, C., HER. ARCH. LXIX. pp. 207-224. *Nachträge zu den Legenden. Evangelium Nicodemi* (MS. Sion. fol. 13-39).

Horstmann, C., HER. ARCH. LXXIV.
pp. 327-365. *Nachträge zu den
Legenden* (Susanna, MS. Chelten-
ham 8252, Adam, (prose), MS. Bodl.
596).

Horstmann, C., HER. ARCH. LXXVI.
pp. 33-112, 265-314, 353-392. *Nachträge zu den Legenden* (Lyf of
Saint Katherine of Senis, Caxton,
1493). *Anhang.* (The revelations
of Saynt Elysabeth).

Horstmann, C., HER. ARCH. LXXIX.
pp. 411-471. *Nachträge zu den Legenden* (containing St. Margaret,
MS. Bod. 779).

Horstmann, C., HER. ARCH. LXXX.
pp. 114-136. *Nachträge zu den Legenden, Kalender in Versen, von
dan John Lydgate* (MS. Douce
322, f. 2, and MS. Rawlinson
408).

Horstmann, C., HER. ARCH. LXXXII.
p. 369. *Jüngere Zusatzleg. zur
Südeng. Leg. Sammt.* (from MS.
Bodl. 779. Sts. Oswin, Lion, Marius,
Stillu(e)rin, Paulin. Ciluestir, Rem-
igi, Anicet, Gay, Sother, Emerinci-
ane, Virg., Damas, Innocent, Felix,
Cimplice and Faustine, Abdon and
Cemen, Ierman, martyrs).

Horstmann, C., ENGL. STUD. I. p.
293. *Die Vision, des Heiligen
Paulus* (MS. Vernon fol. 229);
Eufrosyne (MS. Vernon, fol.
103).

Horstmann, C., ENGL. STUD. III.
p. 409. *Tomas Beket, Epische Legende von Laurentius Wade,*
(1497) *nach der Einzigen Hs. im
Corp. Chr. Coll. Cambr.*

Horstmann, C., ENGL.STUD. VIII. p.
275. (3) *be pope Trental* (MS. Vernon, fol. 230 and 303).

Horstmann and Furnivall, *Minor
Poems of the Vernon MS.,* E. E. T.
S. No. 98. 1892 (containing, (xxxiv),
be Pope Trental, with version from
MS. Cott. Cal. A II. fol. 86).

Kölbing, E., ENGL. STUD. I. p. 215.
(1) *Zu Chaucer's Cäcilienlegende.*
II

(2) *Die Zwei Englischen Cäcilien-
leben vor Chaucer* (reprinting cod.
Harl. 4196, fol. 191a ff. (3) *Chaucer
and Caxton*).

Kölbing, E., ENGL. STUD. I. pp. 16, 186,
and II. p. 281. *Die Jüngere Englische Fassung der Theophilus-
sage mit Einer Einltg. zum
Ersten Male Herausgegeben.*

Köpke, *Passionals. St. Cecilia,* pp.
629-642.

Kaufman, A., *Erlanger Beiträge
zur Eng. Phil.* Leipzig, 1889. *St.
Gregory* (in two versions, from
MSS. Vernon 230, Vernon 303,
Cott. Caligula A. II. 15, Lambeth
306, and MSS. Advocates Lib.
Edin., Cambr. Univ. Lib. Kk. I. 6).

Knust, H., *Geschichte der Legenden
der H. Katherina von Alexandria,
und der H. Maria Aegyptiaca nebst
Unedierten Texten.* Halle, 1889.

Krahl, Ernest, *St. Margaret,* Berlin,
diss. 1889 (in four versions).

Massmann, *Sanct. Alexius Leben.*
Leipzig, diss. 1843.

Metcalfe, W. M., *Legends of the
Saints.* Sc. Text Soc. 35-37, 1896
(MS. Cambr. Univ. Libr. Gg. II.
6, in three volumes, with notes).

Miller,Thomas, *Bede's Ecclesiastical
History* E. E. T. S. No. 95, 96,
(containing *The Life and Miracles
of Saint Cudberct, Bishop of Lind-
isfarne*).

Morris, R., *OE. Homilies.* E. E. T. S.
No. 53. 1873 (from MS. B. 14.52.
Trin. Col. Cmb., including St. John
the Baptist (2), Mary Magdalene,
St. James, St. Laurence, Assumpt.
of St. Mary, St. Andrew).

Morris, R., *Blickling Homilies.* E.
E. T. S. No. 58, 63, 73. 1880 (includ-
ing, St. Mary, annunciation of;
Virgin Mary, assumpt. of; John the
Baptist, birth of; The Story of
Peter and Paul, St. Michael's Church,
Festival of St. Martin; St. An-
drew).

Morris, R., *Specimens of Early English*. Pt. I. p. 96 (from Life of St. Juliana, MSS. Royal 17 A. 27 and Bodl. 34).

Morton, James, *St. Katherine of Alexandria* (for Abbotsford Club, London, 1841, from MS. Bibl. Cott. Titus D. XVIII).

Neuhaus, Carl, *Adgar's Marien-Legenden*. Heilbronn, 1886.

Perry, Geo. G., *Religious Pieces in Prose and Verse*. E. E. T. S. No. 26, 1867-1889 (containing, IX. p. 88, St. John the Evangelist, from the Robt. Thornton MS. (1440) in Lincoln Cathedral).

Pfeiffer, F., *Deutsche Mystiker des 14ten Jhrs.* (with prose version by Hermann von Fritzlar. Leipzig, 1845, containing lives of about seventy saints, including St. Cecilia).

Schipper, J., *Alexius, Englische Legenden aus dem 14 u. 15 Jhr.* Erstes Heft. Strassburg, 1877.

Schonbach, Ant., ZEITSCHR. FÜR DEUTSCHES ALTERTHUM, XVI. p. 165. *Saint Cecilia.*

Schultz, Fritz, *Gregorlegende*. MS. Auchin. Konigsburg, 1876.

Schwarz, M., ENGL. STUD. VIII. *Kleine publication aus der Auch. Hs.* LIV. *Die Assumptio Mariæ in der Schweifreimstrofe.*

Spencer, F., MOD. LANG. NOTES, (5) 1890. pp. 141-150. *The Legend of St. Margaret* (from Camb. text p. 213-221 and York MS. XVI. k. 13).

Small, J., *English Metrical Homilies* (1330). Edinburgh, 1862.

Surius, F. L., *De Vitis Sanctorum*, ab Aloysio Lipomano, episcopo Veronæ a F. L. Surio emendatis et auctis Venetis, 1581 (*Cæcilia*, p. 161).

The Surtees Society, LXXXVII. 1889. *Metrical Life of St. Cuthbert* (including versions from MS. Laud 108, and MS. Bodl. 779).

Voragine, Jacobus a, *ed.* Grässe, Th., *Legenda Aurea*. Dresden et Leipzig, 1846. 2nd ed. Grässe, 1850.

de Worde, Wynkyn, abridged by Pynson, 1516.

Wright, F., PERCY SOCIETY, 1844. *St. Brandan, a Medieval Legend of the Sea.*

Wright, Th., *Specimens of Lyric Poetry*, p. 101. *St. Bernhard* (from MS. Harl. 2253, in Vol. 4 of the Percy Society).

Zupitza, J. ANGL. I. pp. 392-410. *Zwei Mittelenglische Legendenhandschriften* (Corp. Chr. Col. Camb. 145, and Bodl. Oxf. Tanner, 17).

II. CRITICISM AND REVIEWS OF MIDDLE ENGLISH EDITIONS.

Blau, Max Freidrich, *zur Alexiuslegende*. Leipzig, 1888. Review of same, G. P., ROMANIA, XVIII. p. 299.

Brandes, H., ENGL. STUD. VII. p. 34. *Ueber die Quelle der Mittelenglischen Versionen der Paulusvision.*

Brandl, A., ZTSCHR. f. d. ÖSTERR. GYM. XXXI. pp. 152, 392. *Altengl. Leg. Samml.*, C. Horstmann, Heilbronn, 1878.

Brandl, A., ZTSCHR. f. d. ÖSTERR. GYM. XXXIII. pp. 684-92. *Altengl. Legenden, ed. Horstmann.* 1881.

Brandl, A., ZTSCHR. f. d. ÖSTERR. GYM. XXXVII. p. 445 *St. Editha*, MS. Cott. Faust. B III. *ed. Horstmann.* 1883.

Brandl, A., LIT. BLATT, 1881. (3) p. 398. *Altengl. Legenden, Barbour's Leg. Samml., ed. Horstmann.*

Brandl, A., LIT. BLATT, 1884. (3) p. 101. *Barbour's Leg. Samml.*, II.

Osbern Bokenam's Legenden, ed. Horstmann.

Breul, Karl, Deutsche Lit. Ztng. 1891. *St. Gregory in Two Versions, Kaufmann.* Beitr. zur Eng. Phil. Leipzig, 1889.

Buss, P., Angl. IX. p. 493. *Sind Die von Horstmann Herausgegebenen Schottischen Legenden Ein Werk Barbere's.*

Einenkel, E., *Über die Verfasser Einiger Neuangels. Schriften.* Leipzig, 1881.

Einenkel, E., Angl. V. pp. 91-123. *Über den Verfasser der Neuangelsaechsischen Legende von Katharina.* (Pt. III. of *Über die Verfasser Einiger Neuangels. Schriften.* Leipzig, 1881.)

Fischer, R., Angl. XI. pp. 175-219. *Zur Sprache und Autorschaft der Mittelenglishe Legenden St. Editha und St. Etheldreda.*

Förster, E., Angl. VIII. p. 175. *Life of Saint Katherine, ed. Einenkel, E. E. T. S.*

Gierth, F., Engl. Stud. VII. p. 1. *Ueber die Älteste Mittelenglische Version der Assumptio Marien.*

Gruber, H., Angl. XVIII. *Beiträge zu dem Mittelenglischen Dialoge "Ipotis."*

Hall, Joseph, Engl. Stud. VIII. p. 174. *Note on Saint Katherine, ed. Einenkel.* E. E. T. S. No. 80.

Hart, J. M., Mod. Lang. Notes, 1889, (4) p. 502. *The Legend of St. Margaret.*

Heuser, W., Angl. XII. p. 578. *Zu Fischer; Sprache und Autorschaft der Mittelengl. Legenden St. Editha und St. Etheldreda.*

Holthausen, F., Angl. XIV. pp. 310-12. *Legende vom Papst Celestin, St. Wenefreda, St. Hieronymus; ed. Horstmann.* Paderborn, 1875.

Holthausen, F., Angl. XV. p. 504. *Margaretenlegende.*

Holthausen, F., Engl. Stud. XIV. p. 104, Angl. III. p. 319. *Marienlegenden,* MS. *Lamb., ed. Horstmann.*

Holthausen, F., Her. Arch. LXXXVII. pp. 60-64. *Antonius-Legende von Horstmann.* Angl. IV. p. 116.

Holthausen, F., Lit. Blatt, 1891. (5) pp. 158-9. *St. Margaret, ed. Krahl.* 1889.

Hoofe, A., Engl. Stud. VIII. p. 209. *Lautuntersuchung zu Osbern Bokenam's Legenden.*

Horstmann, C., Her. Arch. XLIX. p. 395. *Die Legenden des MS. Laud* 108.

Horstmann, C., Introductions to Legend Collections, (1) *Leben Jesu* u. a. 1873. (2) *Alteng. Leg.* 1875. (3) *Leg. Samml.* 1878. (4) *S-E. Leg.* 1887.

Keidel, Geo. C., Mod. Lang. Notes, (8) pp. 296-300. *The St. Alexis Legend.*

Koeppel, E., Angl. XIV. pp. 227-233. *Chauceriana.* (iv) *Die Entstehungszeit 'Lyf of des seynt Cecyle.'*

Kölbing, E., Engl. Stud. II. *Alexius. Herausg. von J. Schipper.* Strassburg, 1877.

Kölbing, E., Engl. Stud. III. p. 101. *Zu Gregorius, ed. Horstmann.*

Kölbing, E., Engl. Stud. III. p. 125. *Sammlung Altengl. Legenden Herausg. von Horstmann.* Heilbronn, 1878.

Kölbing, E., Engl. Stud. III. p. 190. *Barlaam und Josaphat. Herausg. von Horstmann.* Sagan, 1877. Progr. 166.

Kölbing, E., Engl. Stud. VII. p. 142. *Osbern Bokenam's Legenden. Herausg. von Horstmann.* Heilbronn, 1883.

Kölbing, E., Engl. Stud. XIX. p. 121. *The Life of Saint Cuthbert* in the Pub. of Surtees Soc. Vol. 87, 1891.

Kölbing, E., Germania, XXI. pp. 437-442. *Zur Mittelenglischen Legenden Litterateur* (Alteng. Leg., Gregorius auf dem Steine, Her. Arch. LV. Horstmann; Gregor Legende aus MS. Auchin., Schultz, 1876).

Kostermann, Karl, *Sprache, Poetik, und Stil der Altenenglischen Gregorius Legende des Auch. MS.* Münster, 1882.

Krüger, A., *Sprache und Dialekt der Mittelenglischen Homilien in der HS.* B.14. 52. Trin. Coll. Camb. London. Reviewed. ATHEN. 3013 p. 110.

Ludorff, F., ANGL. VII. p. 60. *William Forrest's Theophiluslegende.*

Merkes, W., ANGL. V. pp. 86-88. *Über die Verfasser Einiger Neuangelsächsischer Schriften, von Dr. Eugen Einenkel.* Leipzig, 1881.

Migne, J. H., PATROLOGIA LATINA. Paris, 1845 (containing Latin Martyrologies and Hymns).

Morsbach, L., ANGL. VII. p. 31. *S. Editha Chronicon Vilodunense im Wiltshire Dialekt. C. Horstmann.*

O'Donoghue, D., *Brendaniana. St. Brendan the Voyageur in Story and Legend.* Dublin, 1893.

Schirmer, Gustav, zur *Brendanus Legende.* Leipzig, 1888. Reviewed in ROMANIA, 1889, p. 203.

Schleich, G., DEUTSCHE LIT. ZTNG. 1885. (7) p. 226. *Life of St. Katherine. E. Einenkel.* London, 1884.

Schleich, G., DEUTSCHE LIT. ZTNG. 1883. (33) p. 1162. *Osbern Bokenam's Legenden, ed. Horstmann.*

Schneegans, Heinrich, MOD. LANG. NOTES. 1888. (3) pp. 307-327, 495-500. *Alexiuslegende.*

Schönbach, A., DEUTSCHE LIT. ZTNG. 1891. (34) 1237-8. *Geschichte der Legenden der H. Katherina und der H. Maria. H. Knust.* Halle, 1889.

Schröer, A., ZTSCHR. f. d. ÖSTERR. GYM. 1885. p. 121. *Barbour's Samml.* 1881, 1882, *Osbern Bokenam's Legenden,* 1883. *ed. C. Horstmann.*

Spencer, F., MOD. LANG. NOTES, 1889. (4) pp. 393-402. *The Legend of St. Margaret.*

Spencer, F., MOD. LANG. NOTES, 1890. (5) p. 121. *The Margaret Legend.*

Stiehler, E., ANGL. VII. p. 405. *Alt-Englische Legenden der Stowe-Handschrift.*

Stratmann, F. H., DEUTSCHE LIT. ZTNG. 1882. p. 99. *Ueber die Verfasser Einiger Neuangels. Schriften. E. Einenkel.* Leipzig, 1881.

Stratmann, F. H., ENGL. STUD. II. pp. 9-14, *Zu Marharete.*

Stratmann, F. H., ENGL. STUD. IV. p. 93. *Verbesserungen zu Mittel-Englishen Schriftsstellern* (including Sts. Marherete, Juliana, Early Eng. Poems and Lives of Saints).

Trautmann, M., ANGL. V. pp. 21-25. *Altengl. Legenden, Neue Folge, Herausg. von Horstmann.* Heilbronn, 1881.

Varnhagen, H., ANGL. III. p. 59. *Zu Mittel-Englischen Gedichten:* (iv) *Zu den Sprüchen des Heil. Bernhard.* (vii) *Nochmals zu den Sprüchen Bernhard's.*

Varnhagen, H., ANGL. XIII. p. 104. *Die Quelle des Trentalle Sancti Gregorii.*

Varnhagen, H., DEUTSCHE LIT. ZTNG. 1884. (17) p. 616. *S. Editha,* MS. Cott. *ed. Horstmann.*

Wissmann, Th., LIT. BLATT, 1881. (12) pp. 435-7. *Ueber die Verfasser Einiger Neuangelsächs. Schriften. E. Einenkel.*

Wülker, R., ANGL. XI. p. 543. *The Life of Saint Werburge of Chester, by Henry Bradshaw. ed. C. Horstmann.* E. E. T. S. No. 88.

W(ülker), R., LIT. CENTR. BLATT, 1882. p. 1077. *Barbour's Samml. ed. Horstmann.*

Zupitza, J., HER. ARCH. LXXXII. pp. 465-467. *Marienlegende von Horstmann's Alteng. Legenden.*

Zupitza, J., HER. ARCH. LXXXVI. p. 405. *Lamentatio S. Bernardi, de Compassione Mariæ.* ENGL. STUD. VIII. p. 93. *von G. Kribel.*

Zupitza, J., DEUTSCHE LIT. ZTNG. 1883. (18) p 630. *Barbour's Legenden Samml.* II. *ed. Horstmann.*

III. OLD ENGLISH VERSIONS AND CRITICISM.

Assmann, Bruno, in Grein's BIBLIO-
THEK DER ANGELSÄCHS. PROSA. *An-
gelsächische Homilien und Heiligenleben*. Kassel, 1889 (including (xv)
Passio Beatae Margaretae Virginis
et Martyris, (xvi) Legende von
der Heiligen Veronica, (xviii)
Drei Leben aus De Vitis Patrum,
(xix) Incipit Passio Beatae Margaretae).

Baskervill, W. M., *Andreas, a Legend of St. Andrew* (ed. with critical
notes and a glossary). Boston, 1885.

Böddeker, K., ALTENGL. DICTUNGEN.
p. 254. *Marina; eine Legende.*

Bright, Jas. W., ANGLO-SAXON READER.
p. 86. *Ælfric's Homily on St.
Gregory the Great* (from MS. Gg.
3. 28. Camb. Univ. Lib. with
varient readings); p. 113. *Legend of
St. Andrew* (MS. Corp. Chr. Col.
Camb.).

Cockayne, Oswald, *The Shrine.*
London, 1864 (including (ii) *Life of
St. Neot*. MS. Cott. Vesp. D. XIV.
fol. 142. b. (viii) *King Alfred's
Book of Martyrs*). Index to the
same. p. 157.

Cook, A. S., MOD. LANG. NOTES, (2)
1887. pp. 117-118. *A List of the
Strong Verbs in Part II. of
Ælfric's Saints.*

Förster, M., *Über die Quellen von
Ælfric's Homiliæ Catholicæ I. Legenden*. Berlin.

Glöde, O., ANGL. XI. pp. 146-159. *Cyne-
wulf's Juliana und Ihre Quelle.*

Holthaus, E., ANGL. VI. p. 104. *Ælfric's Lives of Saints*, ed. Skeat. E.
E. T. S.

Kluge, F., ENGL. STUD. IX. p. 217.
Andreas, ed. Baskervill. Boston,
1885.

Kühn, Paul Theodore, *Die Syntax
des Verbums in Ælfric's Heiligenleben*. Leipzig, 1889.

Lefèvre, P., ANGL. VI. p. 181. *Das
Altenglische Gedicht vom Heiligen
Guthlac.*

Morris, R., and **Skeat**, W. W., *Specimens of Early English*. Pt. II. p.
19. From the *Life of St. Dunstan.*
MS. Harl. 2277, leaf 51.

Napier, A., ANGL. X. p. 131. *Ein Alt-
Engl. Leben des Hl. Chad.*

Napier, A., MOD. LANG. NOTES,
1887. pp. 378-9. *A Fragment of the
Life of St. Basil.*

Ott, J. H., *Ælfric, Über die Quellen
der Heiligenleben.* I. Halle, 1892.

Pearce, J. W., MOD. LANG. NOTES, 1887.
(3) p. 186. *Concerning "Juliana."*

Skeat, W. W., *Ælfric's Metrical
Lives of Saints*, in four parts, E.
E. T. S. Nos. 76, 82, 94, (1881, 1885,
1890). Pt. IV. in press.

Stratmann, F. H., ENGL. STUD. IV.
p. 94. *Juliana. Textemendationen.*

Sweet, Henry, ANGLO-SAXON READER
(containing Life of Oswald).

Thorpe, Benj., *Codex Exoniensis*, p.
242. *Legend of St. Juliana;* p. 107.
St. Guthlac.

Wells, Benj. W., MOD. LANG. NOTES,
(3) 1888. pp. 178-185, 256-262. *Strong
Verbs in Ælfric's Saints, I.*

Zupitza, J., ZTSCHR. DEUTSCHES
ALTERTH. XVII. pp. 269-96. *Bemer-
kungen zu Ælfric's Lives of
Saints.* I. ed. Skeat.

ERRATA.

P. 23, n. 3, for 'Origin' read 'Origen.'
P. 27, l. 27, for 'layed' read 'laid.'
P. 35, l. 17, for 'Ashmolian' read 'Ashmolean.'
P. 41, l. 20, for 'dependant' read 'dependent.'
P. 68, l. 15, for 'Cicill' read 'Cecill.'
P. 70, l. 32, for 'þor' read 'For.'